The Boy from the Back Streets of Bolton

And the Girl from Deane.

Norman Longworth

1

Preview

This is the story of how a lad born into a workin
England town of Bolton was able to make a diff
he managed to influence the advancement of lifeiong
growth of learning cities around the world through his books and wo...
lectures, his presidency of the European Lifelong Learning Initiative, the
international learning projects he managed and his innovative ideas, charts and
diagrams. It charts his life story from the back streets, through his schooldays,
national service, as a school teacher, manager, Professor, educator and
campaigner in Asia, Australia, Africa, North America and most countries of
Europe.

At the same time it is a rags to riches travelogue, where the riches are not
measured in monetary value but in the extent to which he, with his wife
Margaret, or Maggie as she is known to all, have been able to experience the
richness of our planet, many of its most beautiful places, the diversity of its
people and wild life and its cultures and customs. While it is the boy's own
autobiography, Maggie also played a large part in it. She has been his rock, his
mentor and his wife for sixty years. In her own way she too has made a difference
for the better to so many people. They had the celebration, such as it was in the
middle of a pandemic, on Christmas Eve 2020. That, not surprisingly is
unfinished business.

Bolton is a town in Lancashire, one of many surrounding the metropolis of
Manchester. At their birth, the second world war had yet to come and to create
misery and havoc on most of the world. Both their parents had suffered the same
misfortune when they were young, and this had a pernicious effect on family
psyche. From the end of Edward the eighth's belle époch almost until its mid-
point the twentieth century had been a disaster. The world was in need of
rebuilding in a different image, not that this was at all in either of their minds
when they were young. They were simply part of that recuperation process as
they grew older.

The lad's own enlightenment began with a laugh by a renowned headmaster at
the Bolton School, a former Direct Grant Grammar school with a big reputation.
Maggie's when acting upon a decision to overrule her father and become a nurse.
They had never met until fate brought them together in Bolton and District
General Hospital later in life. All of this is chronicled in this book. The boy from
the back streets who made a difference, the girl who came into his life and
changed it forever. Neither of them are standard celebrities, nor ever have been,
nor ever will be, but they have both, in their own ways, made a real difference to
many people throughout the globe. These two stanzas from a poem written by the

lad a couple of years ago act as a metaphor for his outlook. The full poem is in the Annexe to this book.

I have climbed the mountains high,
I have watched the eagles soaring
I have heard the planet sigh
For thoughtfulness imploring
I have smelled the flowers of spring
New birth then re-emerging
And I feel my heart should sing
With the joy of life now surging

I have sailed across the seas
Horizons new exploring
I have flown to lands afar
Their diversity adoring
I've resolved to never stop
Understanding and discerning
I've determined to embrace
The universe of learning

Their journey isn't in the history books and no-one will read it in the press. but they are two of many who have tried, and to a small extent succeeded in making the world a better place. In their own way too, their children followed in their footsteps.

So please read this as an example of what ordinary people, no matter what their origins, and given an open mind and wide horizons, are able to do. It is dedicated to our parents, our children and grandchildren, and everyone we have come into contact with during our long lives, many of whom have unknowingly been our inspiration.

Norman Longworth

Chapter One

The Beginning

'On the day of our birth, everything is possible'

(But only if you make it so)

Little is so banal as the announcement of our entry into the world.

LONGWORTH. At Townleys hospital, Bolton, on 19 March 1936, To Fred and Louie, a son Norman.

A new life unkindly deprived, like his parents before him, of a middle name to enhance his future prospects. A new baby, born into the back streets of Bolton to navigate the storms and upheavals of a war-torn early mid 20th century.

Fred

My Dad, Fred, was the eldest of five children, his values and attitudes shaped in the reality of the slums of Bolton, and moulded by the horrors of an epoch of bitter carnage on the battlefields of France and Belgium at which his father fought. He left school at the age of thirteen in the middle of a post-war pandemic, the Spanish flu, with little chance of obtaining a job suited to his skills and prejudiced later by the misery and unemployment of a world recession. A sickly child with a first-class brain that was never-developed because of the absence of the means of developing it. Ambition was thus destroyed, but in the early thirties he recovered some respectability by landing a job with an insurance company, collecting the premiums in an area of fifty square miles around Bolton. This he did for forty years come rain or shine, up and down the hills around the town, often meeting abject poverty and an inability to pay even for the penny premium among his clientele. Typically he would pay it himself from his own wages.

This work was interrupted by a two year stint in the RAF during the second world war when he signed up in spite of being medically unfit to serve, having had pneumonia which badly affected his lungs. He lost two brothers to the war. He spent it himself in the NAAFI at RAF Weston-super-mare playing the piano for the airmen. This is not to decry his commitment. It is what he was only fit enough to do and he brightened the lives of many. Indeed he was an accomplished pianist. He could play the songs of the century without music and by ear, though his own father had taught him to read music. This came in very useful when he needed extra cash, for, later in life, he led a three piece dance band for many years playing waltzes, foxtrots and quicksteps in halls throughout Bolton. My mum and I went to some of these, though I spent much of the time behind the piano reading a book.

In 1951 his lungs gave up the ghost due to the challenges of cycling in the Bolton weather. On top of his boyhood pneumonia it almost killed him. According to my mum the doctor gave him one more year. But he recovered, bought himself a car, did the job with that, and retired 16 years later with a full pension.

He had little knowledge of politics but always took the side of the underdog. One day when I was older, enthusiastically supporting a political party on a platform of slum clearance he reminded me that what we were proposing to knock down were not houses, but homes. That was one of the few times he confided any political orientation, though he erred on the conservative side in his attitudes. As far as travel was concerned he enjoyed his family week by the sea at various holiday resorts around England. This took place always during the last week in June during the Bolton Wakes week, when almost every Boltonian quitted the town. But when my mum proposed a holiday abroad he took the line that 'there's nowt foreign can touch what's in England.' His recreations were snooker and crown green bowling, at both of which he won medals, even to the extent of reaching the prestigious Lancashire inter town bowling final in Blackpool.

He read very little. Books and magazines bored him. But neither was he a well man. He would return home from a work, pockets bulging with the money he had collected, have his evening meal and spend most of the rest of the evening fast asleep in front of the fire. At bedtime he would have to lie over the end of his bed emptying his lungs into a bucket because of the bronchiectasis he suffered daily.

His relationship with me was fairly distant. It was a North of England man thing, where the children are the wife's responsibility, unless its sport, and the husband is there to pay the bills. and not get too involved with their upbringing. Thankfully that attitude is now declining. There were times however when he would come out into the back street and bowl a few balls while I pretended to be Don Bradman or Cyril Washbrook, cricketing icons of the age.

He would take me to the local cricket grounds or to his bowling club occasionally, but in the main he considered his function to be the family provider. Even when I gained a scholarship to the grammar school I cannot remember any real joy from him though I am sure he was proud in his own way. For him education was education wherever it was carried out and my mum told me he really wanted a girl. But I loved him. He was my dad for all his faults.

Although children were not his barrel he was a gregarious man. He would take up conversations with anyone whether he knew them or not. None were deep political conversations with hidden meanings – he would nod and agree whatever the subject and whatever his inner feelings were, though I suspect that he had no deep opinions on anything except the need to feed his family. And that is why he was very popular with the locals.

Despite his anathema to travelling he came quite often to our houses when we lived in London and, later, to Lymington, to see how the grandchildren were

7

faring. He died at the age of seventy five, twenty four years after he had been given that one year to live.

Louie

My mum, Louie, was the fourth of five children and also deeply influenced by the early twentieth century's abominations. She was imbued with the strength resulting from an autocratic, but loving, upbringing. Reserved, even timid, yet fiercely ambitious that her one and only child should have, and take, the opportunities opening up in the post second world war environment, she put education above all else and encouraged me in my learning. Unlike my dad she was an avid reader of both books and magazines. In the days before television this, and the radio, were the only home entertainments available.

She lived first of all with her brothers and sisters in a two up two down house in the Halliwell district of Bolton, not the most salubrious corner of the town. There were only two bedrooms. Every house in the block of 15 houses was the same. Every block on both sides of the long street likewise. They were built in the early part of the twentieth century, mainly to house the families of cotton spinners who worked in the two hundred plus cotton mills in Bolton at the time to take advantage of the damp weather. Such crowding was normal since most families were large, to compensate for the high infant mortality of the time and to service the mills in the town.

Ablutions for all were carried out at the end of the back yard, next to the ash pit into which the remains of yesterday's fire were thrown, ready to be collected by the ashpit men each week. The coal shed was opposite the toilet. Taking into account the extreme cold of winter and the customary wet of summer this was hardly ideal but it had to be endured. It was said that constipation in winter was a blessing.

The oven was adjacent to the fireplace in the front room and heated by the coal fire. Cooking was a fragile occupation and depended on the intensity of the fire. The washing tub and mangle were in the kitchen and the wet clothes were put out to dry on a rail hanging from the ceiling above the kitchen table. The front of the house abutted onto the street. Upstairs were the two bedrooms and a small bathroom over the stairs. No toilet in sight.

Gradually her elder siblings left, two sisters went to Canada just after the war and one brother to London. All of them seeking work. When she became of working age at fourteen she didn't experience the scourge of unemployment as most of her contemporary youngsters did. She went to work as a cotton spinner, the only thriving industry in the town. It didn't pay well but it paid. I have

8

pictures of her as a swinger in the costume of the late twenties. She went dancing and participated in the activities of the local Unitarian church. Regrettably I have no knowledge of how and when she met my father but I do know it was in the early thirties. How much we all wish that we had asked the right questions when our parents were alive.

Into this environment the baby Norman was thrust, screaming and puking from the consequence of a long and painful breeches birth. Like every baby ever born, he would make a difference, good, bad or indifferent to those who came into contact with him. He almost had a sibling but she died in the womb shortly before birth. We lived in the same two up two down which my mum had inherited when she married. Her father had taken a posher semi-detached house with a garden in Doffcocker, a more middle class area of Bolton. The three of us were to live there until I left to perform my national service in 1954.

Some years after the second world war was finished, bliss of bliss, the municipality upgraded the bathroom by installing an indoor toilet. What celebrations that caused. No more dashing down the yard to a cold loo in a freezing temperature. Furthermore the fireplace was completely re-designed, the oven disappeared and became a separate entity in the kitchen, the fireplace rearranged. Modernity had come to Arnold Street.

Chapter two

Childhood in the Back Streets of Bolton

'Education starts from the womb and should never end'

(But often it does)

Early days

My childhood was typical of a working class family in Bolton. However there was one small difference. Between the ages of three and nine a world war was creating bloodshed and slaughter throughout the battlefields of Europe, a regular occurrence through many centuries as European country fought European country. While my father went to do his bit, Mum and I went to live with the grandparents three miles away for a couple of years. I knew it well. One of my earliest memories is of riding my tin tricycle at the age of three to see my grandmother. I was an adventurous child.

One can imagine the consternation this caused in Arnold Street. There were no telephones, no way of knowing where I was, or even that I was safe. Grandma was ill, Grandad was at work as was my Dad, my mother had no transport and couldn't bring me home, even if she had known where I was. So when I cycled the three miles back home oblivious to the mayhem I had caused, I remember the greeting well. It was a mixture of relief, hysteria, opprobrium and joyousness. Somehow the tin tricycle disappeared from my life thereafter. But for me, this trip was the forerunner of a long life of globetrotting though I didn't of course know it at the time.

The war didn't really affect me very much. Of course my family frequently discussed its progress and, as children in school, we were required to contribute to the war effort by raising money, providing clothes and singing for victory. But it was a far-away event for a youngster growing up in Bolton. Cotton mills weren't a prime target for German bombers. More the vast ports of Liverpool and Manchester. Every now and then the sirens blared out to signal danger and we cowered under the tables and staircases just in case they knew where we lived and wanted to bomb our house, but by and large the war passed us by. The ugly concrete air raid shelter they had built in the back yard was hardly ever used for the purpose it was intended. Indeed it stayed there long after the war was over and became a playground for the young horrors my mates and I were growing into.

To School

In 1941, while Hitler's fascist army and airforce were terrorizing Europe, I was despatched during the day, to my mother's great relief, to Oxford Grove junior school. It did not live up to its intellectual eponym, being a bog-standard two storey school building in the heart of another working class area a mile away from home. My mother had determined that I could already read and write from the age of three and so I had a head start. The basic English lessons were something of a bore, but history, geography and music fascinated me.

I read profusely, books were an enchantment. Enid Blyton and Richmal Crompton were my favourites at an early age. I soaked up everything they wrote. The fabulous five, Just William and Paddington bear became my best friends. The Beano and Dandy were my intellectual advisers, Lord Snooty, Denis the Menace, Desperate Dan my role models. My world was a fantasy adventure. I also found that I could sing. In tune. 'Dashing away with a smoothing iron' was my favourite at school, largely because Mr Morris, the headmaster, insisted on the whole school singing it every Monday morning. A hundred and fifty young voices murdering 'Twas on a Monday morning , when I beheld my darling, who looked so sweet and charming in every high degree' without really understanding the adult implications of what we were singing about.

Unitarian

But my voice was being developed elsewhere. Outside of the school, another centre of my existence was the Unitarian church on Halliwell Road. The minister there, a certain Mr Irvine Hodgson, was popular with the kids. He doubled the church's complement of children as news of his kindness, and propensity to freely distribute sweets, rose in the district. We sang the Sunday morning children's hymns with gusto. My personal repertoire increased to the classics – 'Oh for the wings of a Dove', some Handel pieces from the Messiah and others. My cousins were also members of the church and we all added our treble voices to the small choir that was run initially by my Grandad.

For a small nonconformist church in the middle of terraced Halliwell it was a thriving establishment. It had its own scout group, an amateur theatre society, a debating chamber and frequent balls where the congregation danced the night away. Nothing too American, just the veleta, the military two-step, waltzes, foxtrots and quicksteps galore. Later, being the oldest, I was elected to organize a youth club on the second floor of the church hall where there was a full size snooker table and a table tennis table. My first experience of leadership.

Playing the piano

I was seven when my mum and dad decided that I should learn to play the piano. I was sent to Mrs Sinnott's establishment once a week to learn the rudiments of music and to prepare for the music examinations that lead gradually to concert pianist standard. Alas, playing soccer and cricket with my friends always took precedence over practicing the music. While I achieved up to level four, mainly through the leniency of the examiners, my dad decided that it wasn't worth the money. He was right but not before he tried again with great aunt Tina. She was a strict taskmistress, a knuckle-rapper for every wrong note. She was spinster of a certain age and firm beliefs who disliked young boys with ideas of their own. Indeed she liked very little of the world outside of her small cottage and that soon led to disagreements that could not be settled. No longer was I required to practice chords and play music badly.

It wasn't until I was fourteen that I tried to salvage what little I knew of key-bashing again. We had a piano in the house and there was sheet music by the score. The one thing I had learned to do with the misses Sinnott and Tina was to read music. So I tried to teach myself with a few of the classics of the day and music we had around the house. The Warsaw Concerto, the Beethoven Sonata Pathetique, some songs from the 19th century such as 'in a monastery garden'. Of course these were well beyond my capability but I had some success with the slow movements and the pop songs. So much so that, later, I was among the musicians who formed a band to play at the weekly dances. I had found an accordion among my dad's musical accoutrements and played that in the band.

Rationing

The postwar forties were hard times. Money in a working class family was always scarce. My mum went to work in the cotton mills and at the dolly blue factory to pay for my education and the occasional luxuries like summer holidays. Rationing was still in full bloom, as it had been during the war. But new goodies not available during the war years gradually made an appearance in the shops. For a D coupon in the ration book I could buy two ounces of smarties per week at the sweet shop in the next street. Austerity did not apply to me. As soon as I received my pocket money of two shillings a week I would race down to the cake shop to stuff my face with a couple of the newly available cream cakes. In the evenings when the chip shop was open I would buy a bag of chips for threepence with a bag of scraps (the scraps of batter that didn't stick to the fish) for free.

In the wider political world change was in the air. The old colonies were agitating for their freedom, sometimes with bloodshed. The pearl of the British empire, India, would achieve statehood in 1947 and be forever partitioned into 3 separate countries. The new state of Israel made its appearance in 1948 and immediately caused bloodshed in the middle east. Upheavals were everywhere. But none of this was in the conscious mind of a young lad growing up in the back streets of Bolton.

Playmates

Oblivious to all this my regular playmates were both call Kenny. Kenny Hayes lived in the next block up and Kenny Wilkinson in the block opposite. Kenny H came from a very poor family with a violent and abusive father and a nervous mother who played the piano like an angel. He had a younger sister who also suffered from her father's temper. They received very few presents at Christmas, and I can remember my dad chastising me on Christmas day for going to Kenny's house to show my new toy. Kenny W by contrast was an only child like me and was the son of a policeman. His family kept themselves to themselves and I cannot remember ever being allowed into his house. Out in the street, the three of us were inseparable and insufferable, well known by every household as the three musketeers.

Sport, especially cricket and football were our specialities. Our first contact with the former game came at an early age. We were all seven years old. This was wartime. We played in our back street using a lamp post as a wicket, a cricket bat shaped piece of wood and a tennis ball that changed direction fiercely in a wind. Since the back street was not more than six metres wide and the lamp post was just one metre from the ashpit cover on the wall to the left certain cricket strokes were discouraged, the off drive being perhaps the only one likely to yield any success.

Furthermore there was a kerb ten centimetres on the right of the lamp-post which made accuracy a prime requirement for the bowlers. The pitch extended to our back gate. Of course being young and undisciplined we were often tempted to hit the ball into air and over the backyard walls. There were three main methods of recovering it. We could try walking round the block to knock on the front door and ask for our ball back. We could try the back gate to see if it was open and quickly retrieve it ourselves if so. The third method was employed if one and two were not viable. Kenny H was always the fall guy for this, since he was the most nimble.

It entailed using a pair of step ladders to hop over the ten foot wall to retrieve the ball and scramble back very quickly up the back of the gate. This was the most risky since, more than once, Kenny was confronted by the owner sitting on the pot because he or she had not closed the toilet door. On these occasions Kenny did not linger. We soon discovered who the nice neighbours and the old fogeys were. Mrs Macnic for example was a witch. She rarely gave the ball back and was constantly complaining to my Dad about the disturbance.

She had a point, though we would never admit it, since her toilet was right next to our wicket and she was not the quietest of people when it came to ablutions. Many is the time we bowled each other out because of the harrumphing noise as the ball arrived. For four whole years this was our cricketing paradise from which I learned how to bowl a good length, keep the ball down and perfect the off-drives. It permeated into my adult life when I played serious cricket for several teams in other parts of Britain. The batting was excellent to the off side and the bowling was always on length and line.

Our footballing took place at the gable end where we had chalked a goalpost on the wall of the house unfortunate enough to be at the end of the block. More than once we were chased off by the house owners who could no longer endure the constant banging of a football on their peace and quiet. Our solution to this was to find another gable end, or to wait until there was no-one in the house.

We three had bicycles and ventured ever further away from our homes up into the hills around Bolton, sometimes camping overnight. On these occasions we had to rise early to make sure that Kenny H was in time for his paper round. It was, in its own way, an idyllic life for three happy young scrubbers with little else to do but enjoy life. Bolton wasn't exactly the Lake District but we could echo Wordsworth's words ' Bliss was it in that dawn to be alive. But to be young was very heaven' if we had known them at the time. As with all things in life it did not last.

Bonfire night

One of the most popular celebrations in our crack was bonfire night. They had been banned during the war for obvious reasons, but we made up for it starting in 1945. For weeks before we would collect any wood we could from wherever we could find it, legal or illegal. It would pile up in our back yard until it reached over the back wall. We would save our pocket money for fireworks for months in advance. We weren't the only ones. Come the fifth of November the back street was radiant with bonfires up and down. There must have been 30 blazing away within sight.

Dads would come out to supervise but had little control over the mayhem their offspring had in mind. Mums would provide a huge bowl of black peas and people would drink these from a cup with vinegar. We never knew where these came from and perhaps it was better that we didn't. Only in Lancashire could they be found. But the greatest fun was with the fireworks. The Roman candles that glowed brightly in the dark, the rockets that we set off from a milk bottle, the jumping jacks, every young boys favourite, to be thrown among the girls and watch them scream as the firework jumped up and down. The bangers that made a loud noise and the sparklers that we could hold and wave about while they were, well, sparkling.

There was always a warning on them. Light the blue touch paper and retire. It was the retiring bit that people didn't understand. The hospital casualty departments were packed with hundreds of youngsters who had misunderstood, or deliberately ignored, the words. And then there was the bonfire itself on which dad kept throwing wood. It was huge fun for us lads. We would throw potatoes on the edge and eat the blackened mess that was produced.

In the modern day the ritual has been homogenized. There are rules where no rules existed. Safety where no safety was accepted. Organisation to replace the chaos. Back streets no longer were suitable for bonfires. They were dangerous. So every bonfire has to be carefully managed and the fireworks set off by a responsible person. Sure we get some spectacular displays at New Year and other celebrations, and they are very impressive, but nothing today can match the mayhem and madness of our old-fashioned bonfire nights.

Chapter 3

The Bolton School

'Don't think of what to make of your school

Think of what your school makes of you.'

11+ and its aftermath

In 1947 I became eleven years old and the dreaded 11+ loomed. In Bolton there were 2 Grammar schools, one for those who passed the 11+, and the Bolton School, a very select posh school which provided a classical education for the elite. It was reputed to be one of the best schools academically in the country. This was well beyond the young clientele of Oxford Grove Junior school, which had sent a few to the first but never any child to the second. Nor would this have happened in 1947 except that the war had ended two years previously and the new British government was determined to show its commitment to a more equitable education system. Walter Beveridge was the Minister responsible. Posh Grammar schools were told to increase their working class intake and given some money to help the process. This was a gamechanger.

I passed the eleven plus as my teachers expected. Then came a letter through the door from the posh school. I had been chosen to be interviewed to see if I had what it takes for a classical education. My mother was ecstatic. Here was her only son being asked for an interview at the Bolton School, one of the most important and successful schools in the land. My dad was less enthusiastic. He could sense that perhaps some payment might be involved.

Came the day of the interview. Mother gave me some last minute advice based on what she knew of my character. Don't show off she said. Don't try to answer anything that you can't answer. Right mum. So I arrived at the school and was first interviewed by a number of senior teachers who seemed to be satisfied that I knew most of the answers to the factual questions they asked. Eventually I arrived at the headmasters office, Richard Poskitt FRS, and one of the most revered headteachers in Britain, although I wasn't at that time aware of this. He shook my hand and then showed me a medieval water clock. 'How do you think that worked'? he said. Remembering my Mother's warning I said 'I don't know Sir.' He asked me again and I gave him the same answer. 'Why can't you guess how it works?' Well sir I said, 'my mum told me not to show off and not to answer any questions I don't know the answer to.'

He laughed aloud at this. I could not possibly know it but that laugh was the single most important arbiter of my life from that point. From it everything else has stemmed. Forget all that, he said, now tell me what you think. So I did have a guess. In this way I passed into the Bolton school. I still don't know how a medieval water clock worked. And my dad was right. I got the bursary but there was also a small annual payment. In that year Oxford Grove was well rewarded since four of us made it to the educational heaven of the Bolton School.

It was a posh school where they had a decent cricket pitch on real grass, with real stumps and corkies, real cricket balls, and proper goalposts and nets. My life changed. My mates went to the secondary modern up the road where there was no such heaven, and cricket was not on the syllabus. I had homework from the school and they didn't. They stopped knocking on the door and we eventually lost touch with each other. The three musketeers had disbanded and I had apparently become Lord Snooty. We met every now and again in the street and exchanged pleasantries but without the Cricket and the football there was little that bound us together. I learned much later from other people that Kenny H had a job playing the piano on the Cruise ships and Kenny W, like his father before him, joined the police force.

The School

The Bolton School is a magnificent sandstone structure on the main road out of town endowed by Bolton's most successful Entrepreneur, William Hesketh Lever, later Lord Leverhulme, creator of the Unilever empire. The central clock tower separates the boy's and the girl's schools. It is a member of the Headmaster's Conference thus giving it an entry into the world of public schools and at the same time takes most of its pupils from the region around Bolton. Most pupils are paid for by their parents but there are many scholarships and bursary's to enable poorer families to send their children there.

The curriculum is wide, all the subjects of the standard curriculum together with compulsory gymnastics, an excellent music department with choirs and instrumental learning facilities, highly successful soccer, rugby, cricket teams at all levels, a thriving scout group, a well-known theatre where plays, mostly Shakespearean, and operas were performed and a plethora of mid-day and evening clubs and societies run by the teachers. Ian McKellen, the well-known actor was just two years behind me. Boys and girls can apply for bursary's to take them anywhere in the world and every holiday has its trips to all parts of Europe on the proviso that their parents could afford the cost. Language scholars have pen friends abroad and frequent visits to their counterparts. It was the 'English School of the Year' in 2019, not only because of its high examination success rate but also for its contribution to the community and its multiple extra-curricular activities.

That is now. In 1947 when I first entered its portals it had many of the same activities though without a rugby team. For a timid, overweight working class lad from a poor family, life at the Bolton School wasn't all roses. First of all there was the problem of getting there. The school was on the other side of town a good two miles away and I had to walk there since cycles weren't allowed. Secondly there was the business of how the new working class lads could fit into a school that favoured middle class families with middle class support systems at home. In my first year it wasn't so much of a problem. Two lads from Oxford Grove, one of them being myself, happened to come first and second academically in the Shell A1 class over the year.

Problems

But as we became older it became harder. I was a small boy with a weight problem and, as often happens in semi-public schools, the weaker were often the butt of the stronger. Nicknames were understandable and could be endured. Everybody had them, including the teachers, though many were simply aimed to hurt rather than to describe. In my time bullying was rife. While it was frowned upon there was no rule against it. As in many public schools it was considered to promote character building. The baiting was both physical and psychological. It was known that it happened by the headmaster and staff but the stiff upper lip prevailed and it was up to the individual student to find a way of coping. It was deemed to be character forming. Anyone who has read books about life in a public school knows the syndrome. Those who are small, naïve and from a different background, as I was, became bait for the stronger, taller and richer. We all had our little gangs to protect us but they were not always successful against the larger and older boys in the school. In their world, bullying and being bullied was part of the experience.

In this environment my overall performance dropped rapidly from top of the class to somewhere below the middle as my self-esteem fell. Some of the staff understood why but could do little about it. The one area where I excelled however was in modern languages. French and German came easily to me. Not to speak it of course, this was the late forties and the idea of language laboratories and language students visiting other countries had not yet been invented. But the grammar posed no problems. Of course other boys from the school went on overseas trips and camping expeditions, and profited greatly from them, but this required funding from parents and mine could not afford it.

Deliverance

Despite this I adapted, as all boys must. I knew that I was receiving a vastly superior education and was immensely grateful for it. It enhanced my outlook on life for the better. I learned the classics, latin (just in case I would be going to Oxbridge, a highly unlikely outcome), World, European and English history and geography, the joy of classical music, the nuances of literature through the ages, the importance of scientific method and the subtlety of great art. I read books that stretched my imagination and tested my perceptions. I determined that the name-callers were not going to win.

I found that I had a voice. Not up to Lorelei standards and not one that would force Odysseus to tie himself to the mast, but one that could stay relatively in tune. Not perfect pitch but close. So I joined the choirs and participated in the mid-day societies, the railway club, the literary and debating society, the music society and more. I became who I am now and not what I might have become had I not experienced such a complete education.

I played cricket for the school team and soccer for the 3rd team. I entered the house swimming competitions. Like every pupil I learned more from some teachers than others, especially from those who would digress from the standard syllabus and talk about practical life experiences. Until finally in 1951 we reached the fifth form and examination time. This was the UK's first year of the GCSE, and later A level, and it was very much a matter of guesswork about how it should be approached. In its wisdom the school decided that the first O levels should comprise only three subjects and then we should take the A levels only a year later with three different subjects, a far cry from the multiple subjects now taken at each level.

Anyway it was what it was. I don't believe that bullying exists now as much as it did. I left the Bolton School at the age of seventeen years and 3 months with three O levels, Latin, Maths and English, and three dodgy A levels, French, German and English Literature, and a thoroughly inclusive education that should enable me to make my way in the real world, if I were ever able to take advantage of it. Or did I? I had little knowledge of business, even less of how to speak in public, or lead others, or a hundred and one tiny things that we meet in real life. I was a highly educated non-practical eunuch. But then isn't that what a classical education is for? It was up me to take advantage and build upon the learning I received for the rest of my life. And that is what I have done.

My middle class contemporaries would spend another year in the school prior to leaving for universities around the country and especially Oxbridge. I, and several others from the Beveridge intake, could not do that because family circumstances could not allow it. Which doesn't mean that we didn't obtain any value from going there. It opened up so many more opportunities for the future, as later pages will testify and I have taken a pride in having been there. I have kept in touch in all the sixty seven years since I left, and when I read 'the bugle' or the school magazine I notice that it has improved even more.

As it happens I first joined a bank aided by the teacher responsible for finding jobs for early leavers. It was in any case only nine months before I would reach eighteen and have to do my duty to my country as a national serviceman.

I paid one more visit to the Bolton School two years later when they asked for old boys to play against the school cricket team. I applied and was chosen. At that time the school team was unbeaten. It contained a young man who would later become captain of Lancashire Cricket Club and play for England and another who was regularly making 50s against other schools and was the key stone of the batting. The old boys team was a motley crew of those who played in the local league and those who hadn't bowled a ball or handled a bat since leaving school. I was asked what I did by the captain and I told him I was a bowler. The game started with the school team batting. The opening bowlers didn't make much headway into the game. Only one wicket went down and the half century batsman was making hay. I was called over to bowl. He put my first ball somewhere into the next county. The second however was on a good length and broke back on the bounce. He moved across the wicket missed the ball and was out lbw.

The umpire was my old English teacher and the first team coach and he gave me a wry look. In came the future England bat. He played himself in and scored only one run in the rest of the over. And then proceeded to knock the next over at the other end to all parts of the ground and beyond. Then came my second over. He had ended the previous one with a single and was on strike. I bowled a standard length on the first ball as fast as I could and he blocked it. Then I served him up with a slower half volley which also turned slightly. He slammed it at great speed toward midwicket who didn't have time to get out of the way so he caught it. No wonder my old English teacher chuckled. I was taken off after four overs with no more wickets. As it happened we lost the game, but I will always remember it as the day when I took out an England cricketer in two balls.

Six things the Bolton School gifted to me

60 years after leaving the Bolton School I wrote this piece which I believe sums up the influence of my school upon my life.

1. Aspiration

Not in the 'Go West young man sense' – when I left school at the age of 17 I had no idea of what I wanted to do, to be. As life continued, an inbuilt sense that there is always more to achieve took over almost subliminally. It pervaded my future careers as teacher, international manager, President of a European organization, author, Professor and consultant to UNESCO, and the EC - a feeling of a higher calling which has never left my now octogenarian mind. This is articulated in the poetry I write.

'The future belongs to those who will yearn
To constantly, easily, willingly learn
Adaptable, flexible, versatile too
And able to keep new horizons in view'
(From Past, Present and Future, 2016)

2. A love of fine music

As a teenager at school I was of course influenced by the mostly American pop music of the day – Johnny Ray, Frankie Lane, Guy Mitchell. Strangers to the modern generations. But the music teacher, PAS Stevens, persevered, inveigled me into the school choir and instilled a knowledge of, and love affair with, classical music, together with an eclectic view of other genres, including Jazz and rock, and that has never left me. I am still singing in a choir and writing music.

3. A sense of Service, of contribution

The idea that we are not here for ourselves alone. That there are many contributions people like me who have been fortunate enough to live comfortably can make. Not, in my case, only as a donor of money or even sympathy, more on a larger world-sized scale. The work I have done for the European Commission and UNESCO in creating learning cities still endures.

If on the other hand your vision is wide
And covers the planet for which you take pride
Become a world patriot and direct your mind
To doing your damnedest for all humankind
(From On true patriotism, 2016)

Treat every human being as your sister and your brother,
Whatever their religion, their culture or their title
Everyone who's born is but the offspring of a mother
In the melting pot of human life, an open mind is vital
 (From Lifelong Learning, 2015)

4. A sense of adventure

Although I never joined any of the wild tours of Europe which were led by one of the school's most forward-looking teachers, Butch Ingham, (my family could never afford it), the yearning to travel, visit exotic places, see everything there is to see that is worth seeing in this beautiful world was planted in my brain at school. I have been fortunate enough to fulfill that longing in my work.

Discover, understand, the world of knowledge and discernment
Every human being has the power to reach the sky
Widen your awareness of your own immense potential
Let the power of lifelong learning allow your mind to fly
(From Lifelong Learning, 2015)

5. Lifelong Values

Although a bursary boy from the less salubrious end of Bolton, the outward-looking inspiration and values that the Bolton School implanted in me has fed me through life, even though, at the time, I was completely unaware of it. And I will be forever grateful for it. It wasn't explicit – no-one told me to accept these values - more they were ingrained in the school's DNA, and eventually my own. When I read the school magazine I am pleased that the tradition continues.

The root of education is giving inspiration
A stimulated student learns with pleasure
The teachers' roles reform into how they can transform
Young minds to value learning as a treasure
(From Modern Education, 2015)

6. An Enquiring Mind

Many travel through life obeying the rules and settling for comfort, a good salary and contentment. The Bolton School didn't encourage that sort of life. It taught me to think, to reason, to be creative in every aspect of living, to value difference and diversity. It doesn't always make for self-satisfaction and serenity but it helps me to believe that my life has been instrumental in attempting to push back the frontiers a little more.

For people to achieve potential
Creative thinking is essential
Mulling all perspectives through
To come to a well-reasoned view
Opinions based on evidence
Encompass every consequence
To make a rational decision
Needs thinking skills and forward vision
Features of self-liberation
Rarely taught in education
(From Banality, 2016)

Would that these attributes were given to all schoolchildren throughout the world. What a difference there would be.

Chapter 4

National Service - Saving Britain

'Toughness turns men into boys'

'And boys into toughs'

Life in a bank

I remember very little of my time in the Swinton branch of Barclays Bank. I remember catching two buses every morning to get there. I remember the salary of twelve pounds per month – not much income into the family considering a quarter of it went on bus fares. I remember the nice Bank Manager and some of his customers. I remember his assistant who, quite rightly chastised me for my lack of enthusiasm for banking. I remember being bored out of my mind. National Service could not come quickly enough.

In the real world, Queen Elizabeth the second was being crowned, the North Sea was flooding large parts of Eastern England and Everest was being conquered by Edmond Hillary and Sherpa Tensing. Rationing had been abolished by the new Tory government and televisions were on sale for the first time to the masses. My Dad bought one specifically to watch the Bolton-Blackpool FA cup final. It was a 12 inch screen with a 2 inch thick magnifier on the front. As we were the only house in the block with a TV, our front room was crowded with neighbours wanting to see the Trotters win the cup. Most of them couldn't see it from the back of the room and relied on those at the front to keep them informed. And Bolton lost thanks to the genius of Stanley Matthews.

Saving Britain – square-bashing

In April 1954 my papers for saving Britain from enemy action came through the door. I was invited to say whether I wished to join the RAF or the Army. The Navy was not an option. I opted for the RAF, not by any sound reasoning but because it sounded a little less onerous than the cinema image of exhausted soldiers struggling through fields of mud in pursuit of an armed enemy. Having made that decision I was given a pep talk at the local recruitment centre on whether I wanted to join for two years under a pittance or for three years under a larger pittance. For no reason that I can justify I chose the latter. Two months later I was called to Cardington in Bedfordshire to pick up my brand new blue RAF uniforms and transported to Hednesford in Staffordshire to start my new adventure as an airman.

The next eight weeks were a real shock to my innocence. Never before in my life had I heard other people scream at me as if I were an idiot, for the sake of screaming, never had I met such obnoxious sergeants treating me as dirt, never had I had to rise before six am, march round a square all day and be slandered for a wrong step, never had I been abused for three specks of dust on my bedpost. To be fair, it wasn't only me, it was all of us suffering discipline, RAF style. Here was the alternative education. There were twenty five of us in the billet from many walks of life, including the then current British tennis

26

Champion Billy Wright, a couple of middle class public schoolboys and many from the very centre of poverty. A mixed bunch in every way. Every now and then Billy had to leave to play tennis for England but he became my best mate when he was there.

The objective seemed to be to remove any sense of self-worth among any of us and to create a group that would respond like twenty five Pavlovian dogs in a final marching contest against other squadrons that were being similarly treated. In that eight weeks I learned a lot by talking to my fellow sufferers. I learned that there were people whose outlook on life was very different from my own liberal theories, instilled in me by my church and my school. I learned that there were nasty as well as nice human beings, I learned to obey without question, I learned fear and I learned that I had a lot more to learn than I could ever contemplate. I grew up. I knew that, despite a classical education, I didn't know the half of it, and determined to do something about it.

The only success was on the day we spent shooting bullets from fairly archaic rifles, and learning how to strip and put them together again. It was the first time I had seen a rifle, never mind shot a bullet in anger and, in the shooting contest, I was lucky enough to get four bullets out of five so near enough to each other that they gave me a cross-rifle marksman award to sew onto my lower sleeve as a badge of pride. I was now eligible, but not inclined, to become trained as a sniper.

Saving Britain - Learning

The next stage was learning the jobs that we would have to do while in the RAF. This was to be in Hereford where beings called Clerks Progress and statisticians were taught the intricacies of standard deviations, regression theory, inferential and descriptive statistics, analytical methodology and econometrics. It had been some time since I had passed my O level in maths and for sure none of this was included in that syllabus. It was well above my knowledge grade but I applied myself to the theory and practice for another eight weeks, took the test and much to my surprise, earned myself a fortyeight hour passage home for passing with honours.

And now we were to be allocated to our respective RAF stations where we would put all this training into practice. Armed with this new knowledge, I was sent to Wattisham, an airfield in Suffolk where the latest fighter jets were housed. A day later I met my new leader, Sergeant Williams, who welcomed me to his group in a voice that seemed to say 'God save me from another bleeding wet behind the ears greenhorn'. Anyway, for better or for worse, my job was to count the airplanes out and then in again, keep tabs on how long they had been out and ensure that they had a service when it was due. I did wonder why we had learned all that complex statistical methodology when this was a task that could have been done by most primary school pupils.

However work was work. In my off days I explored the Suffolk countryside, often cadging a lift in another airman's car. Frequently too we would take the coach to London for a weekend in the flesh pots. There I would stay with my Uncle and Aunt, the latter a strong Methodist who made absolutely sure that I did not stray from righteousness. I played soccer for the station team and hung around in the Naafi, but mostly I read avidly and, to pass away the boredom, took another A level in Geography for the hell of it. I didn't get much help for this locally so I read my cousin's notes on the subject and, again much to my surprise, obtained a B pass.

Close to death

Then came the event that was to change my life forever. I had had a bad feeling in my stomach for a few days and mentioned it to the station doctor. He immediately assumed that I was trying to avoid the parade planned for the following Saturday, gave me an aspirin and dismissed me. I went on parade that Saturday but during the week the pain grew worse. The following weekend I had a 48 hour pass and decided to make the long journey back to Bolton to see the family. I took the train to London and then from Euston station to Manchester. The pain grew worse until somewhere between Crewe and Manchester something seemed to explode in my abdomen. The pain was not just intense, it was excruciating.

The other passengers showed sympathy but not much could be done in the half-hour left to reach Manchester, nor on the connection to Bolton. I caught the bus to home, crawled from the bus stop to my parents' house and collapsed on the doorstep. My mother, practical as she was, immediately contacted the doctor, by what means I do not know since we had no telephone in the house. And anyway I was out with the fairies. He arrived after half an hour and straight away called the ambulance. I was blue-lighted to the Bolton and District General Hospital and within fifteen minutes was in the operating theatre. The explosion that I had felt was peritonitis of the abdomen caused by a ruptured appendix. I later learned that another thirty minutes and I would probably not have survived. The doctor who had saved my life was from Cyprus and I am forever in his debt.

Enchantment

But this in itself was not what changed my life, though it certainly threatened it. This second explosion, of a different sort, happened in C recovery ward run by a fearsome ex-army matron called Sister Porter. The danger from the peritonitis was not yet over and I was still knocking on death's door. Shortly after I had

28

been laid sideways in my new hospital bed I noticed through the mist of pain a pair of black silk stockings coming towards the bed. The stockings stopped, sorted out the blankets, stuck something sweet in my mouth and then retreated. The pain eased.

Two hours later the same stockings turned up by my bedside, and fed me food. This happened every day several times. I found myself looking forward to the visit of the black silk stockings, indeed it was the only thing on earth that made keeping alive worthwhile. At this stage I had no idea who or what was motoring the stockings or even if this had perhaps only been the last mirage of a dying man. More days passed, and the owner of the stockings took shape as I was more able to look upwards.

It was a young 17 years old nurse, new to the ward, who had been assigned by sister Porter as my guardian angel. Her name was Margaret. I believe such nurses were called primroses at the time though I never understood why. It was she who made life worthwhile again and my recovery was accelerated while she attended to my every need. Came the time to leave the hospital two weeks later and I knew that I could not bear to be without this angel of mercy. So I asked her for a date for when she wasn't reviving dying airmen. For the next eight weeks, before I had to go back to Wattisham, I escorted her from hospital to home every working evening. We laughed and talked and discussed and eventually kissed. She lived in Deane, an area of semi-detached houses , albeit still two up two down, but with indoor toilet. So, in a sense, she was above my station. In the ensuing years I wrote poems to proclaim her beauty of body and soul. This lady has now been my wife for sixty years.

Back to education

On my return I was being posted to other places The first of these was back to RAF Hereford. They had been asking for someone to teach statistics to new recruits and I had applied. In spite of my lack of teaching experience it was accepted and I was on my way back to a more easy-going existence in the spring of 1954. Or so I thought. Teaching is not quite the sinecure people believe it to be, especially when you are nineteen years old without experience. And even though you think you know the subject matter you have to find a way to get it over to the people you are teaching. And many of these were older than me, not always with the mathematical skills for the course and well able to make life difficult if they didn't understand.

Equally there were people with degrees, even masters degrees, far more qualified than a mere holder of three, now four, dodgy A levels. At least I now had my own room at the end of the billet, as I had been promoted to Corporal, And my own record player. Here I learned to cope and often entertained those with a love of classical music like me in musical evenings in my tiny hovel. I was introduced to the delights of Beethoven's Missa Solemnis, which we played over and over again for lack of much else, except a small repertoire of music of all kinds that I had never experienced. It was a limited musical education. All in all, this was an atmosphere I thrived in. I played cricket for the Station team as the demon fast bowler, mostly with public school officers. I visited the 3 Cathedrals in Herford, Worcester and Gloucester, joined a choir, frequently ate out with my students in Hereford and dashed home every other weekend to meet my darling Maggie. Nirvana had arrived. As Plato wrote 'Happiness springs from doing good and helping others.' And that is what I was doing.

But paradise rarely lasts forever. The need to have statisticians dashing about the RAF declined and I was redundant, posted once more, this time to Weston Super Mare in Somerset where the RAF trained its drivers, and where my father had spent some of the war years. Since I could not myself drive it was not a teaching job. Indeed it was hardly a job at all. Certainly I was surplus to requirements for the most part and spent much of my evenings drinking the scrumpy in the local pub and staggering back to barracks as high as a kite. Weston Super Mare was a nice enough town with cafes and dance halls but this was 1956 and the haute cuisine of the standard café chef was corned beef with chips and beans. Don't get me wrong, I actually like corned beef. After all I had spent the postwar years eating it and acquired a taste, but there are limits. It seemed that I was simply passing the time waiting for demobilization.

Which came in Spring 1957. I handed in my RAF badge and paraphernalia and headed back home to Bolton. It was a strange feeling. The RAF had been my baby sitter for 3 years and it felt like I was being unleashed onto a hostile and unknown world. I had no job, few prospects and no idea what I really wanted to do, except marry Maggie.

Chapter Five

Adventures in Europe and Teacher Training.

'Buy a cycle and see the world'

'Become a teacher and forget the world'

Cycling through Europe

So I looked for an adventure beyond the shores of England, a dangerous place where monsters lived and danger always loomed. I tested my fitness on a bicycle ride. Not any old bicycle ride, you understand, but one which took me (and my friend, another Norman) from Bolton to Lucerne in Switzerland where there was a conference of young unitarians in the mountains above. It was an epic journey using the youth hostels in Germany, Belgium and France. We set ourselves a punishing schedule, often arriving at the hostel well into the night. For most of the journey through Germany we cycled down the motorways, illegal of course, and we were often honked but rarely stopped. Stoos, the conference centre, was high above Lucerne in the high mountains. It had to be reached by cable car. Neither of us had ever seen scenery so beautiful and fresh. We walked on a cloud of wonder at what nature could do to stimulate the senses.

At the conference there were young people from many countries, including one young lady, the daughter of a Hungarian pastor in Budapest, who had been shot in the foot the previous year during the Hungarian uprising against the Russian occupiers. We all joined in the discussions on leadership, life, love thy neighbor and how to create a perfect world before parting, ready to transform the world into a better place and vowing to keep in touch with each other, a promise that was never kept. We cycled back through France and Belgium to my darling Maggie. It was such a pity that she could not have been there in that paradise, but she too was already making the world a better place in the hospitals of Bolton. This was a journey which, later in life, I replicated in a car with Maggie and the children. And it even inspired me to write inspired but excruciating poetry about cycling on foreign roads. Here's a couple of examples. Prepare the sick bag.

A Bitter experience on Belgian Roads

Bumping, bouncing, deeply sighing
Nerves on edge and swear words flying
Jumping, jangling, mending, making
Now and then wild tempers breaking
Wheels revolving, onward battling
Saddles squeaking, mudguards rattling
Cycling upwards, onwards, downwards
Pedalling hillwards, windwards, townwards
Forward rolling, never stopping
Valleys passing, hills-a topping
Still the cobbles cut the tyres
Loosen spokes and sever wires
When they made these Belgian roads

They didn't allow for heavy loads
An aching back and blistered hands
It's hard to ride in foreign lands

©Norman Longworth 1957

Swiss Bliss - A tribute to Swiss Roads

Smoothly on with softly whispering sigh
Hills and valleys all glide swiftly by
Softly murmuring winds sing sad refrains
Harmonise and echo 'gainst the lanes
Fields of rain-soaked green a happy sight
Glistening lakes reflect the gleaming sun
Beauty all around for everyone
Nothing stirs, save birds and circling wheels
Village bells sound out their joyous peals
I owe this present state of perfect bliss
To these pressed-sand smooth roads built by the Swiss
©Norman Longworth

Teacher Training

It was 1957. Elvis Presley was in full voice, Dwight D Eisenhower was US president for a second term, Britain was recovering from the ill-advised invasion of the Suez Canal and the New Prime Minister, Harold Macmillan, was telling us how we had never had it so good under his government even while the IRA was bombing targets in Britain. And the Russians launched Sputnik, the first ever spacecraft. The European Economic Community was born comprising six countries, thus starting the healing of a thousand years of war. Many other things happened that year that would impact on the future but we didn't know it at the time.

I returned fitter than I had ever been since square-bashing. And now was the time to make a firm decision on a new life course by finding work. It was a casual conversation with one of my aunts that gave me the idea. Teaching she said. Long holidays and a regular income. And Britain is short of good teachers. Good idea. I already had some experience of that in the RAF, so I applied to the nearest teacher training college in Chester, a Church of England establishment, and was accepted for a two year course in preparation to be let loose on the children of Britain. Once more my Maggie, the girl from Deane, and I were separated by distance.

33

Chester really is a beautiful city. Its Cathedral of St Werburgh, its roman remains and amphitheatre, its medieval covered shopping centres, a racecourse, the ancient church of St John the Baptist, and the ramparts around the old town are well worth visiting. It was into this proliferation of historical monuments that I came in the September of 1957. The college was situated just outside the western side of the town within easy reach of the centre. It comprised an Anglican church, two halls of residence and a large area of sports ground, often waterlogged in rainy weather. Since that time it has become a full blown University, much enlarged with a syllabus that extends far beyond the training of teachers. At the time teachers were in short supply, hence the shortened course time for preparation.

The two halls of residence were insufficient to cope with the number of students and about half of us, including me, were farmed out to various houses in the vicinity. Mr and Mrs Turner welcomed me gladly into their house. I was the source of much-needed extra cash. Mr Turner was a retired bus driver and his wife had been a secretary in a local firm. They were a delightful couple always eager to help me, and they had a piano that neither of them could play. It had been bought for one of their children who had married and gone to live many miles away. They were delighted to hear that I had some rudimentary knowledge of music however bad, and I rewarded them, if that's the word, often with my recitals of the pop songs of yesterday plus the classical repertoire I had amassed in the old days at home. It wasn't pretty, certainly not as good as my Dad could have offered, but it was well-received, I think! Here I renewed my love of music and improved as I persevered.

There were about two hundred students, young aspiring teachers with, like me, absolutely no sense of what they were letting themselves in for. Everyone had their own subject specialisation, mine was Geography and French, plus additional lessons on sports, the theory of education and of course, religious education, this being a Church of England college. In the latter, unknown to the hierarchy, I was a heretic because of my Unitarian upbringing. I would tease them by asking which council of Nycaea they wanted to support.

(In effect there were two councils of Nycaea in the fourth century. It was a gathering of the bishops to determine whether Jesus was an outstanding prophet or the Son of God. The first council decided for the first, but the Emperor Constantine who was the chief convert and propagandist for the new Christian company declared that the masses would not be attracted unless that verdict was changed and called a second council packed by his followers to change it. A bit like the way the American republicans do things. Hence the Nycene Creed. Well that's my simplified story or conspiracy theory whichever way you want to take it). In the event it didn't cause much debate since no-one knew what on earth I was talking about.

Chester was my sportsground. I played soccer, cricket, tennis, table tennis and basketball for the college and ran the chess and geographical societies. For this latter I organized visits to companies and places of geographical interest and even a trip to London. Strangely, by popular demand, twenty-five percent of the visits, much in demand, were to breweries. I wrote poetry. I sang in the Llangollen Eisteddfod with the college choir. We came twenty eighth out of twenty nine in our class. That was put down to the fact that we weren't Welsh but I have doubts about that. Maggie visited me from time to time when she was not working weekends. The academic work was not terribly onerous but I learned much that I hadn't known before from the subject tutors, especially how to make the subject more interesting for children and how not to be an intellectual prig.

School Practice

There were two sessions per year of school practice and these were perhaps the most intimidating. Each time I was working with young children eight to ten years old and, unsurprisingly, they were very different from the adults I had taught in the RAF. The trick was to gain their attention, every one of them, not easy in classes of thirty five to forty. I had too to stick to the school's syllabus. But I was given carte blanche to do it my way, within reason of course. We were bussed early in the morning to the school where we were working. They were mostly schools in the Wirral area of Cheshire. One school in Birkenhead I remember well. I was working on a history lesson with thirty children aged nine and decided that we would create a medieval village with a gigantic castle in the middle of the room.

Each group of children had responsibility for a different part of the castle, the ramparts and its surrounding houses. We worked to a large blueprint which we all agreed upon. The walls, the keep, and other buildings would be created out of wood and glue and a great amount of plasticine was involved as well as other building materials. We improvised a lot. They loved it and every child was a part of the whole. There were some casualties as little girls got stuck to the wood and clumsy lads knocked down the wall they had just built.

The usual class teacher was fascinated. Then in walked an inspector from the government. He took one look at the edifice we had constructed and said 'Architectural work hey, old boy? ' Then walked out again. I never saw him again, but I think that he approved. I just wondered about the calibre of government inspectors and their qualifications for the job. The whole point was not the result but the camaraderie among the kids working together to create the village.

I made many friends in Chester and we stayed friends for a long time. The camaraderie of teachers. One in particular, another Dave, whose room in college I used when I was farmed out, and who used mine in the second year when he was roomless. He visited us regularly in our various homes abroad until a few years ago when his wife, also a teacher, contracted dementia. We are still in touch and visit occasionally when we are in England, but it is sad to see a once bright and vigorous lady in her present state. She barely recognizes us now.

But we graduated with various levels of success and were let out into the big wide world to do our worst on the children of Britain. It was a strange feeling for me. As if a new unknown responsibility in an unknown place with an unknown outcome had been placed upon me.

Chapter Six

Bullington School

'Educating is a two-way learning game'

'If the teacher wins the children lose'

A Proper Job

The two years had passed quickly, as they do when one is having a good time, and it came time to find a proper job and to exercise the skills and knowledge I had acquired at college. I was invited to an interview at the Bullington, a new school just opening in Bury, six miles up the road from Bolton. It was a mixed secondary modern school, a groupage for which I had not been trained, but starting with the two lower years from eleven to thirteen years old. I took it. And what an experience it was. Firstly the older cohort had been taken from other secondary schools and was a mixture of those whose parents had been dissatisfied with the education their children were receiving and wanted more rigour and those whom the other schools in the town were extremely glad to be rid of.

Secondly, it being a new school, and me being a raw teacher straight from college come to enlighten the pupils on the delights of geography and French, there was the small matter of providing books and other teaching aids. This had certainly not been on the college curriculum. I had now become head of two departments (unpaid) with absolutely no experience of teaching in a secondary school or what the tools of the trade were. The Bolton School had provided no help – this was far from being its world - and nor, for that matter, had Chester college. The books used there would not have been useful even if I could have remembered what they were. It was time for much research into the offerings of the various school book companies to find reading materials for an entry level I had no knowledge of and had never met.

Choosing Books

The choice was not easy. The majority were standard text books written by revered geographical experts with vast experience, providing all the essential facts about every aspect of the geography exam syllabus, boring as hell for the kids I would be teaching but guaranteed to force feed enough information to ensure a pass. The school had no examinations policy and, at that time, no decision on which examinations would be chosen. It was a period when there was a choice, each one having different requirements. City and guilds, the CSE, a sop for children of so-called lower intelligence, or the full blown O level in common with other schools. They chose all three.

I chose what I thought were books that would be both understandable and partly entertaining, though I was working from guesswork most of the time. The new head teacher was taken from an academically successful school some miles away to fashion Bullington into its image. There were four streams – level A those who were deemed to be reasonably intelligent bearing in mind that the grammar school had taken most of the intellectual talent, level B those who were deemed to be less intelligent, level C those who were not deemed to be intelligent at all, and finally the D stream - those who were said to be either a nuisance, mentally disabled, dyslexic or bordering on psychopathy.

Life in the lower regions

Into this pedagogical pit I was thrust as a rookie teacher with responsibilities. There were another two straight from college like me but the rest of the teachers were from other schools and it showed. It was not at all like the Bolton School and was underfunded every year by the Local Education Authority which controlled a family of six other underfunded secondary modern schools and two well-funded Grammar schools. It was a challenge in every sense. But in general we were all ready to make a success of this new venture whatever it took. The PE teacher was an energetic young man determined to make every child super fit and to ensure that the school football team would make its mark. For this he needed the help of others, and so, because games was another of my teaching responsibilities, I was appointed as the first year soccer coach.

This entailed fashioning a team out of a rabble, training them in the games lessons, taking them to inter-school matches and watching them lose to bigger, stronger and more disciplined teams. Over the years this changed as will be seen. The head teacher was a small, strange man who issued edicts on how to behave and administered corporal punishment to those who didn't. This was still the age when children could be physically assaulted by teachers. He believed in academic and sporting success and in examination achievement. Thus those children who were likely to pass the GCE, City and Guilds and the CSE examinations, were entered into their appropriate slot and those who might not pass at all were not entered. In this way the reputation of the school for examination success would be maintained.

Real geography

His deputy suffered badly. An honourable and empathetic man, he often had reservations about the educational policy of the school and did his best to mitigate the excesses, acting as a go-between between headmaster and staff. He became my mentor and fed and watered me when I had to stay behind for further punishment in an evening session. As for me I had my own interpretations from the training I received. I tried as much as possible to engage the children in the learning they were asked to do. I printed thousands of 'banda' sheets with questions and exercises so that they could study themselves, and then come together to discuss the results while I would expand on the content. I also recognized that Geography has never been inside a classroom and devised lessons to take the kids out to find it locally. Posses of children from my classes could be found wandering the streets around the school with their clipboards searching for geography. In this way they came to enjoy the lessons, but it is no longer an activity that would be allowed in these more restrictive times.

In the holiday periods I took groups of children to the Lake District staying in youth hostels and to the Isle of Skye camping, to climb mountains and learn about the geology of the land. I organized learning weeks in North Wales for lessons in Geography, History and English and took parties of children abroad to Austria, Holland and Italy. Those who could afford these outings loved it. They were my best pupils. As usual those families who couldn't afford it, of whom there were many were unable to profit from the insights the trips provided. For those in the lower streams who could only learn within the classroom I ordered geographical films and devised geographical games. Geography was always about discovery wherever it happened and the children were rarely bored. In the absence of cash to buy enough books I used the brochures that holiday organisations created to publicise their region.

Football Scouts

My football teams improved over time and started to win. Word got around the country and professional football scouts would turn up to watch always on the lookout for young talent. Don Revie, once the manager of Leeds United and eventually England appeared on the school football field, having heard on the grapevine that I had a couple of potential professional level players, and the manager of Bury football club paid the school several visits. The headmaster was delighted and ordered the girls domestic science department to make him eggs and bacon. You could tell he wasn't too happy about this, especially since no-one else was eating, but the head insisted and we all sat around the table watching him eat it somewhat self-consciously. Out in the playground during the summer I organized cricket practice with artificial wickets and gave lessons on bowling and batting. It was only what my own teachers had done some years previously albeit on a proper field with proper cricket balls and wickets.

Emulating the Beatles

The outside world was also changing. We were into swinging sixties, the Beatles, the Stones, the boybands proliferated like swarm of locusts. I was reminded about that when asked to be one of four teachers in a pupil-driven scheme to emulate the TV programme Juke Box Jury in which experts forecast if the song would be a hit or a miss, referring of course to the songs that were being written it seems by everyone between sixteen and twenty five. So I dressed the part with a Beatles wig, a Rolling Stones jacket and a guitar. They had contacted the local record shop and played a number of new items. I remember that one of them was 'The Mighty Quinn' by Manfred Mann. I gave it a miss and of course it became a number one within the next two weeks. Likewise all my hits seemed to be never played again.

When asked why at the end, I said that none of them were as good as Beethoven's ninth, which produced some puzzlement as to which boy band was singing that at the time. Elsewhere Kennedy had become the President and within three years was assassinated, as was Martin Luther King later. And in 1964 Harold Wilson was elected the first labour Prime Minister since the Attlee Government after the war.

Teaching French

Back at Bullingdon, teaching French was another story. Some of the children were eager to learn but it didn't come as easy to them as they hoped. We did organize speaking groups where they practiced what few words they had learned but language booths had not yet been invented and nor was the idea of visits or months abroad with another family possible in such a working class area. The intellectual effort of learning a new language without such support was beyond them. It may be because I was a lousy languages teacher, though I did meet a couple of old pupils years later in Paris. They spoke English.

Abused kids

Pastoral care was also a project of the future. Many of these children were from one parent families and others were abused at home. I knew because they confided in me what their parents had done to them, whether it be fathers abusing daughters, beating the kids or mothers on drugs. There were families with multiple children that could not cope and at least a third of the school intake would be the subject of social service visits. The home environment in the catchment area was not exactly conducive to good educational standards and pupils brought some of their damage to school. Most of these kids were down in the C and D streams. They had no interest in learning and were only there because they had to be. Motivating them to learn was a constant struggle.

There were at least eight children with sociopathic and even psychopathic tendencies who bullied and led their classmates into rebellion. A little like a certain American President in 2020. These were a terror to teach and impossible to discipline. Sometimes they would be away in a young person's prison. Some teachers did not turn up on the days they were due to have these classes and it was up to the rest of us to cope instead. Most of these children were not unintelligent, indeed some were very capable of being much higher in the school hierarchy but they chose to remain where they didn't have to conform.

There was however among those in the D stream a quiet boy who would write reams and reams of what seemed to us to be gobbledy gook. When asked to say what it meant he gave a perfectly valid explanation. Indeed much of it was of a high level of perception. This was my first encounter with dyslexia. That the boy was highly intelligent was obvious but, because he could not write it intelligibly, he was banished to the D stream. I wondered how many of these lost clever children there were throughout the country because of ignorance of their condition.

Married at last

To back up a little, to the biggest change of all. On Christmas Eve 1960 Maggie and I were married in the Unitarian Free church on Halliwell Road. It was a happy affair for the hundred or so people who packed the church and even more so for the guests who stayed behind to partake of the food afterwards. Maggie looked gorgeous in her wedding dress and even I remembered to wear a tie. Neither of us came from rich families but our parents did us proud. There were the usual speeches of goodwill and the afternoon was spent in my Uncle Cecil's car on our way to our honeymoon in the Strand Palace Hotel in London. Although not the Ritz this is one of the posher hotels in the capital city and certainly way beyond anything we could normally afford. We could afford only three days exploring London before we needed to return to the daily grind back in Lancashire, but they were certainly very enjoyable. We returned to our semi-detached and our various callings with renewed energy.

Helping bruised kids

Bullington was still the centre of my working life and it wasn't easy. In other places, such as Finland and the Far East where education is taken very seriously, there are psychologists, specialist teachers and a whole range of professional aids to detect and ameliorate the lot of children with problems. In the Bury of the early 1960s they didn't exist and in most places in the UK they still don't. Education at this level has lower priority in Britain. But we did what we could. One boy in my class lost his father at the age of twelve. He transformed quickly from being a very good pupil to being a horror. He refused to do homework and threw tantrums in the classroom. At home his behaviour became unacceptable.

His mother came to me to ask what could be done since I was his favourite teacher. I had long chats with him, but what brought him back on track were the Lake District excursions. He became a different person in the mountains. He enjoyed the buzz one gets after achieving the top of Scafell Pike or Helvellyn. He washed the dishes at the youth hostels. He was always the first to lead others up a steep hill. Gradually he settled down again and returned to normal. Eventually he passed his O levels and the last time I met him much later, I was thrilled to know that he was the village policeman in Patterdale in the Lake District.

Leonard

The tale of Leonard is also a tribute to the power of mountains. Leonard was from a one parent family in the terraces near the school. He had several siblings and spent much of his time out with his mates in the street. They were well known to the local policemen. At school he was in the C stream, the not unintelligent but not very motivated by education section. I was organizing a trip to Skye to climb mountains. Leonard said to me that he might like to go. This was a surprise since he had never shown much enthusiasm for anything at school.

The family had no money so I paid for him, not difficult since we were travelling in my own converted Ford Transit (that too of course would not be allowed today). We arrived there after a 12 hour journey and erected the tents in a field near Broadford. The first day after breakfast we were to climb Beinn a Caillach, not one of the Cuillins but still over 3000 feet high. We set out. The rest of the lads started up the path. I was half way up to the first bend when I noticed that Leonard was still at the bottom. So I walked back and asked him why. 'I'm not bloody going up there' he said. 'Why not – all the others are going' 'Just not going up there.' 'Look I can't leave you here on your own' I said, 'Tell you what, just come with me to the first bend and let's see.'

Reluctantly he agreed to that. We got to the first bend and I showed him the way to the second bend. 'Look if you can do that you can get that far' I said. Grumbling and cursing to himself he walked to the second bend. 'Look we're nearly half way now' I said lying through my teeth. 'You might as well go the rest of the way.' More grumbling but he set out on the third, fourth and fifth bends and decided he might as well go to the top. At the top he sat on the cairn and surveyed the stunning scene. Mountains on the mainland , a view over to the Cuillins, lakes, blue sky and a new sense of achievement. It was so obvious that he had experienced an epiphany. He saw and recognized beauty perhaps for the first time. 'Bloody 'ell Sir' he said 'I'm glad you got me here.' Thereafter we had no further problem either on the trip or in school. And that is what teaching is all about. Changing perceptions, inspiring, opening minds, widening horizons. Would that this happened to all youngsters.

Home thoughts

Not that that was the school ethos. The be-all and end-all of most schools, including Bullington, is getting pupils through examinations. That is what parents want. Something to open the doors to a job. I have no quarrel with that. But in my mind education is about something much greater and that is a theme I will elaborate later. Maggie was working during the day as assistant to a general practitioner, while at the same time bringing up our children. We lived in a three bedroomed semi-detached house near to her mother and overlooking a park, and a view to the Croal valley, Bolton's only river, in the distance. It had a fairly large garden in which the children played with the dog. A cat and a rabbit in a hutch made up the whole menagerie. It had cost us the princely sum of 1500 pounds. For me it was very heaven.

Maggie was a conscientious worker and, being a nurse, was forever trying to make the house spotless. This is not easy with two young children and a husband with no sense of tidiness. Apart from a little trouble with the local teenagers who congregated around the park entrance, as teenagers do, and sometimes kept the children awake it was an idyllic place to be. Every morning early I would wait for one of my colleagues to arrive and then drove us both to work. Every evening late I would return, often with a bag of books to mark which took me into the small hours.

Back to real life. To make ends meet I took up another job three evenings a week in a youth club in Westhoughton, a village close to Bolton. I tried playing the piano in a pub but they weren't enamoured by the music I played, much of it classical and I wasn't able to play by ear. I taught night school geography to the local constabulary. In the holidays, as we have seen, I took the schoolchildren to exotic places. I was neglecting my own family in the name of education. I was a becoming a stranger to my own children. We did have family outings and kept in touch with friends but it wasn't satisfactory. Not that sweet Maggie complained. She was always busy on one thing or another. But it was time to move on. I left Bullington after six years. The pay of a teacher for creating miracles is not what it should be. By this time, I had a wife and two young children and we found it difficult to make ends meet. Time to move on into pastures new.

Chapter Seven

IBM UK

'Contrary to common belief, Computers can't do your thinking for you'

'You have to do the thinking for them'

A change of life

I looked in the advert pages for a better paying post and eventually spied one from IBM requiring an education developer. I asked around about the company and received positive answers. This was one of the world's foremost companies and looked after its staff royally. Despite having no knowledge at all about computers I applied. My first interview was in Liverpool. This was with a recruiter who didn't know much about the job itself, only that it had something to do with developing courses. I told him about my experience and my novel approach to education including the discovery methods I adopted in school.

This seemed to please him and I was sent to London for the second interview, all expenses paid, to meet the departmental head of education in IBM UK. Here I was grilled. IBM sets high standards in its education effort. He told me about the job, which entailed creating written courses on new hardware and software so that the ever-increasing expenditure on instructors could be kept under control. Programmed Instruction was the buzzphrase, and it seemed to fit my discovery learning experience. I was required to teach a model lesson to a group of the instructors, so I taught them about the continental shelf through the eyes of a diver who eventually fell off it into the deep ocean. This caused amusement for some of the spectators, though one of them without a visible sense of humour thought I was being flippant. I confessed to a lack of knowledge of computers which my future boss said was no problem since that would be provided. And the job was mine.

Now came the task of persuading Maggie that this was a good thing. She had her own career in nursing and to move the family lock, stock and children to London would be an enormous upheaval for a Bolton girl, born and bred. The children too, were now five and three years old, and would have to adapt to a new school in a new environment where people spoke in a funny dialect. But she agreed and we searched for accommodation in a city where houses were more than twice as expensive and travelling to work was a pain in the neck.

Harrow

We found a house in Harrow within our inflated price range. It entailed a larger mortgage and a long trek to work, on the metropolitan line into the city. It was a terraced construction but had three bedrooms in a respectable area and a fairly large garden. At five and a half thousand pounds it was double the price we obtained for our semi-detached in Bolton, and with no view of either valleys or hills, just houses upon houses. We found a good school nearby for the children and Maggie quickly found a new job. After working in A and E at a large hospital up the road, she became the district midwife for the London Borough of

Harrow. Thus, although our outgoings had more than doubled our income had tripled. IBM paid well.

It was January 1966 and I was thirty years old. Maggie was 28 and leaving Bolton for the first time, though she had had many holidays in Ireland at her Grandmother's house. We moved into our new home in the middle of one of the coldest winters in memory. I became a commuter together with another hundred thousand people strap-hanging their way to work on the Metropolitan line from North Harrow to Baker Street, and walking to my place of work in St John's Wood near to the Lord's Cricket Ground. Here I was to learn what it takes to be a systems engineer in the largest and richest computer company in the world.

New Challenge

The course was tough, very tough. Mathematical thinking had atrophied in my brain, even if it had ever existed, and the talktalk way of learning how to programme computers was boring and yawn-making. My colleagues on the course were almost all straight from university with first class degrees in mathematical science and often with an early computer knowledge far superior to mine. Nor were there any who had had a back street education. Educationally the methodology comprised long boring lectures from experts who knew their stuff, but had little clue on how to get it over. I could certainly see how the system needed improvement. It was all so strange and, at times, mysterious.

It was here, among these high flyers, that I met George, a colleague of my own age but with a physics and mathematics background from Cambridge and the brain of a genius. He, more than anyone helped me cope with the new concept of making computers do what they were built to do. We still converse after more than 50 years. Of course there were practical lessons when I had to create machine code and subject my efforts to the computer for verification. I could just about cope with that and eventually some of the other aspects seeped into my reluctant brain. There were also practical lessons when we were attached to people who were actually doing the job, often in the customer environment throughout the night.

Eventually the course examination loomed and we all braced ourselves to parrot back the concepts we had learned and prove practically that we could be let out with real customers without bringing their precious machines to a halt. This of course was not to be my fate. I was recruited to work in the educational department writing self-study modules that would speed up the time needed to learn, and to reduce the burgeoning number of people in the educational schools. IBM was at the height of its power and number one company in the world. As it happened, I did pass the course and became a systems engineer in name though not in practice.

A job for Maggie

Back in the home Maggie was searching, and finding, nursing jobs. To repeat, she first joined an A and E department in Hillingdon hospital, dealing with a variety of ailments that usually result from stupidity, and later returned to the branch of nursing she had trained to do in Bolton. She became the district midwife for Harrow. It was, if you'll forgive the pun, a harrowing job. But first she had to learn how to drive a car and, rather than pay for a professional, I was elected as principal instructor. It was another harrowing time. I began to understand why driving instructors have such a permanent look of terror.

We spent time inadvertently parked on pavements wondering how we got there, and the number of times we threatened oncoming motorists is legion. But she was a quick learner. She had to be. It was quick or dead. For the actual driving test Maggie wore her midwife's uniform as a large hint that the new babies of Harrow would lose out if she didn't pass. She did. And to be fair she was one of the safest drivers in London, a city with more lunatics on four wheels than normal. Except when pursuing ambulances containing patients to the hospital.

In the pursuit of her vocation she spent long hours on call, a hundred and twenty in a week followed by a week of fifty. She could be, and was, summoned at any time of the night or day to help bring a new entry into the world, sometimes for a long period of time if the birth was difficult. When not doing that she had a punishing round of visits to pregnant ladies in houses from mansions to hovels, mostly the latter. She was the foremost district midwife in the borough, with a responsibility for teaching young nurses on the job. She bore that burden with a an energy that would put teenagers to shame. Often I would come home to a message that said 'dinner in the oven' and be awakened at two in the morning by her need to attend an impending birth somewhere on her watch. She made light of the job, considering it her pleasure as well as her duty. She was, and still is, that sort of lady.

The children

As for David and Jeannette, our children, they must have wondered what sort of planet they had landed on. A mum who frequently dashes through the door to attend a pregnant patient and a dad who spent long hours in the smoke and evenings and weekends at sport. More of that soon. Luckily there were fallbacks. They both had plenty of friends in Harrow and when there was no-one at home they would spend time with them. They were both intelligent kids and self-sufficient at an early age. They had to be. Of course we also had frequent family outings, taking advantage of visits to the treasures of London, playing in the local parks and, during the summer holidays camping in France and other exotic places, or driving to cheap hotels in Spain.

RPG

Back in my workplace, things changed. Having made the grade as a computer expert I was now eligible to do the job I had been recruited for. I was moved to the brand new IBM Education Centre in the next borough to Harrow. It was certainly very different from Bullington School. On the first day I was thrown the manuals for a new software program called RPG, Report Program Generator, which used the concepts of Boolean algebra to get the machine to understand what was required of it. It was a simple concept based on the logic of and-or, not and-or. If this sounds difficult, it did to me before I fully understood.

The next step is to make the computer understand through punched cards that convey the message to the machine. For mercy's sake I won't elaborate further. My task was to thoroughly understand how the machine could be programmed in this manner and then write a programmed instruction book for others to replicate this understanding in the workplace. Simple! I was then told to become the country expert on this programming language. Very different from Geography and French with class 3B. More learn it yourself using the manual and then getting others to learn it themselves using Programmed Instruction. I accomplished the first part of this task within the month I was allocated, and moved on to complete the second part within the next 2 months.

Baby-sitting the boss's son

Then came another challenge. The son of the IBM worldwide boss in America was sent to the UK to learn about computers. He had no knowledge at all from his privileged education at an American private school. He came with his wife. The UK company pondered over what to do with him that was worthwhile. Then one of the Directors had this great idea of creating a new accounting system that any company could use using RPG as the methodology. And no prizes for guessing who was given the job of baby-sitting the son and teaching him the language.

This was a task of huge proportions. RPG was not the right computer language for such a complex exercise, I didn't have the knowledge of accountancy and, worst of all, the son was not really interested in learning anything. For him this was a jolly in London and an opportunity to visit the nightclubs and enjoy himself. The project was doomed before it began. I could get round the RPG bit by recruiting George to help but I couldn't do anything about the reluctance to learn. We did have several lessons and I did teach him the rudiments of the language. But he had no intention of doing anything that stretched the brain beyond the pursuit of happiness.

We also had some great conversations about such arcane subjects as skidooing in the Allegheny mountains, American food (he found the average British meal insufficiently large), his college experiences, where he was going to take his wife in the evening and so on but he was not at all committed to the task he had been set. Which of course affected my situation in the company. I became his chauffeur in my Austin 35 which was three times smaller than the cars he was used to and frightened him to death with my London-necessary driving.

I visited him in the hospital where he was confined for a week for an operation on his foot which he had kept until he could have it free on the National Health Service. After six weeks he returned to the USA, still computer illiterate, to take a place at the Harvard Business School thanks to the wealth of his father. I never heard from him again but I do know that he didn't take over from his father as the boss of IBM. Which was a blessing for the company.

Psychocybernetics

Another of my responsibilities in the education development department was to assess new methods of learning. I had always regarded learning as a holistic process involving finding a new dynamic from the brain, using different ways of self-motivation and exercising the body. So every time a new methodology came around I was encouraged to pursue it. One such was 'Psychocybernetics' an import from the USA run by a self-styled guru called Dr Maxwell Maltz. He described it as 'the power of self-affirmation and mental visualization techniques using the connection between the mind and the body.' Which is gobbledy-gook for treating the brain as if it were a computer.

He recommended techniques to develop a positive inner goal as a means of developing a positive outer goal and applying the cybernetic theories of John von Neumann with methods of self-stimulation. Which is more gobbledy-gook. He came to London to advertise the power of his theories and I was elected to take the course. I attended his lessons for ten weeks and even wrote a book for him describing how a computer takes in information and processes it as an analogy for human learning. The class went through exercises to activate body with brain, but in the end I found it was more snake-oil than a scientific stimulator and ended my connection with it.

Success in sport

Harrow was also the centre of my greatest sporting achievements. I joined a cricket and tennis club not far from my home. I played for the tennis team and in the club competitions during the summer evenings and for the cricket team on Saturdays. Although I had won a few trophies from my time in Bolton I found the standard of both sports much lower in Harrow. In the North sport is more like war than a game. It is played with an intensity that puts winning as the only worthwhile goal, although the war is over after the game is done. A little like Rugby.

In Harrow the objective of sport was to obtain gentle exercise and to play the game as good sports, gentlemen and ladies alike. I became the club singles and doubles tennis champion for each of the six years we were there and headed the bowling and batting averages at cricket. Maggie and the children occasionally came along to watch, though it's not certain what they were thinking while they were watching Daddie running around a tennis court while swinging a bat with strings on it. They were all certainly there at the ceremonies on presentation night. I also took up playing squash in the education centre gym. Here I was out of my depth against the former public school champions who also played there. It was great exercise, but also a sober learning curve.

Friday night was bridge night. Many of my colleagues at work played the game and came to our house to practice. It started around 8pm when the children were in bed and went on to the small hours. They were all so competitive that they were reluctant to leave until they were winning. Maggie supplied the snacks and drinks and went to bed leaving us to fight it out. At that time the IBM team was Number three in Britain and occasionally members of the team would also join in. We gave them a good run for their money, and occasionally, when the cards were on our side, beat them.

A new challenge

IBM believed in its inmates changing jobs every three years. In this way everyone could have a knowledge of many parts of the company prior to becoming a knowledgeable director if one ever achieved that status. And so, after three years in education development I was transferred to the public relations department that operated from the centre of London. It was still education but this time I was tasked with increasing IBM's image in the schools of Britain. There was no guidance mostly because it had never been done before. It was up to me to find ways of achieving that as a goal.

Computer education was just then increasing in the mathematics departments of the schools and IBM wanted to be a part of that, even though the schools could not afford the IBM prices for computers. Other British companies had developed small affordable computers for use in schools whereas IBM was still the big machine company. It wasn't until 1984 that the company brought out its first PC. This was 1969. Neil Armstrong and his co-astronauts had landed on the moon, the Beatles had sung their last song together, there were riots in Northern Ireland and Bob Dylan came to the Isle of Wight Festival together with 150,000 other people. Monty Python's Flying Circus first hit the BBC.

I was now representing the company on several national committees. One of them was the UK subsidiary of the prestigious International Federation for Information Processing (IFIP) and others were more concerned with business development for young people. It was through the former that I instigated regional IBM schools cup competitions. We would choose a subject such as programming, or computer knowledge, publicise it through the Local Education Authorities and on the day of the competition a group of us would turn up as judges. It was highly successful and enhanced the image of the company as supporters of education.

Schools were always short of learning materials in the subject. I trawled through what was available from the company and there was a surprisingly large number of publications that would be usable. So I created the IBM Schools and Colleges information service, a free source of reading materials for ages eleven to eighteen. I also wrote several books on computing for youngsters to add to the mix. It was very popular. Schools were not used to receiving reading materials free of charge. I travelled around the country giving lectures on computers and information processing and displaying the bits and pieces of a computer, printing mechanisms, memory, motherboards, CPU boards, valves, transistors, integrated circuits etc showing stages of development and much more.

It involved much travel to all parts of the UK and speaking to high level government and local government people about how to improve computer education in the schools.

Chapter eight

Back into the Learning Fold

'What we see and consciously remember in our environment is only a tiny fraction of what we see'

A change of scenery

This period from 1969 to 1973 was a happy time of my life. I had carte blanche to do anything I wished within reason, a budget with which to do it and a successful time educating teachers and lay people alike. I often went to schools to talk to the children, including some of the poshest in the UK. I had excellent colleagues both inside and outside of IBM. However life changes frequently. IBM then had one of its periods of austerity. A new leader in the USA who reduced the budget of what he considered to be unnecessary activities. My department was asked to reduce its manpower by one means or another. I took this as an opportunity to fill a huge gap in my life, that of never having been to university or obtained a degree.

I suggested that I could serve the company, and myself, by spending three years at university on full pay. I had already prepared for this with a friend from the IFIP committee and ascertained that I could follow a Masters degree without first having a bachelors, subject to the agreement of the university that I was capable handling the intellectual challenges, which I ostensibly was. I found a place in the education department of Southampton university to pursue a research based Master of Philosophy degree, though philosophy had little to do with the actual subject. Immanuel Kant, Voltaire and Bertrand Russell could rest secure in their graves.

A Lymington Paradise

It was the period of the oil shortage, the three day week and the resignation of the American President to avoid being impeached. Northern Ireland was in Turmoil and Britain was in the process of joining the European Community. And so the family found itself on the move once more, much to the chagrin of my son David who had just passed the 11+ and spent the first term in Harrow Grammar School. Jeannette was much more amenable. But Maggie, being the wonderful wife she was, agreed and off we went to live on the South Coast of England. The company paid the removal fees.

Lymington is a one of the main centres for yachting in the UK. At the mouth of the River Lymington it has two harbours and a ferry service to the Isle of Wight. The harbours are awash with yachts ranging from racing boats to the Gin Palaces that cruise the seas and oceans. The one and only High Street is a Georgian delight with shops of every type. It extends into a cobbled passageway down to the waterfront where the yachty boutiques can be found. There are pedestrian footpaths along the Solent, the water passage to the Isle of Wight and eventually to the English Channel. The surrounding countryside is every walkers idea of paradise.

Nearby, the New Forest, its beautiful villages and its wild ponies. Further along the coast are the villages of Milford on sea and the stony beach out to Henry the Fifth's castle opposite the Needles. According to the Daily Telegraph, Lymington is now reputed to be the number one place to live in Britain with house prices to match.

So into this paradise one day in August 1972 we established ourselves in a detached house with the eponymous name of 'the Captain's Cabin' near the waterfront of Lymington one of the prettiest towns in Hampshire. We established the children in appropriate schools, David in Priestlands Comprehensive and Jeannette in Lymington Junior. The one thing that had survived the upheaval was the schools and colleges Information Service. That was outsourced to the room behind the garage with Maggie as chief, and only, Librarian, for which she was paid by IBM.

Information into insight

It was an eighteen mile drive to Southampton University but when I turned up at the department of Education I was given a room in one of houses across the road. I had discussed beforehand what the research I would be doing would be. It also included a great deal of development work in creating and testing course modules for secondary schools on the subject of information processing in all its facets, much as I had been doing for IBM but with a different audience and a much modified subject. It seemed to be appropriate given the increased interest in schools in the subject and the importance that information handling had attracted. We found a school in Winchester that was willing to test the output and for the next three years my Master of Philosophy project was en marche. I would provide the subject matter and advice on how to approach it and the teacher I was working with would pass it on to the children.

As an example the introductory lesson 'Information all around us' took the children in small groups out into the vicinity of the school to document all the information they could find. Back in the classroom they would relate what they had documented. It was interesting to see their results. Some had focused on the houses, the streets they were in, their architecture, addresses, even the door knockers. Other groups had concentrated on the streets themselves, the signs of civilization, the grids with the name of the manufacturer, the electricity wires, the water board indicators.

They were then asked to describe their new insights about information, how it is all pervading around us without us paying much attention to it. Or as the module introduction describes it 'What we see and consciously remember in our environment is only a tiny fraction of what we remember.' It was all a lot of fun and a lot of learning. And that learning was generated by the children themselves through the exercises they were completing. It followed my educational philosophy of discovery.

Over the months and weeks that followed there were activity lessons on how information was handled with and without computers, how each different person would obtain and use it, how it could be sometimes misused, how the police collected and used it, What information was in the school and how the head teacher would use it, how companies needed it to survive, how information is classified. The national Transport and Road Research laboratory was nearby and the course ended with a visit by the children to learn how they gather information, what information they gather and how they use it to improve conditions on the roads.

There were nine long modules in total and each module had five or more lessons - more than seven hundred pages of notes, exercises for the children and recommendations for teachers. At the end of the course children were much wiser about the impact of information on everyday life and this followed through to the other subjects they were learning. All of this experience over three years was written up into the M.Phil research thesis describing what happened, why it happened, how it happened and where it happened. The adjudicator, from a different university, recommended it for a PhD but that apparently was impossible for someone with no first degree. The boy from the back streets of Bolton was now a Master of Philosophy, whatever that implied.

As always there was the difficulty of making something that was not on the standard school syllabus more available to schools. Especially since there was no examination in information studies and parents were very reluctant to condone anything that wouldn't provide a certificate, as we had discovered during the trials. And, after all, this was only a research project for an M.Phil degree no matter how much the children had profited from it. However, after the research had been published in the university journal, as were all such projects, the course found its way by mysterious means to Australia and the USA and was taught, without my knowledge, in schools there. I discovered the Australian connection during my first visit to Australia much later in 1984. The course written in 1976, now resides on the shelf in my office in the South of France next to the thesis.

There is still much more to be written about information and the way the all-pervasive misinformation in today's politics and press, has corrupted today's society. I would suggest that, if everyone had taken that course in school since 1976, they would be much more inclined to make sensible decisions based on their ability to interpret the information. The ever accelerating pace of change has left many behind. But then that is only my opinion. And I could be biased.

Councillor Maggie

Meanwhile back at home, Maggie had become ever more bored with her job as librarian. So she decided to enter into local politics and stood as an independent for the Lymington Town Council. She was duly elected and her energy in supporting the local population led to her becoming the chairperson of the community section, organizing sports and leisure facilities for all ages. Eventually she was offered the chance to become the first female Mayor of Lymington in nine hundred years.

However, by this time she had passed on the IBM schools and colleges work to an IBM centre in Hursley and started to do what she knew and loved best, nursing. The uneven hours made it impossible for her to accept the offer and it went to yet another man. Midwifery was not one of the specialities of Southampton General Hospital, one of the foremost research hospitals in Britain, and so Maggie retrained as a neurological nurse, eventually climbing the ladder to the sisterhood. She once again worked odd hours, often with split shifts between morning and evening. But she was in her own habitat, the hospital and very happy with it.

Home chores

This period of working locally and spending more time at home meant more time with the children. David was doing well at school and had made many friends. When not doing homework he was out meeting his mates. He joined the local Sea Scouts which met in the hut at the bottom of the lane twice a week. He was, too, becoming more interested in cricket and we spent several hours batting and bowling in the path up to the garage. It reminded me of the back streets of Bolton, though in a different theatre. The offdrive was still the only possible stroke available. Jeannette had now joined him at Priestlands school and was making her own elite clique of inseparable friends, a bit like Enid Blyton's fabulous five. She was also learning to swim under the tutelage of the British Swimming coach in Southampton. Twice a week Maggie would take her at 6am to the swimming pool for lessons. Although she never made it to the Olympics, she is still an excellent swimmer.

What neither of them were doing was to help me in the acre long garden. I had overturned a large area at the end as a potagerie where I grew forked carrots, strangely shaped cabbage, limp lettuce, onions, curly kale and tons and tons, or so it seemed, of broad beans. These were our staple diet, except for Jeannette who hated them with a vengeance. We always had a surplus to give to anyone who would take them. I also made home grown wine from the bounty of the garden. Plum wine, apple wine, carrot wine and of course bottles and bottles of broad bean wine. Visitors were treated to copious quantities of the latter, and we wondered why their number seemed to decline. Plums were the other crop that produced a super-surplus. We could have opened a plum shop with the bounty of the plum tree.

Sport again

Shortly after arriving in Lymington I joined the tennis club and a Cricket club from one of the villages up the road, Hordle. The tennis didn't last long. The courts were not well kept, the membership was low and only occasionally was it possible to play. In the first year I reached the final of the annual tournament and just lost. There wasn't a second year, not because I lost but because there wasn't the variety of players that there were in Harrow. That was the last time I played the game until I went to Belgium in the 1980s. The cricket however was different. We played in all the beautiful, and sometimes weird, cricket grounds in the New Forest league and beyond. One of these, I remember was situated on a hillside. While the pitch itself was on a flat plateau, the rest of it was either well above or well below. Furthermore it had a large thorn bush behind one of the wickets, so that when the ball went into it, there was a reluctance for anyone to go and find it. Meanwhile the batsmen were running between the wickets. It's the only pitch I ever played on where 12 runs were scored while the ball was being retrieved. I played in the New Forest for eleven years and as soon as he was seventeen David joined me in the team. Modesty forbids me to say how many trophies came my way in that period.

Chapter Nine

Return to IBM UK

'Whatever you do, do it well'

'Well, as well as you can do it!'

But all good things come to an end and in 1977 I had to return to the company that was paying my salary. I was forty one years old and unwilling to leave Lymington because of the upheaval to the childrens' education at such a sensitive age. Elvis Presley died at the age of forty two, though millions claim to have seen him since, Jimmy Carter became President of the USA, The Clash released their first Album and France renounced the guillotine. I was offered a job in New York which I declined for the same reason and returned to London at IBM's smart new London Office near to Waterloo station.

I commuted the one hour twenty minutes from Brockenhurst to Waterloo on the 7.10am train and back again on the 5.30pm. In the morning I slept most of the way. In the evening there was a party almost every trip, business commuters from Winchester, Southampton and beyond taking advantage of the train's bar to empty the whisky and the gin bottles. I travelled as far as Winchester with my boss and he could certainly put it away. Several times I would join in, go to sit down and find myself in Bournemouth 30 miles past my destination of Brockenhurst. Whereupon I had to catch the next train back that stopped there.

The IBM-Woodberry Down project

As for the work I did, the work with non-IBM organisations increased. My equivalents in the other large companies, British Petroleum, Marks and Spencer, ICL, British Telecom and more had frequent meetings with me to discuss how we could cooperate. I was co-opted onto the Government's microelectronics in schools project and worked well with the directors of that. I retained my links to IFIP. The IBM cup programme was lost but I started a brand new project that linked just one IBM location with one school with difficulties in Inner London.

The IBM-Woodberry Down school link was my major project. We called it schools-industry twinning. Woodberry Down, an inner city school, had a rich ethnic mix within its catchment area and a high proportion of one-parent families. It is situated in a difficult area of inner London with an unenviable local crime record, where only the suicidal policemen patrol alone at night and where there is very little background of learning success. By contrast, the city location of the mighty IBM, three miles away, was situated in one of the richest areas in the world, employed seven hundred highly trained professional people – systems analysts, salesmen, managers, experts on all aspects of computing, many of them commuting in from their four-bedroomed houses with large garden in the more affluent suburbs of London.

Michael Marland, a well-known Headteacher in the inner London Authority was the driving force and he worked with me to establish the boundaries. These two apparently incompatible organizations began to explore how one could help the other. So meetings were held at both places and a social evening was arranged.

60

As a result of this, a coordinator, actually the wife of one of the IBM managers, formerly a social worker, was employed to actually organize the links. She talked at length with the staff of the school and with the managers in the IBM location and how the skills and knowledge of one could be used to improve the situation of the other. The IBM people, who had the right spend five percent of their working time on community projects, were given the opportunity to volunteer to work with the school. Seventy of them, ten percent, said yes.

As result a series of joint projects and events took place over the next two years which changed the outlook of teachers and IBMers towards each other, broke down the stereotypes and provided valuable human, intellectual, social and financial resources for both the school and the work location. For example, teams of IBM people met with school-leavers to advise on interviewing skills, running mock interviews to point out to the youngsters how they could improve their performance.

The company commissioned and paid for a large collage to be constructed by the art class for display in the foyer of the city location. This provided a talking point for visitors (which included the then prime minister, James Callahan, who I met at his visit – he showed a great deal of interest in the project) and an increase in schools industry activities by other city companies. Each term a discussion session between teachers and IBMers on a particular topic – leadership, management, computing in education etc – was held at the school and at the IBM location for an exchange of views leading to action, for example, teachers attended IBM management courses to extend their performance, computers were donated and expertise was extended to teachers and children, children visited the IBM location to give them a better understanding of the work environment, mentoring, and so on.

My favourite was when members of Covent Garden Opera, with whom the company was working on creating a new ballet, gave a demonstration at the school and got the children involved – this was great fun and changed their minds about music and musicians. In all there were thirty different projects during the four year period of the link. They revitalized the school, inspired the children, gave new insights about education to the IBM people, opened minds and widened horizons. It stopped when Mrs Thatcher closed down the Inner London Education Authority. If this can be done in one small part of a city, how many children could be rescued from a life of crime, poverty and disruption by similar schemes throughout each country. The cost was negligible – it relies mainly on the contribution of time, talent and ideas by many people on both sides of the education/industry divide.

Having originated it, it was now my task to expand the methodology to other companies and schools in the UK. I wrote a book about the experiment and organized seminars for companies around the UK. I became the chairman of the national schools-industry committee. Those who attended my seminars became convinced about the need for companies to help schools but not always in this way. Their ethos of contribution to the community was not as well-developed as IBM's, nor did they have a scheme to release people from work for a period in the week. While the incidence of Schools-Industry cooperation increased it was not always through twinning. In this period I also responded to demands for public speaking in many parts of the UK and abroad, mostly from local authorities eager to improve their knowledge of the computer revolution and the ways it would affect education, and of course schools-industry cooperation.

Musical interludes

It was during this period that both Maggie and I extended our musical experience. The colleague in the next office to me was the events manager, in charge of obtaining tickets for musical and other performances for use by IBM managers to entertain key customers. I exploited this connection with fervour. Maggie and I entertained some of the key educationists in Britain to the opera and other concerts and events. Covent Garden became our second home. We enjoyed particularly opera – Benjamin Britten's Peter Grimes twice, Verdi, Puccini, Bizet, Gounod, Rossini. We would ride by train to London, meet our customer of the day, attend the performance and then entertain them to a slap-up meal at the poshest restaurants in the vicinity. If necessary we would stay in a hotel and Maggie would return alone while I went to work. Then there were the performances for university Chancellors and key educators around the country, concerts at Ely Cathedral, the Bodleian at Oxford, Birmingham, King's College Cambridge and more. We entertained directors of education at Glyndebourne. Ballet too – Prokofiev, Tchaikovsky, Delibes. Marlowe's 'Perfect bliss and sole felicity' were ours for the taking.

Danger in Marseilles

The 1978 conference of IFIP took place in Marseilles. It was my first trip abroad connected to my work and I had been asked to deliver a keynote speech on information handling skills in education. However it started with something of a shambles. Delegates turning up at the University halls of residence on the Sunday found no-one there to open up the rooms. Eventually in the late afternoon someone did arrive, apparently surprised to see so many people waiting at the entrance. The organisers had not taken into account that they would arrive at all parts of the day. The conference started the following day and I was scheduled to speak on the third day. The previous evening a group of us sallied down to the famous harbour to sample a bouillabaisse, the famous fish soup of the city.

We did enjoy it, but on the way back to the halls of residence the stomach rumbles started and I barely made it to my room. For most of the night I was in and out of the toilet and I wasn't the only one. The famous fish meal had taken its toll. Come the time of the presentation I was but a pale image of myself having spent a miserable night deprived of sleep. The keynote was certainly not the best I had ever given since the now thankfully silent urges to be somewhere else were still in motion. I took two questions and gave my apologies as I dashed out of the hall before the worst could happen. Since then I have always carefully selected the pre-presentation meal before speaking.

So once again my job was keeping me from my family at a time when they needed it most. Maggie took it all in her stride. She was a glutton for punishment, combining a full time stint at the hospital with her municipal duties, with ferrying David and Jeannette to their various activities and household cleanliness. She had the energy of a nuclear plant. The family still travelled the continent during the summer holiday and went on trips to places in England. David by now had passed his O levels and left Priestlands for the sixth form college at Brockenhurst. He was studying maths, physics and history. He had also fallen in love, which somehow distracted him from his studies. We saw less and less of him. Jeannette was coming up to O levels and expected to pass as were the other members of the fabulous five.

Chairman of the School Governors

I had now taken on a new task as Chairman of the Priestlands school board which entailed regular talks with the headteacher, a knowledge of the frequent changes in educational legislation and an increasingly onerous commitment to solving the school's problems. In this duty I had joined my wife as a pillar of the Lymington Community. It was the early years of the Thatcher government and schools all over the country were having trouble in affording the books their children needed. The head and I called a meeting of interested parents to highlight the problem. We received some sympathy but, this being Lymington and a very conservative area, most were not willing to hear criticism of anything she did.

So I initiated a 'fund a book' scheme for the school, inviting parents to make up the shortfall. We named the books needed in each subject area. This was highly successful. One donation was for a thousand pounds and in total we raised twenty thousand. The head then asked me to present the awards at the school prizegiving ceremony, which I did. I presented my own daughter, and of course others, with her O level certificate. She was not impressed by my speech but then she always. quite rightly. set the bar extremely high when it came to appreciating what her dad does. Thereafter Jeannette joined the A level students at Brockenhurst College.

The children

Our children had grown up. David's A levels were not as good as he had hoped. It took some phone-calling on my part to a colleague at Bradford University to find him a place on the degree course 'Science and Society.' I had previously recommended this course during my presentations since I believed that, as a mixture of several scientific disciplines, it would be a good preparation for very different future. He was the first in our families to go to university from school. He reluctantly left Lymington because he was leaving his girl-friend behind. However in his second year she joined him on the same course, which, in terms of getting work done was both a good and a bad thing.

He completed his three years and, in 1983, achieved a degree for which we all went to Bradford to see him receive. The photograph still stands on our cupboard. It remained to find a job suited to the degree, but at this time there was a downturn in the economy and no openings in the career he wanted, journalism. He spent the next year back at home, unemployed and taking odd jobs as he could find them, including a spell with IBM, which he hated. Finally he decided on the only course open to him by applying to a teacher training college to follow the one year course for degree holders.

Jeannette meanwhile had settled down at Brockenhurst. Her heart appeared to be set on the theatre, a calling she had craved since appearing in a play at Junior School. And so her A levels were geared in that direction. She was now learning to drive. and every now and then I accompanied her in my car. As with her mother it was an interesting time. It would have been safer to clear all the other cars off the road. But we survived with nothing more than a putative heart attack which never happened, and she got one up on her brother by passing the first time. She passed her A levels and, taking after her dad's restless spirit, immediately decided to explore the wider world by taking up a child minding post for a family in London for a few months before going to stage college.

Riding the USA

1981 was a busy year. I had now become an expert on the way that computers could enhance education in schools and the software they could use. IBM had been very slow in responding to this challenge both in Britain and the USA, and since I seemed to be one of the few people taking it seriously in the company. I used a visit to the IFIP conference in Norfolk Virginia to add on an extra meeting at the software development centre in Boca Raton, Florida. The IFIP conference was the usual mixture of presentations and discussion. my contribution being a talk on schools software which raised much interest. I was accompanied there by two other IBMers, one from Denmark and the other from the UK.

After the conference we decided to hire a car and drive for three days southwards through North and South Carolina to Georgia. That was a sober learning experience. Although I had previously visited IBM Headquarters in Connecticut, this was my first encounter with the bible belt. Each time we stopped for a drink or overnight stop we attracted attention. People would come over to us and ask who we were and where we were from. And if we were born again by accepting the Lord as our saviour.

My Unitarian upbringing had given me a particular knowledge of Christianity, though certainly not one that required a rebirth, and my colleagues had no religion at all. We needed to be very careful in our answers because the questions were veiled in a mildly threatening way which boded ill if the answers were not what was required. Nonbelievers had been hanged in these parts in the past. Even to this day religion determines politics. And their interpretation of Jesus's message is certainly not mine. However with a lot of nodding and weasel words we made it to Georgia, from where my colleagues flew back to Europe and I flew to Miami in Florida, and eventually to Boca Raton.

Here I spent a couple of days with the software developers describing how schools were being taught, Geography, English, History, Languages and other subjects by computer. It was an alien concept for them. They already had ideas about using it for reading and writing, and teaching children about spreadsheets and word, but the possibility of expanding further into school subjects had not crossed their minds. In addition this was before the launch of the IBM's small PC and there wasn't really the suitable hardware for such uses. It was a wasted journey but I did leave some ideas for the future.

Back to the USA

Later in the same year, IBM Headquarters in Paris was investing in a new educational project and I was chosen to prepare for it by touring the USA visiting the places that had already implemented it there. I was accompanied by my colleague from Southampton University, and Maggie came along to make sure we didn't lose our way. Being so tidy-minded she is perfect for that. At the same time this was to be our annual holiday. We all paid a hundred dollars to Republic airlines for a ticket that would take us all around America for thirty days. This was a real eye-opener. The first stop was to be Princeton University deep in the heart of New Jersey. We were given instructions how to get there from the airport. Hire a car, take the road south, then the first right and the second left.

What they didn't mention were the distances. The first road right was fifty miles from the airport. We wondered whether we had missed half a dozen roads on the way. The first road left from there was forty miles and the second eighty. Another ten miles brought us to Princeton University, whacked and weary. It was evening and we were given an exuberant American welcome and typical American meal, twice as much as an English one, as compensation. The following morning, after a huge breakfast, we were treated to a presentation of how the university was implementing the project in New Jersey. We discussed the pros and cons all day and went to bed tired and happy.

The following day we were off to Atlanta in Georgia, where I had two years previously spent two days. This time we were housed in one of the luxury hotels in the outer belt of the city and warned not to go to the inner city at any price because we may not return alive. This was another taste of the two Americas, the wealthy suburbs and the neglected and crime-ridden inner city. It was true of most large cities and based largely on racial lines. Even after two hundred years the white supremacists have not given up.

The hotel was palatial and expensive and the staff had their own sense of values. My colleague gave the bellboy a five dollar tip and it was torn up in front of him. In the evening we met our hosts at Georgia State University for another gigantic meal and pre-prepared for another day of presentation and discussion. By this time we must have added pounds in weight and resolved to hold back on the food in future. So when we took only the cereal at breakfast time the waitresses could not understand why we were not stuffing our faces like everyone else. The morrow arrived and we were transported to the University in luxury cars to be entertained by a full screen presentation and project members from university and companies. It was fascinating. Hospitality and brain food combined.

Our third hosts were in Florida and much the same happened. We were all regarded as special guests. This is where we decided to take a holiday. One of the lecturers had an apartment in St Petersburg on the Gulf Coast and offered it to us free of charge for however long we wanted. We took a plane to Fort Lauderdale, hired a car, drove through the Everglades and up the east coast of Florida to our destination. The apartment was an opulent condominium right on the beach. We sent several days there. Each evening we would walk along the promenade and watch a huge sun disappear into the gulf.

The camera was at its busiest. Pelicans crossing the sun, the luxurious buildings, the views. During the day we drove to EPCOT at Orlando where multinational companies compete with each other to present their latest inventions to adults and children alike. Here were large IMAP screens, rides to create every sensation, lakes, pleasurable, exciting education in every sense. We called in at Cape Canaveral (Now Cape Kennedy) to tour the space centre. Three days later we caught the plane to Arizona and marvelled at the Grand Canyon for two days.

Then back to work for a couple of days. My colleague from Southampton had left us at this point. Our next schedule was San Francisco where we were booked into the Grand Western luxury hotel.. This was the life of the elite and it was happening to a couple of escapees from the Bolton back streets. We spent a day at the University and then flew to Los Angeles to visit another university there. Back to San Francisco and on to Seattle for the start of another holiday with Maggie's uncle Harold who transported us into Vancouver. He had emigrated there many years previously. This was my first meeting with Harold although Maggie had met him several times in England when she was young. We were entertained as if we were royalty. Meals in the Chinese quarter, visits to a luxury retirement home to meet Maggie's great Aunt, tours of Stanley Park, to the ski stations at Whistler, boat trips across to Vancouver island and more. Vancouver really is one of the world's greatest cities and we were mightily impressed.

We had one more visit to make for the company, the capital of Minnesota, Minneapolis-St Paul and its university. This is a typical American city, skyscraper buildings with little charm, dedicated to mammon and showing apparently even less culture, though I am probably maligning the place since we spent only one day there..

Thereafter we had eight more days before the Republic Airlines expiry date, so we flew to Toronto, sampled its delights by lake Ontario, hired a car and drove to Niagara Falls where we stayed a couple of nights in the Honeymoon hotel, and then from Buffalo through New York state to its Capital via the Finger Lakes. In New York we took the lift to the top of the World Trade buildings, no longer there, having been destroyed on 9/11 and walked along Broadway and through Central Park. Three magic days before we had to return back to England and home. We had done America in thirty days, sixteen thousand miles for hundred dollars each, and learned even more about the project and the country. It only remained to write my report for Headquarters. The following year Republic Airlines went bust. We were not surprised.

Chapter Ten

Paris Mon Amour

'See Paris and Die'

'But not just yet – it's a great place to live'

Paradise in Paris

But now came another major upheaval. As a result of this work I was asked to go and work in the IBM Headquarters for Europe, Middle East and Africa for a term of three years. It was a hard earned and welcome promotion and I was very keen to take it despite the fact that Cricket was in short supply there. The drawback was that Maggie, who had just been appointed sister in Southampton General Hospital, was understandably reluctant to give up her hard-won promotion. The children were now off our hands making their own way in life, Jeannette as an actress with a partner in her own schools theatre company operating from Lymington, and David as a teacher in Kent.

I went to Paris to arrange accommodation in a seventh floor apartment in the much sought after sixteenth arrondissement near to the Bois de Boulogne, the French Rugby ground and the Roland Garros Tennis Club. Here I lived alone for three months, commuting by metro to the recently opened La Defense 'Carrefour du Monde', a vast expanse of multinational company headquarters built by the French government while Mrs Thatcher was practicing TINA (There is no Alternative) austerity in Britain.

Maggie joined me in July 1984. Unlike me she had no French at all. It wasn't ever on the curriculum of her school in Bolton since good obedient housewives were not normally required to speak French. So, courtesy of IBM she was given a permanent French teacher with whom she made great friends during the three years we were in Paris. It was street French. They went everywhere around Paris while I was working until Maggie could speak French much more easily than me. American companies didn't work in the language. Having made the decision, she fell in love with Paris, as all its visitors do. We made friends with the neighbours across the floor and explored everything Paris had to offer when I wasn't at work. It was like working in a film set. A long way from the back streets. Bolton may have its charms, but nothing like this.

Two months later I was asked to go to South Africa, then an apartheid nation, to supervise the distribution and use of the gift of twenty million dollars of small computers to schools for the black majority, together with the software on reading and writing that would enable people of colour to catch up. This was the time when American multinationals were putting the squeeze on Apartheid in order to transform South Africa into a Democracy. Maggie would not go because of her deep principles against the system. So I spent three weeks in Johannesburg and Capetown talking to government ministers, visiting the schools and preparing the conditions for the delivery of the computers. I visited schools in Soweto where classes of seventy children were taught in a field near to the school building with little equipment and two dedicated black teachers. I also visited privileged rugby mad white English and Afrikaaner schools, where classes of fifteen pupils had every opportunity open to them.

The comparison was stark. We negotiated with governments in Johannesburg and Capetown and eventually agreed the terms. They would pay fifty percent of the cost of installing the computers and provide an additional teacher in each recipient school to ensure that they were used properly. My job was done and I returned to Paris. I learned fifteen months later that the computers had not reached the schools after all because the South African government had reneged on the agreement. Such was the morality of leaders whose origins came from the Christian religion. It seemed to me that such behaviour was far from the tenets of the Christianity I had been taught as a youngster. It reminded me of the bible belt in America where similar distortions of what normal people call integrity, honesty and decency are commonplace in the name of Jesus.

Adventure in Saudi

My job description was fairly vague. My territory covered Europe, the Middle East and Africa. I was to provide support for an existing series of high level educational seminars in the high mountains of Austria, add one more dealing with schools and Universities, and organize seminars in other parts of my territory as I, or another government, deemed necessary. The second part was easy. I organized speakers, including myself, for seminars in, among other places, Saudi Arabia, Israel and Cairo in Egypt at their invitation. The Saudi one was mainly for the sons of the King and his cousins.

Two people from IBM France, one of them female, accompanied me. The seminar took place in Taïf, the King's summer place in the mountains behind Mecca. In order to get there we needed to fly from Paris to Jeddah on the Red Sea coast. Never have I been to a place so hot and steamy. I spent the night in a hotel gasping for breath, before we were driven in a luxury car around Mecca (we infidels were not allowed to enter the holy city) to Taïf, where the atmosphere was much clearer and fresher. Arab architecture was quite new to me but the city and the palace presented a pleasing sight.

So here was the boy from the back streets of Bolton running a seminar in the King of Saudi Arabia's palace to twenty of his approved relations, all male of course. None of them objected to the presence of a female. It would have been impolite to do so. The first surprise was how well educated everyone was but that was simply a symbol of my own ignorance. I should have known. They had been to universities throughout the world, but mainly in USA and the UK. All spoke impeccable English and surprisingly to me all were well informed politically and intellectually. Not all toed the Saudi line of gender inequality and authoritarianism, though I had to tread carefully when discussing such subjects.

There were indubitably government spies among them. The seminar went very well. They learned much from us speakers and raised intelligent debating points. In the end they agreed that computers could do much to raise standards in Saudi education. It was then up to the salesmen to profit from it.

Came the end of conference meal, everyone seated on the floor around a superbly woven carpet. A whole lamb on a spit was placed in the middle of the carpet. One of the eyes of the lamb was presented to me on a plate. I was ready for this. I had been warned. The meal cannot be started until the guest of honour has eaten the eye. I smiled, what alternative did I have? bowed my head to everyone and swallowed the eye whole. I cannot say what its taste was – it went down in one, though I did make a munching gesture which I am sure they all recognized as false. So now the feast could begin. There were no knives, forks or spoons. Just a plate in front of everyone and hands.

The Saudi leader started by grabbing a handful of hot meat from the lamb and putting it upon his plate. Whereupon everyone joined in and the lamb was eventually consumed by hand. The meat had to be taken from the lamb with the left hand because everyone knows what most human beings also do with their right. There followed a sweet dish which I could not identify but was delicious. I do not remember what we drank, but it was alcohol free and strong. We retired to bed well fed and watered.

The following morning we were let loose in the Taïf Souk, its local marketplace. I could find several mementoes to take home but thought that they were rather expensive until the French lady, whom I had come to call Fifi (without her knowledge) arrived and explained to me that I was expected to bargain to reduce the price. I wasn't very good at this and so Fifi bargained for me and knocked everything down to less than half the price they first offered. The vendors seemed very happy with this which made me think that perhaps they could have gone much lower. In the afternoon we Europeans left in the car back to Jeddah after shaking hands and receiving good wishes from every participant. I for one had been educated too. This was my Saudi Arabian adventure and one I will never forget. Having spoken with these well-educated young men I still do not understand why the country is so firmly inflexible. But then I don't live in the Middle East.

Fun and games in Israel

The Israeli seminar was equally eventful. After landing at Tel Aviv I was driven up to the IBM research centre in Haifa near to the Lebanon border where a war was being fought against Hezbollah Guerrillas. The uneasiness was palpable but I was given a right royal welcome by the staff there. The following day we had a short seminar where I gave my standard presentation and they asked questions and made additional suggestions. Then it was down to Jerusalem where I had been booked into the famous King David Hotel. I was given a tour of the city and all the Jewish and Christian holy places, including the wailing wall.

It seemed strange that I should now be seeing with my own eyes, in the flesh as it were, what I had frequently seen on television. I had been joined by colleagues from IBM Israel for the next installment of the journey. In the late afternoon one of them, a larger than life and very friendly Arab strangely enough, thought that it would be a good idea to hire a car to see the dead sea. It probably wasn't but I acquiesced and four of us jumped into the hire car for the journey.

This was where I saw the real paranoia at work and not for the first time. We were stopped four times by armed soldiers each one with his finger on the trigger of his gun, every time treated as dangerous subversives. We were advised four times not to proceed any further. I am not easily frightened but it was obvious to me that this trip was not a great wheeze. However, stupidity prevailed and we eventually reached the Dead Sea in pitch blackness unable to see any water. The return journey was the same. Tenacious interrogations at each checkpoint. Israel really is a country under permanent siege and these soldiers were taking no prisoners.

I was grateful to be back in the hotel for dinner. After a meeting and a presentation with people at IBM Israel, all of whom were warm-hearted and friendly, as were many of the people I met, I left the country. At the airport I had the most disagreeable experience with two members of the EL AL airport staff who seemed to assume that I was a terrorist with a bag full of bombs which I would set off on the plane journey back to Paris. They were nasty, arrogant and irrational. I could understand why they have to be so suspicious of everyone, given the hostility around them but I can't help thinking that they brought it on themselves by the violent treatment of their neighbours. But then who am I? I don't have to live there permanently.

To Egypt

Egypt was very different. I stayed at the luxury hotel near to the Geiza pyramids where the seminar was taking place, right opposite the Sphinx. It was an amazing experience. The proceedings were enhanced by a belly dancing exhibition and a magician. The seminar was tame by comparison, but I received the usual polite response, and a sign that many at least had listened in later conversations. Naturally we wanted to examine the ancient relics of Egypt's rich history. But whatever time we left the hotel to do so, be it six in the morning or under the stars at midnight, so we were swamped by the persistence of people wanting us to hire them for a tour of the pyramids and the naughty bits they thought all westerners would be interested in.

A simple No was not enough. It seemed that by doing so we were depriving an Egyptian family of food that day. One cannot blame them. They had no other income and scores of these poor people went home unhired and hungry, in contrast to the excesses and profligacy in the hotel. I forget how many donations I gave to them, even the smallest amount was accepted gratefully. I left Egypt the sadder for their plight. As always the seminar was successful, maybe more because of the belly-dancing than the presentations and discussions.

Loose in Australia

During my period in Paris I organized conferences and seminars in many European countries, including Greece, Spain, Germany, Hungary and more. But the biggest surprise was from a country far away from Europe, Middle East or Africa. I had made a keynote presentation on the information handling in schools research at the Paris meeting of IFIP in 1984. Just afterwards, the leader of the Australian delegation came up to me and asked if I could say it all again in Sydney, Australia, so impressed had he been. All travel, accommodation and meals paid. What could I say but yes, if my manager would allow it. My best man at our wedding had emigrated there two years after the ceremony and it would be an excellent opportunity to meet him and his Australian family twenty two years later in Melbourne where he lived. I asked and my manager was delighted that European expertise was being exported to the antipodes. This time Maggie accompanied me. We boarded British Airways flight 98 on the 6th June 1985, flying to Sydney via Singapore. It was Maggie's first long haul flight.

After a stop at Singapore, we landed a day later for the first time on Australian soil. We were met by a lady who announced herself as the Head of Catholic Education in Australia. She was honoured she said because most catholic schools were following my research course on information handling. This came as a great surprise to me since I was not aware that it existed outside of the university of Southampton library and no-one had ever sought permission. I wasn't sure of the law on using research theses even though it was a great boost to a Bolton boy's ego. She further said that she had fixed a meeting the following day to meet the Australian Minister of Education. Surprise number two. I had no idea that he had ever heard of a boy from Bolton. We found our hotel and crashed out after our eighteen hour journey.

A journey to Canberra

The following day a limousine arrived at the hotel to take us to Canberra. I was still more than a little jet-lagged but managed to survive the journey without falling asleep. We arrived at two pm and were taken to the great man's office. There he was sitting and chatting to a colleague. Both of them gave me a hearty

Aussie welcome and we had a little chat about Australian education. Then surprise number three. He threw open an adjoining door and there was a long table surrounded by thirty people. The Minister's introduced me to his subject and political advisers who all waved their hands in greeting. I was gob-smacked. No-one had prepared me for this. I was obviously expected to say something wise and eye-opening.

So for the next twenty minutes I ad-libbed about my educational experiences and in particular the philosophy behind the information course. They knew about it and they knew that I was in Australia to talk to the conference. We then broke up in the tea-room for a drink and a bite to eat. Sandwiches. By this time I was so hungry that I could have eaten the Australian flag on the wall. And so was Maggie. The last time we had eaten was on the plane and we had been in the country for less than twenty four hours. We all chatted, they asked questions, I answered and then the car came to whisk me back to my hotel in Sydney. This was my baptism to Australia and I was once more knackered. We slept the sleep of the dead once more.

The conference

The following day was the first day of the conference. I was scheduled to give my keynote in the afternoon. Although this was a computer conference and I worked for IBM the subject matter was very geeky. I hardly understood a word they were saying. Maggie had gone off to explore Sydney while I was trapped in Australian accented computer jargon. I said my piece first thing in the afternoon, starting with a few pom jokes and mentioning my cricketing experiences.

That got them on my side so long as I didn't remind them that the Australian team, which at that time was in England, had lost the first test match. The presentation received a bigger ovation than it deserved. I think that they were so relieved to hear someone not talking about computer languages, bits and bytes and the latest software marvel. From then I was free to listen to whichever presentation I thought I could understand. I rang Maggie and sneaked off to meet her on the harbour.

Exploring Sydney

Sydney is a superb city with much to pass the time. We ate in one of the harbour restaurants that evening. An Australian fish meal of Moreton Bay crab and Barramundi, both of them for the first time ever and delicious. We retired slowly to our hotel which was at the top of the hill on the main street to the harbour. The following day the two Bolton scrubbers cruised the harbour, past the tall ships, and the iconic Sydney Harbour Bridge, close to the Opera house, described typically by Australians as a few whales humping each other, and past the luxury houses to Manley and back.

It was a magical experience. We booked to see a show at the opera house. It didn't matter what it was. We wanted to see the interior of the whales. It was the Sydney Opera house. As it happened it was a modern ballet which was excellent. As we exited the theatre we notice that it was not just raining cats and dogs, it was more cows and horses. Already it was ankle deep outside the theatre as the water poured down the streets leading to the harbour. The noise of rain on concrete was deafening.

As we waded up the street to our hotel it became deeper and deeper. At knee level we had to watch out for the cars floating quickly past on their way to a watery grave in the bay. Much higher and we would have been joining the cars. Swimming gear would have been more appropriate. We reached the hotel and walked through the door, clothes clinging, looking and feeling like wallabies after a cold bath and crossed the lobby to the lift. The gates opened and two young ladies dressed to the nines looked at us and said 'Ouh is it raining.?' We nodded. Little did they know what they would encounter as they left the hotel.

Melbourne Ed

The next day we flew to Melbourne to stay with our long lost best man and his family. It was an emotional greeting at the Airport before we were transported to his home in Kew. Norman 'Ed' Bailey had also been to the Bolton School and had been a member of the same Unitarian Church as me. We became great friends. When he was fourteen I taught him a few notes on the piano. Much to my surprise and chagrin, within three weeks he was playing jazz and popular songs by ear far better than I could ever dream. He lived in a much posher house, a fully detached dwelling not in Halliwell but close to it.

He was the guy who accompanied me on the cycle ride to Switzerland, who sneaked into the upstairs room at church through an attic window to play snooker and who formed a band with me to play at the church dances. He, of course, played the piano and I played the accordion at his side since we only had one piece of music for each dance. He attributed the deafness in his left ear to that experience.

After he emigrated to Australia he joined IBM, then set up his own IT company with a partner who, after ten years, decided that he would disappear with all the money. He became a lecturer in IT at Swinburne University just down the road from his house. He had two children and an Australian wife. After twenty two years we had much to catch up on. Outside of work his major activity was a childrens' theatre which he set up with his wife. For this work he received a medal from the government.

With us he became a tour guide. He showed us around Melbourne. The city centre, the beaches, the river walks, Puffing Billy in the Dandenong hills close by and down to the Mornington peninsula to see the fairy penguins rise from the sea and waddle their way to their nesting sites. We prospered well on the Australian Chardonnay, reminisced on times past and told many a tale of our experiences in the past twenty years. At departure time we professed eternal gratitude and the hope that we would be back, a hope that has been realized many times in the years that followed.

An Austrian Interlude

Back in Paris I continued to prepare the Austrian seminars which required me to identify the major European players in schools computing and invite them to pass some of their valuable time with their peers in the Austrian Vorarlberg, courtesy of IBM. Maggie meanwhile had made friends in the American church and was taking tours of Paris with them, as well as following her French lessons with her mentor. In the evenings we would stick a pin in the metro map travel there and eat in one of the restaurants that was certain to be there. Or we would go to the cinema. This being Paris, our friends and relations suddenly developed the urge to visit us and we spent many a weekend, and Maggie many a day, in showing them the city. And many an evening in alcohol-fired conversation.

The Austrian IBM seminars took place during the summer at one of the many ski resorts. It was an idyllic setting with fabulous mountain views, a luxurious conference centre and Michelin star grade meals. There were two seminars in successive weeks, the first for universities and the second for schools. I had to help with the first and be the organizer, agony aunt, director, producer, keynote speaker and orchestrator of the second. Maggie came along too and helped out.

The delegates were all high level administrators, educational politicians, heads of schools and hangers on from all over Europe so this had to be useful and entertaining for them. The seminar went well. We transformed the educational scene of Europe in one week. The scenery and the ambiance did its magic and so did the bar in the education centre. It seemed to me that the route to the top in European education was an ability to drink copious amounts of alcohol without falling over or making a fool of oneself. Whatever, everyone left reluctantly having learned from the Bolton backstreet lad, each other, exchanged ideas for greater cooperation and consumed vast amounts of food and drink.

Luxury in Monte Carlo

Back to Paris. My three years were coming to an end. I was offered a job in the sales department of IBM London and was not looking forward to it. However I did get a taste of it before I left Paris. I was invited to speak to those members of IBM UK who had been successful in the sale of computers in the UK. They were having a jolly down in Monte Carlo as a reward for a successful year. Maggie and I drove there from Paris and were housed in the Hotel de Paris just opposite the Casino. Normally rooms here would cost at least four thousand pounds per night and more, and probably did, except that we were not paying it. It has a brass bear at the entrance which the punters rub on their way across the road to give them good luck.

So here was the boy from the back streets of Bolton and his wife, the girl from a two up and two down from Deane, living for 4 days in the most expensive hotel in the world. How our plebeian hearts did beat with a certain self-reproof at the thought of the poor citizens back home. The only sad thing about it was that we could not afford the entrance fee into the Casino. It seemed too that even IBM could not afford the Casino de Monte Carlo since the proceedings took place in the Sun Casino down near the beach. Here I said my piece and tried to make it jolly though I couldn't compete with the two real comedians who also were on stage. This was after all a celebration of success. Afterwards Maggie and I had a little flutter on the machines. I lost fifty pounds and Maggie won thirty. So we didn't come out poor but neither did we break the bank at Monte Carlo.

One wedding and two funerals

While we were in Paris our son had competed his course and was now a fully-fledged teacher. David had met a new girl-friend, Karen, in his teacher training college and in 1987, they were married in the picturesque church at the end of our road, followed by a rave up of the many guests in a posh Victorian pub in the New Forest. It was quite an affair. They both obtained teaching jobs in Kent and took out a large mortgage on a small house there.

There were also sad days. My two cousins, Dorothy and her brother Michael, the children of my dad's brother, who died during the war, both contracted cancer and died within a few years of each other. We of course flew home for both their funerals and to try to console my Aunt, who had now lost both her husband and her two children. They were all stalwarts of the unitarian church and as a teenager, we had played tennis in Egerton Park near to Bolton.

Chapter Eleven

Over to Belgium

'Be the change you wish to see in the world'

'But only when it makes it a better place'

Goodbye Paris – Hello Brussels

Salvation came in a strange way. The IBM Europe education centre was based in Brussels in the Forêt de Soignes, an area of mature forest on the Eastern outskirts of the city. IBM and several partners from the open universities had won a European Commission project to explore the uses of satellites to distribute education at distance. It was called DELTA. The centre needed a project manager with a knowledge of distance education and I was asked to be that manager. It entailed another move, to Brussels, the centre of the European Commission. I was sent in haste to start the project before we could make arrangement for the move. Maggie stayed in Paris while I rented an apartment in the suburbs of Brussels for two weeks and drove to work in the IBM centre.

When she finally came to join me we hired a house in Waterloo near to the battlefield. We had acquired a dog while in Paris, a Briard, Artur, who was large, affectionate, and noisy. The Belgian neighbour was not the world's greatest dog lover especially when Artur broke through the fence into her garden and left her a present. So rather than spend the next years arguing with the neighbour, we changed to a house nearer to the forest and stayed there happily for three years. In the next two years of the project I learned a great deal about satellites, which ones could be used and where. The IBM technical development centre in the south of France were experts in satellite matters and they advised on the specialised high-tech aspects. We paid them several visits. Then there were the pedagogical issues which were more in my line and these were added to the mix so that finally we were able to present to the Commission a complete dossier on the use of satellites for education.

IBM Education Centre

The education centre was a multinational organization in itself. It was situated in a beautiful spot, the Forêt de Soignes to the West of the city. While the majority were Belgian there were experts from many European countries, Germany, France, Holland, Romania, Sweden, Armenia, UK, Ireland and more. There was also a cohort from the USA. Maggie and I made many international friends while we were there. My office in the centre was on a corner looking outwards in both directions to the trees. There was a swimming pool and a tennis court in the grounds and I used to play the latter every lunchtime.

There were some excellent players including an ex-regional champion from France and a state champion from the USA. The standard was therefore far higher than I had been used to in Harrow tennis and Cricket club. Although I was now fifty three years old, my tennis improved immensely. In the centre competition I made it to the semifinal, being beaten only by the French star in three sets. True to form Maggie needed something to organize in order to keep herself busy. She formed an IBM wives association from the partners of the non-Belgian workforce and organised trips and visits to museums, theatres, and other cultural places in Brussels and its hinterland.

It was here that I met Bill Weimer. He had been a contender for the big job in IBM worldwide but had missed out and decided that he wanted to extend his knowledge base in Europe. He was a strong leader running a small external projects department and his personality pervaded the whole centre. We always seemed to obtain the funding for new projects. He was one those oxymorons, an American gourmand, his knowledge of fine food and wine was legion. Maggie and I became great friends with him and his wife and accompanied him to the epicurean hotspots throughout Belgium.

It hardly made a dent in his salary but it certainly made a large one in mine. Thanks to him I became the interface between IBM and the European Commission. Persuading bureaucrats that working with an American multi-national company as was natural in the United States, was not the easiest task in Belgium. There was always the suspicion that the private sector had ulterior motives. But the knowledge that I had was useful to them. I made many friends there and we worked well together without rancour, providing expertise where it was needed.

Back again to the USA

The largest project was decided after Bill's arrival. It was 1978 and a slight downturn in the world economy. He was convinced that this was an opportunity to improve education in European Industry and persuaded twelve major tech companies, including British Telecom, Hewlett Packard, Philips, Thompson and eight other giants to dig into their warchests to fund a project that would tap into the leading edge researchers in European Universities and enable them to provide lectures and lessons by satellite to the companies, building upon our expertise in the DELTA programme. It was called businesssat and was one of the largest of such projects in Europe. The addition of UNESCO in Paris provided integrity. Once again the experience of the Bolton boy as leader of a previously successful satellite project came in useful. I was the deputy project leader advising twelve of the major European companies how to invest in their future.

The first step was to find out what was already active in this area and the only example, which Bill had already known, was the National Satellite Education Programme in the USA. So off we went. I led a posse of three company representatives and the head of the Paris UNESCO department to the USA to discover how they did it. Our first stop was in Denver Colorado, the headquarters of the organization. Here we learned the extent of the programme, how the satellites were used, the advantages for industry and some of the technical details. It was commonplace in the USA for industry to use satellites for distance education, though the pedagogical issues were not always well carried out. Then we flew to three examples, one provider in Atlanta, and two receiving companies in New York and Rochester .

We returned with ideas for a strategy that we believed would suit Europe. Meetings were held in all the countries involved, universities with relevant expertise were contacted and companies made ready. But where should we house this new organization? In theory it was not very attractive. We were offering only twelve new jobs at a time when millions were out of work, but in practice such was the lure of a new high-tech company that many cities were prepared to pay to have it based there. We contacted several cities. Now came a very pleasant exercise. Four of the project leaders including myself toured a selection of the cities that had offered a base.

We were wined and dined and treated like people who would single-handedly rescue the economy in Paris, Amsterdam, Brussels, Strasbourg and Toulouse. They all offered free accommodation for the new company. Additionally some offered to provide secretarial staff. And they also offered fine dining and luxurious hotels. Eventually we chose Paris as the new centre, at the technical facility of La Defense and near to the IBM building I had occupied four years previously. The head was a certain Bill Weimer, who left IBM to manage it after forty years with the company.

A World Tour - Tokyo

I had only a few more months before I was due to return to the UK after six years away. I was therefore given the task of marketing the European satellite methodology to other countries of the world. Needless to say Maggie came with me. Firstly Japan, where we stayed in a brand new fifty storey luxury hotel with thirty restaurants and ten lifts. We arrived at Narita airport in Tokyo jetlagged and tired and were then transported by taxi for an hour to the hotel. It was evening and we were hungry. Japan is a very expensive country and, while the expense of my meals would be picked up by IBM, those of Maggie would not. The average meal was around the equivalent of a hundred and fifty pounds per person and rising. We eventually went down to the basement snack bar where the cheapest item on the menu was egg and bacon for thirty pounds. We took it. And very good it tasted.

The following morning I was due to be at IBM Japan. Breakfast was an all you can eat for a reasonable price. I took a taxi to the address I had been given and found that it was also the centre for expats in Tokyo with a lounge and drinks as required. Brits, Americans, Europeans and Australians, many retired who hadn't bothered to go home, whiled away the passing hours in a permanent state of inebriation. So while Maggie lounged the morning away I met the boss with a bow which I hoped was low enough and discussed with him how, where and to whom the presentation should be given. He was very pleased to see me and to help strengthen the company's relationship with the university. He allocated a Japanese employee to ensure that we were able to negotiate the language and the places we may want to visit. Everyone was extremely courteous and eager to help. In the afternoon we were taken on a trip to the Royal palace which was only ever open to honoured guests. It was a long way from the Bolton palais.

Maggie joined me in the afternoon, and we were introduced to the famous Senbikiya shopping centre ,where we made our first acquaintance with the concept of 'the perfect fruit.' Classical music played throughout the store and uniformed members of staff were politely attentive, ushering the customers to chairs and taking their orders. And yet Senbikiya is simply a greengrocers owned by an entrepreneur who, in the 19th century followed the Tesco model of piling them high and selling them cheap. Then the wife of the second-generation owner astutely realised the real money was to be made by inverting the business model, and Senbikiya became the most expensive fruit shop in the world.

There are apples, the size of a child's head, with evenly red, blemish-free skin on sale for fifteen pounds each. Strawberries come in boxes of twelve perfectly matched fruits at fifty two pounds. Even on a slow day they sell fifty boxes. Melons, each perfect, of course, sell for two hundred and sixty four pounds fifty for three. I was hoping that, as honoured guests, we were not expected to buy at these prices but I need not have worried. Maggie was presented with a perfect apple as memento of the visit. When we returned to the hotel we ate it. It tasted like an apple.

In the evening we were taken to a Japanese restaurant where the menu was in pictures for those, like us, who couldn't read kanji characters. Indeed we discovered later that almost every restaurant in Tokyo did the same.

The following morning I was again driven to the university where I delivered my piece to much applause, and once again given a memento with which to remember the occasion. I have no idea how many of them understood a word I had said, But it didn't matter. This was an opportunity for listening to a presentation from an honoulable visitor and increase the university's profile. In the afternoon I was shown around the grounds and its perfect Japanese gardens. The same day, Maggie had taken herself off to the Tokyo Zoo using the city underground system. She spent much time admiring the animals, but when it came time to return to the hotel she left by a different gate. So there she was, lost in a strange country unable to speak a word of Japanese and not knowing what to do to find the underground station.

So she used her initiative by stopping several Japanese people to ask them if a) they spoke English and b) if so, where was the train. She quickly found a young man who had a few words of English and who then not only told her where the station was but personally took her to it. We found this to be the norm all over the country. The people were incredibly polite and helpful. They would insist on guiding us to wherever we wanted to go even if it wasn't in their own direction. It was the same in the underground system. We made a point of remembering how to pronounce the station near to the hotel and a copy of the first three of a row of kanji characters in its inevitably long name. Often this was enough to see us in the right place but if we had made a mistake there was always someone to take us back to the straight and narrow.

Kyoto the Beautiful

Gradually we learned how to travel around the city. We had our personal minders for some of the time and when I had to give a seminar in Kyoto they accompanied us there via the bullet train. Before the meeting, they recommended a trip by plane from Kyoto to Nara, and flew with us there, explaining the history of this holy place. **Nara was the capital of Japan during the Nara period from 710 to 794 as the seat of the Emperor** before the capital was moved to Kyoto. It is home to eight temples, shrines, and ruins and was added to the list of UNESCO World Heritage Sites in December 1998, nine years after we were there. It was very beautiful in a Japanese way with statues of buddha, gardens and many ancient Japanese buildings.

Back to Kyoto, another tourist's delight. While I was doing my bit at the university, Maggie was given a free tour of the temples, of which there are one thousand eight hundred in the city. She swears she saw them all, so exhausted was she that evening. We spent another day looking round this spectacular city before our minders directed us to a Ryokan on the way back to Tokyo. A Ryokan is a special Japanese hotel where everything is laid on for the visitor, an opportunity to experience the traditional Japanese lifestyle and hospitality, such as **tatami** floors, **futon** beds, Japanese style baths and Japanese style haute **cuisine**. There are very few of them in Bolton, in fact none. Or even London. They are places where the rich go to relax and are usually very expensive. Ours was paid for by our hosts as a reward for my presentations.

Michael Jackson

We were both sad to leave such a beautiful and friendly country but we had to fly to Australia for the next leg of the trip. My ticket on the jumbo jets was in business class, but Maggie's was in the cheaper seats since we couldn't afford the higher prices. Inevitably that turned completely round when we actually got on the plane. The eight hour flight to Sydney was an example. Maggie was in the upper layer of the jumbo jet while I was relegated to cattle class at the back of the plane. But this was a special journey in the upstairs part of the plane. The regular passengers were invited to change seats to the lower cabin because upstairs might get quite noisy. Maggie stayed where she was, curious about this. Gradually the empty seats were taken by young people some with instruments.

She turned round to the seats behind and asked a young man what this was all about. 'Have you ever heard of Michael Jackson?' he said. 'No' said Maggie. "well that's me' he said 'and we are practising for a concert in Australia'. So she was regaled with music for at least half the journey, and given a ticket for the concert, which she couldn't use because we were due to change planes on arrival in Sydney. Maggie tells that story with pride to everyone who will listen. The day the girl from a two up two down in Bolton met Michael Jackson and told him that she had never heard of him.

Hello Melbourne again

We arrived in Melbourne and once more we stayed with the Ed Bailey family. Our daughter Jeannette joined us. She was spending a year back-packing in Australia after her schools company failed because of yet another Thatcher era depression. She had taken work wherever she found it, including at the Brisbane World expo. The Baileys took this invasion by the massed family of the Longworths in their stride. I had several appointments in the country to tell the businesssat story and the first was at the Royal Melbourne Institute of Technology in the centre of the city.

This I accomplished and received the usual expressions of thanks and dying love, though I suspect that I said nothing they didn't already know, since they were already using satellites for education, though not with industrial partners. We passed a few days in the Mornington peninsula relaxing, imbibing, meeting friends. making excursions to the ocean where in 1967 Harold Holt, a former Australian Prime Minister walked out to sea never to be seen again. Returning to the city we went to the theatre where one of Ed's childrens' performances was taking place. It was very professional and indeed several of his young players later became well-known people in show business.

To Hobart

Before moving on to my next port of call Maggie and I hopped onto a plane to Hobart in Tasmania. When I was in Paris another of my responsibilities had been to babysit an accountancy lecturer who had come to the city with his wife to research the French monetary system. They were excellent company and we had enjoyed entertaining them. We were simply responding to his invitation to visit him in Tasmania, which I am sure he offered with tongue in cheek, thinking that it would never happen, as indeed did we. It did happen.

He met us at the airport and took us to his palatial house in a twenty acre spread in the centre of the island. Land is dirt cheap in Tasmania. He took us to the tourist spots in the south of the island including the first convict settlement at Port Arthur. This was a solemn place replete with emotion. We learned how the convicts had been (mis)treated, how they lived , how they had been punished. They were not well treated and the regime was harsh. Those trying to escape were hanged and their bodies left hanging as an example. The buildings are still visible and in this two hundred year anniversary from the first landing it was particularly poignant. Jeannette was especially moved by Tasmania.

In the lounge of his house there was a grand piano which our host said was the one played by Nyree Dawn Porter in The Forsyte Saga, a very popular tv series in the late sixties from the book of that name by John Galsworthy. What it was doing in the outback of Tasmania I have no idea. Of course I had to show my lack of prowess on the piano by playing it endlessly. Had I been thirty years younger I could have settled in Tasmania.

Moving West

Once more we said goodbye to my old friend and moved on to Adelaide, where I gave my presentation at the University and onward a further two thousand one hundred miles to Perth. This was a city I had always wanted to see. So isolated from the rest of Australia, it was growing rapidly because of the minerals, iron ore, gold, coal, precious metals, oil and more along the west coast and in the desert . When we were there in 1989 it was a smallish city of about five hundred thousand souls. It has now grown to a large metropolis of more than two million in twenty years. thanks to the urgent needs of China for its minerals.

We found it to be a charming place with houses and offices on each side of the river Swan. It had a good cultural life with three universities, now five. We went to a new opera-cum-spectacular named 'Australia' in honour of the bi-centenary. It was excellent. We took the boat down to Fremantle, home of Western Australia cricket, stared out at ten thousand miles of sea before the next landfall, and looked up the old convict settlements. My work took me to Curtin university, internationally reputed for its research and its joint work with Asian partners. Their isolation from the rest of Australia and indeed the world of cities gave them a particular interest in what I had to say about the use of satellites for education. Afterwards we were given a tour of the university and taken for a gourmet meal, Australian style on the Barbie. Regretfully I never discovered if they had responded to my presentation.

A new home

The time came to return to Belgium. It was October and my three year attachment was almost over. I had amassed several weeks of holiday time which could only be spent while we were in Belgium, We passed the first 2 weeks in the Pyrénées Orientales. near the French border with Spain with my old friend from Chester college, Dave and his wife. It was our intention to buy a holiday home while prices were so depressed. We wanted to cement our connection to Europe. During our spell in Paris we had explored every inch of France and fallen madly in love with the country. So France was where we decided to eventually lay down our aging bones and impose our rudimentary language skills on the natives. But where? The obvious answer was as far as we could get from the UK and still be in France.

So late October 1989 found us near the med, spending a thoroughly blissful couple of weeks researching the whole area of the *Pyrénées Orientales* and the *Corbières* for potential permanent accommodation wherein to lay down new roots. I can thoroughly recommend this as a geographical and cultural pastime. How else can one afford the services of a free daily guide to the sights of the local region, inspect the habitat and ways of life of the local bipedal fauna, and be frequently entertained to meals? It's a much under-rated activity and it's free. Even if the dream-house hits you in the eyes on the first day, better to feign continuing interest in order to continue the whole pampering experience. In a rustic region like this one, rarely does your first choice go quickly.

Our excursions into the stunning hinterland took us into well-preserved mediaeval towns, narrow limestone defiles and gorges, singular outcrops and splendid mountain-top views and some of the most precarious and picturesque roads on the face of this earth. Villages perched perilously over thousand foot drops, sunlit hamlets on bare hill-tops, settlements hidden in deep chasms. We saw houses large and small, mansions town and country, *maisons de maître* and *de village*, fortified *bastides,* poky habitations built into town ramparts, and secluded dwellings miles from the nearest loo let alone electricity, gas and water. Life here must have been one long search for urgent relief. We observed buildings without walls, studied residences without roofs, researched barns without doors and occasionally examined edifices with all those missing parts.

One house in the village of *Davejean* in the *Corbière* mountains was blessed with eight bedrooms, an enormous kitchen and living room - and those were just on the first two floors. Two more undeveloped floors rose above this, capped by a massive terrace which opened up a superb view over the surrounding limestone countryside. The estate agent apologised for the outrageous price - £9,000 - but pointed out that we could probably knock the owners down since it needed some money spent on it.

Indeed it did. It was a veritable bank-buster, though an even greater drawback was the remoteness of its situation in a small hamlet forty five kilometres from the next habitation. For a family of seventeen attracted to the idea of eternal solitude, delighting in its own company and prepared for a mountain of DIY it would have been perfect. For our more sociable spirits it held little attraction,. Eventually however we were to be seduced by the house we now live in, a perfect *mas* in a perfect setting. But more of that story later.

Russian Roulette

One other assignment remained. The Berlin Wall was down, Russia was opening up to the rest of Europe and IBM smelled business there. I became the educational representative of the company in a visit to Moscow with three other members of the IBM staff. It was an interesting trip. I loaded up with roubles and flew to Sherematievo airport in Moscow. We landed and I tried to get a taxi to my hotel only to meet a refusal from every taxi driver because they wanted dollars, not roubles. Pounds might have done but certainly not the currency Russia was noted for. I eventually found a limousine driver who would transport me for a considerable sum well above reason but then IBM would eventually be paying the bill and they could afford it. Moscow was dull. Only Red Square with the Kremlin building on one side and St Basil on the other seemed to have any architectural merit, although I wasn't there long enough to discover others.

I was ferried around a couple of schools. Both reminded me of Bullington. Children seated in rows at their desks, teachers with chalk and blackboard. Solemnity, never a smile from pupil or staff. No computers to be seen. It was the greyest of the grey in education, though in one of them there was a language laboratory. Back at the hotel with my colleagues we wondered where to eat. We were told of a cabaret restaurant in the centre of town, to which we made our way. The bruiser at the door asked our names, apparently one needed to book at this highly regarded restaurant. One of my colleagues asked to see his list to see if we were on it. He found a non-Russian name and said 'that's us.' And so we were led to a table for four near the stage.

Personally I didn't think this a very good idea in a Russian city with a high level clientele probably including many from the Kremlin. I had visions of being carted off to the Lubyanka for questioning and torture. However it seemed that this was the new mother Russia of glasnost and Perestroika à la Gorbachev. Visitors from other countries, except perhaps Chechen, were now to be tolerated and even welcomed. Another table was found for the people we had displaced and the food was good. The cabaret was a real education for a well brought up boy from Bolton, somewhat reminiscent of the anything goes days in the Berlin of the twenties.

The meeting with the Russian bureaucrats on the following day was intriguing. We, the representatives of a previously hated American multi-national company presented our various expertises round a large table to a tight-lipped group of fifty something functionaries and our wish to open up discussions. It became obvious that glasnost had not seeped into the executive brain. Perhaps the translator had misunderstood our intention. In turn some of them expressed an unfavourable opinion while others were more conciliatory. In the end it was agreed to continue the connection and a intermediator was appointed. It was the most we could have hoped for at this stage. We all flew home the following day, me to pack our furniture and other accoutrements ready to return to the UK. I was returning after a fascinating six years with three exceptional achievement awards and a lifetime of stories to tell.

It remained only to spend the other 2 weeks holiday, which we did in a chilly November in Brussels. Except that we decided to drive down to southern Italy where it was much warmer. Passing through Italian paradises such as Florence, Assissi and Pisa, we arrived at our hotel in Sorrento ready to make the most of our last days working in Europe. It was fascinating. We visited the beautiful Isle of Capri, the stunning Amalfi Coast, Pompeii and Herculaneum, climbed Vesuvius and let the Italian countryside work its magic before returning to Brussels to load the removal lorry with our European booty and crossing the channel.

Chapter Twelve

Back to Blighty

'It's great to be home, but our memories of Europe will never fade'

Back to Blighty

Our return to England was notable for the lack of any job within the company that could use my skills, knowledge and talents. IBM was drawing back. The day of the large computer had come to an end and the company had far too many people on its books In addition I had been absent for six years and had lost all the potential pathways to promotion in the UK company. So once more I suggested a compromise. Increasing awareness of climate change and sustainability was growing. But it was not yet in IBM's field of vision and this needed to be corrected.

I had made friends with several people from UNESCO and even helped them to develop a UNESCO professorship programme. I suggested that perhaps a new IBM/UNESCO professorship at Southampton University would be a way of keeping me off the books and at the same time provide valuable information that the company could use. They bought it. I had already discussed this with my friend the Professor of Education at Southampton University and he too was keen to make it happen.

And so it came about that the back street boy became the IBM/UNESCO professor developing a 'Centre for Education and Research in the Educational Sciences,' CERES, the goddess of grain and harvests. I was given an office, a colleague who was the biology lecturer and a secretary who was his wife. Nepotism exists in Universities too.

The return to our Lymington home was strange. We contacted all our old friends, hoping to start again where we left off. But somehow the old magic had gone. We had moved on and become that figure of tabloid hate, lovers of Europe. We had a vision of a connecting, collaborating continental future, we had experienced it and we were excited about it. There was little of that in Lymington. Maggie returned to Southampton General Hospital to resume her nursing career. David had married and lived in Kent. Jeannette had returned from Australia and was living in Cornwall. Our social world had changed. I joined the Brockenhurst golf club and spent my leisure hours beating the bejasus out of a small white ball, trying encourage it to enter a small hole far away from the starting point on the tee, 18 times per round. I had played a few games with my dad on the municipal course in Bolton when I was fifteen years old and later on links near to Lymington in the New Forest but was still a rookie at the game.

A Spell in Kenya

Down at the University we had meetings about the parameters of CERES and how we could persuade other companies and organisations apart from IBM to support it. We arranged a meeting with the CBI and spoke to its environmental

90

officer. We gained some interest but zero support. I went to Nairobi with Professor Blunt to give a presentation at the United Nations environmental centre on how information technology could enhance their work. Nairobi was an eye-opener. We were entertained by the education officer at his house. It was a building surrounded by a huge fence and he employed a security officer. I understood why. Nairobi had an enormous unemployment problem and people were desperate. All foreign homes were also prisons. At the centre my presentation was well received but they had little to spare for supporting research outside of their own needs. The Reagan USA had had one of its sulks. The delegates were taken to the elephant rehabilitation centre, a place where baby elephants were brought up because their parents had been killed by poachers, a sad reflection on humanity, but also a poignant indicator of poverty in Africa..

We also spent a couple of days a five hour drive away in a game park in the rift valley. Although I had spent time in Johannesburg and Capetown, I had never seen a wild, African animal. This trip soon put that right. Elephants, Giraffes and an abundance of Hippopotami in the river. Kenya educated me once more in many ways. I saw abject poverty which would make Bolton a luxury holiday resort, and the United Nations at work trying to solve these problems while trying to address one of the world's severest problems that could only make it worse. The imminent scourge of climate change.

To Halifax

As a result, I was also invited to attend and speak at a United Nations Environmental conference in Halifax on the East coast of Canada. So off I flew, this time without Maggie who was busy at work. Since schooldays, and as a geographer, I had always been fascinated by Nova Scotia and the extreme tidal differences in the Bay of Fundy and here was a chance to perceive the reality. The conference was one of a series of early meetings to highlight the upcoming problems of climate change. It included many speakers from around the world and highlighted the situation in each country. My contribution concentrated on the use of information technology, the need to keep people informed and how this might be achieved through education and the use of computer software. It seemed to be well received but there was so much to take into account from so many people that it is doubtful if real progress was made from the conference. I received no feedback in the following days and nor, I believe did the other speakers. But I did make many friends and saw the tidal phenomenon.

But back in Southampton there were problems. My colleague and his wife were wary of professors who had not gone through the university mill. It didn't sit right with them and led to resentment. And my knowledge of biology was certainly lacking which became another bone of contention, though I was always

91

willing to learn. Nor did they have the background in industry which entailed marketing an idea or a project. After eighteen months it was obvious that the centre wasn't going to work. It could have been my lack of leadership skills in the university environment but I would have needed to have a magic touch to make a difference. Instead I also worked with another professor on staff development and helped him organize seminars and meetings in the UK and at La Hulpe in Belgium. He did not have the same outlook as my colleague and we made a great success out of the work we did together.

Goodbye IBM

IBM was shedding its employees by the thousands. They called it right-sizing while the rest of the world called it down-sizing. However it offered a good termination package based on a lump sum and a much reduced payment for the rest of one's life. Not one that could sustain a lifestyle but attractive, provided one could find something to augment it. I took it and said good bye to the company after twenty four years. We had Maggie's salary. We used the lump sum to pay off the mortgage, Maggie went to work each day and I retired to the golf course improving from a handicap of twenty six to one of fourteen in the three months after leaving the University. But this was not to last long. My successor in Belgium, Keith Davies, had also retired and, with some help from the European Commission, was setting up a European Organisation promoting lifelong learning throughout the continent and based in Brussels. The topic was just coming into Europe's radar and he asked me to support him.

ELLI

The association was called ELLI, the European Initiative on Lifelong Learning. It didn't pay much but the work was fascinating. This was my third career. Fourth if you count the RAF. I worked initially with a Don from Oxford University to organize a European conference there on the subject. It was fascinating work and perfectly suited to my background, since I had had to adapt to new knowledge and understanding throughout my life. This was a Europe wide conference with speakers from the European Commission, high level politicians, academics and leaders from Industry. It took place in Oxford in 1992 just after a new Prime Minister, John Major, was surprisingly elected to succeed Margaret Thatcher. The conference generated some interest in lifelong learning in the UK which extended to the European Commission. A few forward-looking local authorities fastened onto the idea and formed an association to propagate the concept.

To Washington DC

Around the same time Keith and I made a trip to Washington DC to meet with Government and Educational leaders there and gain their support for organising a world-wide conference on lifelong learning in Rome. So very little work had been done on this subject and it was our task to increase awareness and encourage action, largely because we considered it to be crucial to the future of the planet. We met with advisors and practitioners there, to whom the concept was unknown. But we managed to persuade them of the importance of learning lifelog and they had access to high levels of government, In this way we received their agreement to cooperate in the planning of the conference.

Chapter Thirteen

Goodbye Britain and Hello ELLI

'Everyone will need to be educated to the level of semi literacy of
the average University Graduate - this is the minimum standard
for human survival'
(Arthur C Clarke)

Lifelong Learning

The rationale behind lifelong learning relates to the increased pace of change over many years. It had been accelerating to the point where it has left many people behind and unable to make rational decisions. Unless learning takes place lifelong, life wide and life deep for everyone, the political, industrial, social and environmental landscape will be compromised. The implications for all of them were, and still are, urgent. It goes to the heart of education and impacts upon the fight for global sustainability, responsible behaviour, integrity, honesty, the opening of minds, the need for international cooperation and community well-being.

It certainly beats ignorance and reminds me of the difference between the education I had received and the utilitarian ineptitude often served up in today's commodified, examination focussed schools. Education, Education, Education, was the mantra of the early Blair days before he was led astray by American revenge politics. He got it wrong of course. It should have been learning, learning, learning – lifelong. One can have all the education in the world and learning does not necessarily take place. We were already seeing the effects of inadequate education then, exacerbated by a communications media that had become a propaganda machine for the rich and powerful and even more true today.

Our first task was to put together a board of advisers familiar with the implications who would meet regularly to help make things happen. This included the Head of the European Confederation of Industry comprising the top forty eight companies in Europe, a visionary Belgian from whom we learned much. His major interest was continuous education in European companies in order to keep pace with new developments. I had done some work for him on learning organisations with which he was very impressed.

We had a Finnish MP who was organizing the lifelong learning effort in his country, Finland, a country always ahead in educational matters. The rector of the University of Napier Edinburgh joined in together with the vice rector of Sheffield Hallam and Head of the IBM Education Centre in Brussels. They were all attracted to the concept of lifelong learning for different reasons and all convinced that it represented the future. The European Commission also was planning to build a similar future for Europe and had already planned to make 1996 the European Year of Lifelong Learning.

Bye Bye Britain - again

In 1993 too, Maggie and I had had enough of the UK and its inward looking ideology. We had both become that tabloid figure of revulsion, European, more open to other cultures and languages, more tolerant of people and customs, more understanding of non-British habits and values, excited by the dream of a cooperating Europe, free of conflict for the first time in thousands of years, able to compete on equal terms with other global super-powers. The Britain of the time appeared to us to have lost the outward-looking idealism which had made it such a special place to live, and we found ourselves out of step with utilitarian governance, xenophobia and tabloid power and values. I love my native country, but as the new soft white underbelly of a nation where holding wider and different ideals seemed to have become a dubious, if not criminal, practice, we had to leave once more. It was Maggie who suggested that we should emigrate to France to live in our holiday home permanently. And this we did, and have never since returned to Britain to live, while the parochialism and insularity has become worse and worse through the years, ending in Brexit, in my mind the greatest betrayal of British values of all.

A Rome Conference

The ELLI world conference I had organized for Rome took place in 1994. It had a star-studded caste and attracted 500 delegates from all over the world. The Americans had done their stuff by identifying three top-level speakers from Government, Education and the head of the educational development organisation we were working with. They had also contacted the US organisations that would be interested and paid the fee to attend. Speakers also included the head of UNESCO and the head of its Lifelong Learning Institute in Hamburg, the head of the Catholic Universities of Australia, whom I had met on my first visit there, and professors and project managers from other countries. Attendees came from 30 countries. There were major presentations, after which discussion groups debated the content and the implications, and then reported back in plenary sessions. It was a defining event. The vision of lifelong learning in schools, universities, industry and adult education as an antidote to biased news and propaganda was established in some delegates with real power in their own lands. Experts stayed for an extra day to write down the proceedings. I edited them and they were made available through ELLI Headquarters. The idea of a world initiative on lifelong learning had been mooted and approved. All was well with the world. The second world conference would take place in Ottawa in Canada and ELLI would help organize it.

As a result I wrote my first book. 'Lifelong Learning – New Vision, New Implications, New Roles for People, Organisations, Nations and Communities.' It included many of the sub-topics that determine a lifelong learning society – new skills and values, new learning processes, new roles for teachers, schools, universities and adult education, the impact on business, examples of good practice and so on. The foreword was written by John Towers, the then CEO of Rover Limited with whom ELLI was working. It was published just in time for the 1996 European Year of lifelong learning, described below. Although I wrote it myself, I also put Keith's name as co-author on the cover as a token of respect for his efforts. It sold very well in the circles where we operated. The European Commission ordered many copies. The boy from the back streets was making a real difference.

Finland

Around this period I paid many visits to Finland. Here was a place that was prepared to embrace educational change, where lifelong learning was encouraged at government level. I did the round of speaking at meetings and conferences and hopefully solidified the journey it was taking to a lifelong learning society. I visited schools and universities noting the great educational and philosophical approaches to learning in that country. Many of our projects would include Finnish cities as leaders in educational thinking. It is not by coincidence that Finland consistently tops the PISA world achievement statistics. Its government supports innovation in learning and the municipalities respond in kind. At the same time I assisted some British towns heading in that direction, speaking at Learning City launch events in Glasgow, Edinburgh, Southampton, Sheffield and others. Lifelong Learning was alive and well and living in Europe, and even in Britain, especially after the new labour government came into power. That is not a political statement – my own politics are often based on what works in education and even the efforts the labour party was making to change mindsets were not enough.

Back to Japan

I was also sent to represent the Commission at a UNESCO conference on lifelong learning in Japan, one of the countries that had embraced its precepts for many years. Delegates to this came from all over the world to discuss developments. This took place in a teacher training college to the north of Tokyo. There were echoes of the Rome conference throughout the proceedings and a determination to embrace change in education. There wasn't much sight-seeing, though the grounds were nice enough. As usual at these conferences, the camaraderie between people of different cultures and experiences worked its magic to create a common outlook.

A group of thirty of us went out on the last night to eat at the local diner. There were no pictures of the meals as there had been during my previous visit. Just thirty scripts of the dishes they were offering in Kanji characters above the counter, which none of us could understand. It could well have included wichiti grubs with whale blood. So to be on the safe side, we ordered one of each and shared it around. Whatever we were eating proved to be delicious. The following day we each went our separate ways promising to stay in touch but suspecting that we wouldn't. Change is always unpopular. Both people and hence governments are wary of it and often reject desirable innovation.

New developmental aids

Back to Belgium and to the European Year of Lifelong Learning comprising many events and celebrations throughout the continent. I had been busy developing visual aids and clarifying the concepts of lifelong learning There are more than a hundred of such principles and they included every aspect of life in the future, including the new skills and values that people would need in order to cope with the changes to come. The following diagram is just one of many charters and diagrams I created at that time.

Skills and competences for a Modern World

Self-management Skills	Being determined to fill your own potential Continuously developing personal skills Setting and achieving personal targets Purposeful introspection Maintaining Perspective and sense of humour
Handling and interpreting Information	Using IT Tools and techniques Collecting, Storing, analyzing information Recognising patterns and links and acting appropriately
Putting new knowledge into practice	Seeing connection between theory and practice Transforming knowledge into action
Learning to Learn	Staying open to new knowledge and learning Identifying and using sources of knowledge Relating learning to personal objectives
Questioning, Reasoning Critical Thinking	Recognising and embracing quality in everything Transforming knowledge into understanding Recognising reasoning from manipulation Never being satisfied with the status quo
Management and Communication Skills	Expressing oneself clearly orally and verbally Persuading others with reasoning Listening to others Helping others to help themselves
Thinking skills and creativity	Using creativity and imagination to solve problems Thinking out of the box Anticipating and developing forward vision Knowing how and where to find inspiration
Adaptability, Flexibility Versatility	Facing change with confidence Adapting to new situations Being ready to change personal direction Keeping an open mind
Team Work	Sharing and receiving information and knowledge Participating in goal setting Achieving common goals
Lifelong Learning	Continuously upgrading personal skills Cherishing the habit of learning Contributing to the learning of others

You may wish to test yourself against all of these by giving yourself a mark out of 5 showing the extent to which you can honestly say you are proficient at. 1 = not at all. 5 = super competent.

There are a few more diagrams like this at the end of this book. They could be charters for all educational organisations wanting to become lifelong learning establishments. But the whole panoply, comprising hundreds of hours of learning aids that I created in the ELLI days, can be found at www.longlearn.info

European Year of Lifelong Learning

1996 became, as promised, the European Year of Lifelong Learning and we were well placed to help the Commission implement its agenda. ELLI was asked to organize the Year's conference and that became another of my many tasks. It took place for four days in Helsinki, Finland, to an audience of five hundred high level educationists from all parts of Europe. The first two days were the standard presentation and discussion elements of the conference followed by the conference dinner. Lifelong Learning was dissected into all its constituent parts. Several people flew back to their homelands at this point. But they missed the most innovative and enjoyable part of the conference. Only two hundred and fifty travelled on the third day, a ten hour train ride from Helsinki to Rovaniemi on the Arctic Circle with features peculiar to a novel way of conferencing, described in the following piece I wrote afterwards in tongue in cheek manner.

Riding the 'LEARN' - An Account of the Journey of The World's First Lifelong Learning Train

It is June 1996. ten carriages of the 'LEARN' - so named because the word train is banned from the Lifelong Learning lexicon, the destination being the learner - emerge hesitantly from the capacious womb of Helsinki railway station to begin a ten-hour odyssey to the Arctic Circle town of Rovaniemi. The Nordic Gods of the weather have not been kind. An angry sky threatens to make the experience a wet and windy one, and already the first droplets of the day are splashing on the speed-gathering windows. Comfortably entrenched on board, more than two hundred and fifty learning explorers, each nursing various degrees of hangover - the previous evening saw the conference Gala Dinner stretch into a long night - watch city turn into suburb into tree-clad, ice-sculpted countryside.

It is the flagship event of the flagship conference. 1996 - The European Year of Lifelong Learning, a time for renewal and change in a whole continent, an invitation to innovation and a search for new horizons extending into a dimly-seen future. This is a voyage to discover, nay to experience, the very meaning of learning. In Rover Carriage 1, the conference organisers gird their loins. From there the LEARN guardian reveals the what, the where, the when, the who and the how of the day in sepulchral, public address system tones. Discussion, debate, deliberation, decision-making and determination are the main ingredients of the travelling agenda and active participation by every passenger the ticket to its success.

Situated at each end of the LEARN, Rover Carriage 1 and Dipoli Carriage 10 are specially designed 'meeting-room' carriages, comfortable armchairs surrounding baize-covered tables which might have been used to sign the armistice of 1918. Indeed they are almost the exact image of that carriage in the 'clairière' near to Compiègne where Weygang, Foch et al forced the signature of that historic document. Here the 'trainstorming' sessions - essentially loud-speaking brainstorming with railway-like noise - take place. Here Longworth and Davies are kings for the day, reigning like benevolent despots, encouraging, stimulating, persuading, cajoling, pleading - converting erstwhile empty space into 'factories - learning ideas for the production of.'

Six times, each in the space of one and a half hours, unsuspecting people will produce more than 150 ideas for creating learning organisations in learning societies, and equally unsuspecting volunteer scribes will scribble them down rapidly, and remarkably readably, onto large sheets of paper. By the end of each trainstorm, the two carriages resemble a billboard advertising competition after a hurricane. Sheets of ideas - sensible and incomprehensible, feasible and crazy, perceptive and ineffectual, balanced and lunatic, wise and wild - are glued to the front and back of the carriage, stuck to the windows, laid on the floor and strewn on the table, while eager groups of delegates both expand and refine them into practical and achievable meaning for their own organisations and for their own learning purposes.

Two hours from Helsinki and the LEARN continues to make that distinctive, monotonous, hypnotic staccato which is the trademark of all real railway journeys - da-da-da-DAH, da-da-da-DAH, learn-ing-to-LEARN, learn-ing-for-LIFE. Every now and then, cameos from Hieronymus Bosch - wandering human strings of the dispossessed and dislocated, faces stricken, gazes blank, shuffling along the corridors hands on the shoulder in front like the survivors in the Poseidon Adventure, looking for the next port, seeking enlightenment from chaos.

It lies in the centre of the 'LEARN'. The world's first internet carriage, boldly proclaimed on its external surface to the trees and lakes of Finland, and sponsored by Telecom Finland. Here is the electronic essence of the journey. Computers inviting all, especially the computer illiterate, to strip themselves of their technological inhibitions, surf the net and communicate with the world. Here is role reversal in true Lifelong Learning style - children, some as young as 9 years old, as learning enablers for adults; accessibility to everyone, including the patronisingly-named 'accompanying persons'; an ambience of learning togetherness to match the best of community colleges. It is popular and well attended by those for whom it is intended. Messages are carefully composed and sent on their electronic way, home pages are constructed for others to read, information sources reveal their secrets and the smiles of children and adults alike demonstrate beyond all doubt that true, enjoyable learning has taken place.

Three hours into the learning journey and our first civic welcome at Tampere, Finland's fourth city. Here the intrepid explorers are given a fleeting opportunity to escape from captivity, to listen to dignified speeches from the city mayor, to be serenaded by the resident close-harmony group, to take advantage of photo- and other calls and to stretch legs unaccustomed to freedom of movement. Here too, by courtesy of the Tampere city authorities, are loaded onto the 'LEARN' the succour, in the form of packed lunches, which will sustain body, soul and mind into the unknown regions beyond the city. But all too quickly the whistle blows, the platform empties and the wheels turn northwards ever northwards towards the Land of the Midnight Sun. Everyone is once more aboard. No-one has taken the opportunity to make a dash for freedom in Tampere. It is, after all, raining.

After a couple of hours to partake of a learning lunch activities restart. Groups, by now bonded strongly into learning partnerships, go about their afternoon commissions - some to trainstorm, some to discussion groups and others to OPH carriage 9 and Rover Carriage 2, where yet more computers can be found. This is the domain of Markkula MP - the kingdom of the 'Personal Learning Plan'. Here also is software cunningly designed to guide wandering learners through the myriad pathways of their inner minds and to stimulate their desire to construct their own learning future. Errant or lost pioneers of the unknown are gently led back onto the more secure tracks where the right structures exist to satisfy their latent desires for knowledge and where mentors can help them appease the Gods of Learning.

Not only is this done by software, but it is also achieved more prosaically, and sometimes more successfully, through the excellent booklets provided free of charge by the United Kingdom Campaign for Learning. Needless to say, every traveller who has experienced this session, and that includes most of them, has emerged more aware of the processes involved in preparing both themselves and others for a more organised learning future. There is no truth in the rumour that people without personal learning plans are not allowed off the LEARN and will forever join the souls of the damned travelling back and forth between Helsinki and Rovaniemi until they develop one.

It is now four in the afternoon and time for another Civic Welcome, this time in the pretty town of Oulu, Finland's most northerly city. The brave Lifelong Learning pioneers have yet another opportunity to escape but none of them take it. Instead they pour out onto the platform to hear the speeches, listen to the songs, take a few photographs and breathe the pure air. The LEARN puffs noisily alongside waiting for their return, and welcomes them back on board within the half-hour allowed - unfortunately no occasion is given to explore the town as a learning opportunity, but then Finnish railways have to run on time and it is a single track from here into the wild North.

The now-flagging trail-blazers are still eager for action and so it is to the final sessions that they wend their well-trodden, weary ways. The discussion groups take place in the Espoo and Nokia Carriages. Here the full conference is exposed for exactly what it is - ie a stimulating display of Lifelong Learning ideas - from the new workplace of the 1990s to proposed Learning Communities of the 21st Century; from examples and Case Studies of Learning Organisations in Industry, schools and Higher Education to the development of national strategies in a European future; from the need for understanding and managing change to the new skills, competencies and values needed for life and work in a Lifelong Learning society. Here is where the strategies, projects and networks for each sector of community in the new learning Europe are discussed and designed. Here is where the alliances of the future are forged.

And so to the last hours of the LEARN, before it arrives in Rovaniemi Station. To the FREELEARN, in which anything goes. The exhausted take the opportunity to rest from the labours of the day, the indefatigable discuss its highlights in small groups or strengthen new friendships and liaisons. Others go dancing in the specially designed disco carriage, or slake their thirst in the ever-crowded bar. The noise level in both is several decibels above the end of the Heathrow runway at Concorde lift-off. A wandering Dutch troubadour offers raucous songs, and songsheets, and everyone who can hear joins in. It is bedlam - and fun - and yet more learning.

8 pm - it is Rovaniemi Station. The courageous path-finders of the LEARN - the world's first Lifelong Learning train - are welcomed by a troupe of young people dancing on the platform to disco music, before being whisked off in buses to their hotels. It is fitting. Learning is fun after all - even when you are part of a captive audience. We have travelled, we have worked, we have learned and we have taken great delight from it. What a stupid idea it was! It couldn't possibly work.....

One outcome of this was that the representative from the Paris OECD at the conference asked me to act as a consultant to the organization and to write an advisory dissertation on how this would affect the future for international economic development. This the Bolton boy did.

Learning Organisations

There were of course many more activities connected with the year of lifelong learning and member nations were beginning to understand its importance and to build strategies to implement it. This increased our work load immensely, but here we were, saving the world, or so we thought, and it was a labour of love. I continued to research the ways in which, schools, companies, universities, local authorities etc could become 'lifelong learning organisations' and developed charters to help them achieve that status.

One of these was the concept of a 'learning company' which I had explored through our contacts with the Rover company in the UK and the academic work being done by universities connected to private companies. The concept of a learning organisation is shown below and gives an insight into how all companies and institutions can improve their performance. It's a little esoteric so ignore this page if it doesn't interest you.

1. A Learning Organisation can be a company, a professional association, a University, a school, a city, a nation or any group of people, large or small, with a need and a desire to improve performance through learning.

2. A Learning Organisation invests in its own future through the Education and Training of all its people

3. A Learning Organisation creates opportunities for, and encourages, all its people in all its functions to fulfil their human potential

- as employees, members, professionals or students of the organisation

- as ambassadors of the organisation to its customers, clients, audiences and suppliers

- as citizens of the wider society in which the organisation exists

- as human beings with the need to realise their own capabilities

4. A Learning Organisation shares its vision of tomorrow with its people and stimulates them to challenge it, to change it and to contribute to it

5. A Learning Organisation integrates work and learning and inspires all its people to seek quality, excellence and continuous improvement in both

6. A Learning Organisation mobilises all its human talent by putting the emphasis on 'Learning' and planning its Education and Training activities accordingly

7. A Learning Organisation empowers ALL its people to broaden their horizons in harmony with their own preferred learning styles

8. A Learning organisation applies up to date open and distance delivery technologies appropriately to create broader and more varied learning opportunities

9. A Learning Organisation responds proactively to the wider needs of the environment and the society in which it operates, and encourages its people to do likewise

10. A Learning Organisation learns and relearns constantly in order to remain innovative, inventive, invigorating and in business

And so, based on this definition, in 1996 I made a bid for a European Commission project to test four European companies in Greece, Italy, Holland and the UK as 'learning organisations.' It was accepted. As project manager I put together a questionnaire for the four companies to assess the extent to which they accepted and implemented the principles. The results were interesting at a European level. The two companies in Northern Europe were aware of many of these tenets and had putative plans to implement most of them. Not all of course, and some only partially. These are quite advanced demands. But it showed how North European companies were constantly examining their procedures and trying to improve them.

However the Southern European companies, coming from a different, more top down, culture, implemented very few of them, and saw no need for change, especially number four. The results of this project were written up and submitted to the Commission and a seminar was held in Brussels for all companies interested in the ideas inherent in the project. The results were filed on a shelf in the basement of the Commission building and life moved on. We continued with our work in other aspects of lifelong learning. This is typical of a large bureaucracy. It funds the research and relies on others to disseminate and implement it.

Welcome Charlotte Megan

1996 was important for Maggie and me because of another happening in the family. We were blessed with the arrival of our first grand-daughter. Not before time - I was sixty years old. Our son had found another lady, Mandy, to share his life with, they had settled down in a house in Hedge End near Southampton and Charlotte Megan was the fruit of their partnership. It inspired me to write a poem as follows. Again if poetry does not inspire you feel free to move on.

<u>Welcome Charlotte Megan – to a new grandchild</u>

Welcome Charlotte Megan, welcome to this earth
You are privileged to be here from the moment of your birth
Your parents love you dearly they're the best you could have had
And they'll always have that feeling through the good times and the bad

We're simply your grandparents, we've experienced many cares
We've travelled through the storms of life and we're passing on in years
But in that lifetime's journey we have learned a thing or two
Of what it is to love and live and what it's wise to do

It isn't our intention to prescribe the do's and don'ts
For what decides your future will be mainly wills and won'ts
Your choice is very simple, to your own real self be true
And know that in the last resort your only judge is you

Our generation's faulty, we have lived our lives in haste
We've bequeathed a world of poverty, we have willed you nuclear waste
Our greed's destroyed the ozone of this earth's voyage through space
Our thoughtlessness has jeopardised the future of our race

But remember that our species is the only one to link
The present with the future through its genius to think
There's a universe of knowledge built by those from every age
Their legacy of progress is your personal heritage

It's the paradox of living in the world where you will grow
That wisdom's true expression is to know that you don't know
So set your own horizons far beyond the daily grind
And accept no limitations to the power of your mind.

Your potential is enormous if your mind be never closed
Realise your imperfections are entirely self imposed
Keep every option open as throughout life you learn
Whatever your profession or however much you earn

Always keep your sense of humour, it's the thing that keeps you sane
And employ life's changing fortunes to re-energise the brain
If you have a love of living, and you're tolerant and just
The crowds will gather round you as a friend that they can trust

You'll meet some charming people and others full of greed
Sometimes encounter misery and violence and need
But if you show compassion, make enlightenment your dream
You're half-way to maturity, respect and self-esteem

So welcome little angel, welcome to our world
By the time you understand these words your life will have unfurled
If you relish truth and knowledge and unlock your inner wealth
Then in living, loving, learning, you'll discover inner health

As you contemplate infinity, as you look up to the sky
Reflect upon eternity as the twinkling of an eye
Be creative and inventive, for the world's not what it seems
Improve it, Charlotte Megan, by fulfilling greater dreams

There will always be a reason for finding things to shirk
For delaying hard decisions, for avoiding urgent work
But keep your wits about you and acknowledge you can do
Just anything you want to if you will determine to

May your mind be ever open to knowledge, wisdom, truth
May your eyes be ever open to the visions of your youth
May your heart be ever open to tolerance, love and grace
May your life be ever open to advance the human race

So welcome Charlotte Megan, another genius come
Another human being carrying hopes for everyone
Be a leader not a follower, stand up tall for truth and right
And life will recompense you with true pleasure and delight
© Norman Longworth

The poem was framed and hung in her bedroom for many years. For all I know
it is still there. But somehow I doubt it.

Chapter Fourteen

Conferences, Conferences

'It isn't what you learn at conferences that counts.

It's what you do with that knowledge when you return. '

The Second World Conference on Lifelong Learning

The Ottawa world conference of 1997 expanded lifelong learning knowledge and practice to the New World. It attracted three hundred people world-wide to the capital city of Canada and most of them were well satisfied with the quality of the presentations. My emails from Canadian cities demanding more information increased tenfold for several weeks. It was refreshing to hear new accents extolling the virtues of learning. The idea of a world Initiative on Lifelong Learning was carried forward and the boy from Bolton became its Vice President. Sadly while the enthusiasm for global learning harmony was high, the willingness to fund it was not. Very few countries would contribute to any organisation outside of their national remit. The United Nations had their own problems and their own lifelong learning drive in UNESCO. Other international events such as the war in the Balkans were taking place. We had outreached our capability to influence change. The global initiative failed to catch on and was disbanded.

Back to Japan

But my workload did not diminish. Some months previously I had accepted an invitation to give the keynote speech at a conference in Japan immediately after the Ottawa conference, this time in the Northern island of Hokkaido. The rector of a university there had read the Japanese translation of my book and decided that I should be the honoured guest. I flew from Ottawa via Detroit to Tokyo, a journey of fourteen hours. Then three hours round Tokyo to the domestic aerodrome where I waited two hours for a three hour flight to Sapporo, the capital city of Hokkaido from where I had to take a three hour train journey to Asahikawa in the far end of the island where the conference was being held. In all about thirty two hours of travel. I was whacked and weary on arrival and, after paying respects to my Japanese hosts, with much bowing and smiling, I retired to bed.

The conference and opening speech was to take place in the following morning. Here there was a misunderstanding. I had been asked to write a paper in advance and had done so. At the same time in my mind a paper is not a presentation and so I had prepared a forty five minute speech with powerpoint support. This flabbergasted the organisers. They had assumed that I would simply read the paper as was the custom in Japanese conferences. And the interpreter had translated that into Japanese ready to echo my words to the audience. I hadn't brought the paper with me. So I borrowed a copy from the professor in charge and did what I was supposed to do. Being Japanese and extremely polite they then allowed me to make the presentation later in the proceedings after some frantic extra translation work. I normally don't stick to the script when I am speaking. This time I did. And the smiles told me that this was the right thing to do.

After the conference I was invited to the celebration of the inauguration of Sapporo, the Capital of the island, as a learning city. They knew my reputation and asked me to speak at it. This was my first meeting with a real learning city festival. It was an eyeopener, more a fair than a festival. A Pacific Ocean of stands and demonstrations promoting every conceivable facet of lifelong learning for all sectors of national and community life, and for all ages. Visitors could find every pursuit known to man from fishing to fiddling, sailing to skiing, knitting to networking. The whole of life was here. The ectoplasm of vitality and energy was phenomenal, and smiling faces showed how much fun there was in learning.

Groups of children snaked between the exhibits from every learning organisation on the island. It was a huge celebration of learning in all its aspects. Japan has always been at the head of lifelong learning development and this was the proof. Sapporo is a provincial city of about a million people and 600,000 of them were expected to visit the festival grounds during the week. A concert was held in the city hall. It included, among many other things, two people with primitive musical instruments and two singers from the Aino Inuit community who sang remarkable and evocative folk songs from long ago.

It was an epiglottal tour de force - all throat and lungs – a vocal tone poem describing the mystical sadness of the sea, the majesty of the mountains, the symbiotic maternal link between man and his environment, the joys and sorrows of community and conflict. Sounds not heard outside of this area of Japan, reminiscent of a Hebridean folk song, an Irish step dance, an Auvergnian mountain call or a Catalan lament. They were sounds I will remember for a lifetime and will never hear again.

Every citizen received two attractively coloured booklets , one produced by the city and the other by the island prefecture. They were 16 pages each, describing the rationale behind the joys of learning, and where, why, how and when it could be accessed. It was estimated that 50,000 new learners joined the learning fold. When it does something Japan does it whole-heartedly and with panache.

After such a tidal wave of learning experiences, I flew back to the UK via Tokyo to Paris and thereon to Perpignan, having made a complete circle of the Northern Hemisphere.

President Backstreet Boy in Bratislava

My colleague Keith however was not well. He had had a heart bypass some ten years previously and was feeling the palpitations that told him all was not well. It was at a lifelong learning colloquium in Hamburg where he took ill and had to return to his home in Brussels. The problem worsened and eventually he had to go back to the UK where he had a second by-pass. He died during the operation. We would miss him for his drive and humour. This was serious for ELLI. For six years he had been the Brussels anchor of the organization and I had been its creative director working from France. It was not possible for me to perform both roles. At the same time we had just landed three European projects including one of them to create learning cities with partners throughout Europe and were preparing a UK conference with the Director of Education for Southampton, another in Bratislava as well as other speaking commitments for both of us. I called a meeting of the Board. They expressed their condolences for Keith's widow and we sent a large bouquet of flowers to the funeral. The boy from the backstreets of Bolton was now a President. Help with the projects was available from both Finland and Sweden. I remained project director of all three.

The organization of the conference in Bratislava was taken out of our hands by the Slovakians so long as I could be there to speak at it. It was my first commitment after Keith's death. It took the format of so many European events. An address by a politician followed by a series of short ten minute contributions by up to twelve experts without questions. It depended where you were in the pecking order as to whether you could get your message over. The first speaker would take twenty minutes, the second twenty five, and so on without being stopped by the arbitrator. Eventually it would run out of time and the last four or five speakers were given just four minutes to comment. This happened to me in Bratislava. So this is what I said in my four minutes.

'Thank-you Mr Chair, I was going to talk about what my organisation has been doing to promote Lifelong Learning in Europe. Instead I now only have time to say what I really think. So since food is imminent, I want to present the first course - that is food for thought.' I waved the morning newspaper. 'This,' I said ' represents today's news' and I listed the national and international doom and gloom of wars, burglaries, murders, crime, divorces and poverty in that edition. 'This is not the sort of world I want to live in. This is a world created by present structures, including the educational ones which you are helping to maintain'. 'What I do not want' I said 'What we do not need, is more of the same. We do not even need better than the same. What we want, and can create between us, is more and better of something different.' I could see the audience puzzled. What is he talking about, and just before lunch?

'So, what is this something different? I have three minutes left to try to change our mind-sets from the way we see things as a progression from what we do now. I therefore recommend a three point plan.' The audience relaxed. Only three points. That we can cope with. 'Number one,' I said 'Close down the Ministry of Education!.' One third of the audience paled and others gave a nervous laugh.

There was even a cheer or two. 'But', I continued 'Only for one week'. Another sigh of relief. 'And then re-open it under an entirely new name.' Puzzlement in the audience. 'I suggest the Ministry for the Development of Human Potential.' Further puzzlement and a few pennies dropping, as they thought about the meaning of what was being said. 'In the week it is closed', I continued 'there should be brain-stormings, creative development sessions, team meetings, new job descriptions for everyone, written and re-written by the employees themselves, and all of this activity focusing on exactly how the human potential of Slovakia's young people will be developed and allowed to flourish.' The audience considered this - mind-sets adjusted a notch. Some even clapped. OK what next?

'Number two, close down the Schools!' Another third of the audience stopped smiling, while two-thirds relaxed. This was not their problem. 'That's everybody's problem', I said 'because during the week they are closed down, they should have the same brain-stormings, creative development sessions, new curriculum development programmes - And they should bring in parents, children and members of the community into all those sessions, ready to re-open as 'Institutions for the development of Human Potential.' focussing on the best ways the youngsters can be persuaded to do that.'

The audience briefly considered this. Mind-sets softened further and insights flashed. 'Lastly,' I said, You know what is going to be closed down next, 'The University section of the audience nodded, 'and I don't have to tell you what happens - simply that Universities now become 'Institutions for the further development of Human Potential.' 'And while we are at it, companies in Industry, business and commerce might become organisations for the application of human potential.' The few business-men in the audience applauded. 'Lastly' I said, now into the dying seconds 'That's what I call lifelong learning. I know you won't do any of this. But at least regard it as a metaphor for what might need to be done to create a lifelong learning society in Bratislava and in Slovakia as a whole. Thank-you and enjoy your meal.' It was a lively lunch.

Money matters

Maggie and I made multiple visits to the UK to see our new grandchild and to deal with other pressing matters. Although our home was now in France, we had sold our large four bedroom house in 1995 and bought a smaller property in Lymington. It was back to the two up two down but this time in a small block of four houses and surrounded by greenery and hedges in a small town. We let it out to holiday-makers when we didn't need it and that brought in some welcome income.

Life with ELLI was not terribly lucrative and much had been done because otherwise it would have been closed and all the work I had done would be lost. I

112

was still receiving my IBM pension and there was the profit from selling the house but it wasn't enough. Sometimes conference speakers get paid but mostly it is only the cost of travel and accommodation. European projects were certainly not the gravy train that people thought. Every penny had to be accounted for and project leaders like myself received less than 5000 pounds per year. Money in the family was getting a little tight by 1998.

A sad affair

Nevertheless there was work to be done even when it was a labour of love. The Southampton/ELLI conference of 1998 came along in November with much fanfare and several ELLI members turned up to help out, together with two hundred people from British cities and many excellent speakers. This was the beginning of Blair's new government and lifelong learning was gaining traction in several cities. There was now an association of learning communities which was supported by as many as seventy interested cities, several of them at the conference. I was helping them to understand what a learning city looked like through the TELS programme. I had also redrawn the ELLI charter to a rotating Presidency with a President annually and a Vice-president who would take over the following year. The meeting at the conference would set that in stone.

Sadly half-way through the conference, my mother, who had Alzheimers and was in a care home died, and I had to dash up to Bolton immediately after giving my presentation. I owed much to her determination and support. My constant travelling from here to everywhere had meant that I had neglected her badly and I felt a pang of remorse and guilt. Not that she would know since she didn't recognise me at the end, but that is little excuse for treating the woman who had given birth to me and encouraged me throughout my life so cavalierly. She had visited us in France just once. Maggie and I attended her funeral and shedded not a few tears.

ELLI on the move

ELLI no longer had an office in Brussels but was still active in many countries of Europe. I still had several months as President and I had the TELS project to complete. Several people on the board offered accommodation and eventually I took up the offer of my committee colleague the Vice-Principal of Sheffield Hallam University to become a Visiting Professor at that university. It entailed being there three times a year for a fortnight, running a couple of seminars for the staff and organising an end of project conference at the university.

The rest of the time I would be on the hoof in various partner countries, for example in Espoo, Gothenburg, Prague, Warsaw, Edinburgh or Bochum in the

Ruhr to mention just a few for meetings of TELS or speaking at conferences and seminars. Sometimes Maggie accompanied me but not often. TELS was a huge project. It entailed finding 80 European cities to complete a long questionnaire that would question their commitment to becoming learning cities, including leadership development, Information and Communicaton, Social Inclusion, Environment, Wealth Creation Networks and more. Within these there were twenty six sub-topics.

Most of the cities I contacted had never heard the term, it wasn't in vogue at the time everywhere. But those who completed the questionnaire could see the advantages and signed up to become part of the network. For the European Commission this was one of their leading edge projects, consolidating what had been learned in the year of lifelong learning and putting it into practice. It lasted two years from early 1999 to early 2001. It ended with two major conferences, called the first and second global conference on Learning Cities. The first took place in Sheffield, where the audience was very supportive and the hall was full.

The second was in Gdansk in Poland, formerly Danzig a Free City on the Baltic Sea. It had had a compelling history, being one of the great Merchant cities of the world and, from the Middle Ages very rich. Because of this, like Venice, it was one of the most beautiful cities in Europe. At the end of the second world war it was 92% destroyed by the Russian advance to prevent the Nazis from escaping to Sweden. But its centre, two square miles, has been completely rebuilt as it was from the documents found buried beneath the ruins of the City Hall. In planning the conference I was taken round the city and also to the shipbuilding docks where Lech Walesa had persuaded the workers to down tools and started a movement which shattered the then Communist Government. He became a hero and eventually the President of Poland. It was in this city that the second global conference on the Learning City took place.

Setting European policy

I sent the project report to the Commission outlining all the cities that had participated in the TELS project and the learning materials I had created for them. When they received it they were impressed. To the extent that I was asked to write the policy document that would be presented to the Executive for approval as European policy at the next Lisbon Summit. This I did. It became a key European policy in 2002. Lifelong Learning and the development of Cities as Learning Cities was alive and kicking in the whole of Europe. The boy from the backstreets of Bolton had done it again.

These were phrenetic years. I was now sixty seven years old but had no intention of wearing the slippers and smoking a pipe in front of the fire. There was too much yet to accomplish. When my term as ELLI President ended in 1999 I became one of the two vice-Presidents and supported the new President, a Swede, by travelling to European cities with him and attended meetings of the Board. I travelled to Australia as representative of a UK association, wrote and published a new book with Kogan page (Making Lifelong Learning Work, Learning Cities for a Learning Century), wrote the Commission's policy document with frequent visits to Brussels, and wrote the applications for two new European Commission projects while putting together the participants from universities around Europe for one of them, and another linking cities from Australia, New Zealand, Canada and three European countries for the other.

Enterprising

I also established a one man French microenterprise called 'longlearn' to conform with new French tax requirements. My fifth career, although the subject matter stayed the same. This was a nightmare. I was suddenly assailed from French organisations everywhere demanding a fee to pay for local taxes, pension rights, solidarity contributions, additional health taxes and more. All of them obligatory. They were taking away more than half of what I was earning. And on top of that they would tax the income I received from clients for the journeys I was making. So if an Australian university paid my fare and accommodation to speak at a conference, as always happened since I could not afford it myself, that would be taxed. That lasted two years and then I closed it down and opened a similar company of the same name in the UK with David, Jeannette and Maggie as Directors. On this I paid no tax at all on my company work. And it was legal provided that I declared the income from the work I was doing to the French tax authorities. Which I did.

On the home front I played Tennis each Tuesday and Thursday when I was in France, at other times for the Prades town team and entered competitions some of which I won. Maggie and I visited the UK frequently to see the family, went to weekly dinner parties with our friends in France, sang in the Eus choir, and also found time to arrange holidays in Venice, Vienna and a tour of Germany. Lastly, in my memory of this period, I came within inches of driving my car over a cliff edge. Had that happened the other way you would not have to read these words.

Almost dead

It happened as I was driving back from a meeting in Toulouse where I had just given a presentation in French. I was taking the mountain way over the col from the Aude valley toward Eus. Near the summit, the road menders in their wisdom had re-gritted the road in places without leaving any message to the motorist that it could be dangerous. As I drove blithely round a sharp bend the car refused to respond to the steering wheel and slid sideways on the grit towards a cliff on the left. I took my foot off the pedal and did what I could to halt the slide. Which wasn't much.

Luckily the car had a look over the edge, had second thoughts, and at the very last second decided that going further could be very painful. Instead it slid back across the road into a large ditch built to collect the rain water at 5000 feet. And there it came to rest, sideways on in the ditch at dusk, up a rarely used road. I wasn't physically hurt but it took some time for my heart to stop playing the flight of the bumble bee. I swear I was not speeding though I had just driven for three hours from Toulouse and may have become complacent. So what to do? I may have to spend the night in a car where the petrol might have been pouring out of the tank. I pushed upward on the driver's door as if I was leaving a tank and crawled out into the road.

The light was gradually fading. I had no mobile telephone and no way of communicating to anyone but the sheep on top of the mountain. The first person to arrive was a shepherd who had heard the crash. He watched me crawl out of the car with a quizzical look. 'Graviers sur la route' I said 'Ah oui' sorry I can't help' he said, 'no telephone' in French. But he invited me to share his hut. I refused politely, saying I would wait for someone to come along the road. He looked sceptical. It was an unlikely prospect at that time.

I waited ten minutes and then – salvation. A couple of mushroom hunters appeared from the opposite direction on their way home. They stopped. I could see the question mark over their heads. 'Graviers sur la route' I said again. 'Do you have a mobile phone?' They did. They rang Maggie who apparently responded with something like 'silly sod. Has he been speeding again.' She rang one of our Brit friends and he drove up the mountain to pick me up. By this time it was pitch black. We contacted the emergency insurance, who sent a pickup truck the following morning to transport the damaged car to a garage in Prades. It was a write-off. That was the fourth of nine lives I had had. Not quite up to the peritonitis but close. Only five more to go.

Chapter Fifteen

Goodbye ELLI

Hello Learning Cities

"Civilization is in a race between education and catastrophe. Let us learn the truth and spread it as far and wide as our circumstances allow. For the truth is the greatest weapon we have." (HG Wells)

Goodbye ELLI – Hello Edinburgh

One of the problems of lifelong learning is that it can be seen as a somewhat vague and wide-ranging concept to those who were not engaged in implementing it. More aspirational than specific It needed to be given a context, more concrete and applicable to everyday life. The context was obviously the city itself where the lifelong learning took place, and the improvement in education that would lead to improved living standards. It needed to be seen as the fuel that would deliver greater prosperity and understanding. In this way my focus was in the building of learning cities – places where education at all levels would be provided for citizens throughout their lives and seen to be the creator of wealth, sustainability and well-being.

The new ELLI had somehow lost that ideal and so I moved on to another stage in my life where I worked with city leaders and the city stakeholders to help create that learning city. I was now a visiting Professor at Edinburgh Napier University managing European projects in which the university linked with other organisations to make learning cities real.

PALLACE

It was still 2001 and both of the two projects I had applied for were accepted. They went under the name of PALLACE and LILLIPUT. Pallace was the most ambitious. It linked cities and organisations in five countries with each other to encourage them to exchange lifelong learning ideas and learn from each other. It was based on a paper I had written where I envisaged a hundred plus projects worldwide linking one city from each continent, each learning from the other. This is an extract from it.

'So now let's imagine that the agreement includes

Schoolchildren communicating with schoolchildren to bring their learning to life, open up minds to an understanding of other cultures and prepare themselves for life in the future.

Universities combining in joint research and teaching to help people and communities grow and to measure and monitor the project locally

Adult and Community Education Centres inspiring adults of all ages to make meaningful, problem-solving contact with each other

Companies developing trade, commerce, ideas , jobs and wealth

Hospitals exchanging knowledge, techniques and people

People interactions to break down the stereotypes and build an awareness of other cultures, creeds and customs

And so on – museum with museum, library with library, city administration with city administration learning from each other and solving problems

Let's imagine further that this is not the only such network, but that more than a hundred such agreements are made between cities and towns globally.

Now imagine the possible advantages…..

Thousands more people and organisations contributing to the solution of social, cultural, environmental, political and economic problems in their own and in other cities

A giant leap in mutual understanding and a transformation of mind-sets through greater communication between people and organisations

Profitable economic, trade and technical development through contact between business and industry

A huge increase in available resource through the mobilisation of the goodwill, talents, skills, experience and creativity between cities and regions

Fewer refugees – developing problems can be anticipated and addressed through cooperation between the cities

It's sustainable – because it's so much more dispersed. Governments and NGOs are no longer the only initiators of aid to the underdeveloped. Action is now shared with the cities and, through them, the people.

Organisations and institutions in the city have a real world-class focus and raison d'être

What an opportunity to make a real difference!

So this was my 'save the world' idea. Of course it was idealistic, but in my mind the only way to stop human beings destroying their own planet is to create learning cities that will make education available and attractive to every citizen so that they can understand the issues that affect their everyday lives. Also in my admittedly optimistic mind this was all about learning and communication, both interpersonal and organisational. The more that people and organisations can learn from each other on a global basis, the greater the chance of breaking down the stereotypes and barriers that divide them. The more citizens that are inspired to become involved in the exchanges, the greater the learning and understanding, the more they will seek problem-solving action. The more such action takes place the greater will be the likelihood that pressing problems such as climate change, racism, hatred and world poverty can be solved, and every Miss World's dream of world harmony can be achieved!'

Well, the Commission bought the idea for a trial in cities in four continents – Australasia, Asia, Europe and North America. Schoolchildren in Espoo, a city in Finland, would exchange ideas with schoolchildren in South Australia on what kind of city the youngsters would want to create when they became adults and what needed to be done now to help it along. A municipality near to Auckland would link with one near to Edmonton in Canada to exchange how one could help the other overcome poverty. City councillors in France would link with those in Adelaide to learn collaboratively about lifelong learning in the city through the learning materials we already had and those we needed to create. And to consider how to implement the concepts. Universities in all the cities would act as research observers.

Beijing joined in also as observers since the Chinese city was considering transforming a neighbourhood of 800,000 people into a 'learning neighbourhood' and was eager to get ideas from the project. It was a great concept but criminally underfunded to the extent that each partner would have to provide the funding for its part of the project. The money, fifty thousand euros, would hardly cover the travel arrangements and the cost of the conferences. More about this later.

So here is the boy from the back streets of Bolton trying solve the world's problems with a fifty thousand euro grant from the European Commission. Of course that's ludicrous, delusional and unlikely, but if there were to be hundreds of such city interactions involving one city from each continent working together, it would have to start somewhere, and this would be the first trial. Anyway that is the mindset with which we entered into the PALLACE project. And it had some success.

An interesting journey

The first Conference was held in Auckland, New Zealand, but we didn't go directly there. Maggie and I had taken a round the world ticket travelling westwards from London. I had been working hard and needed the diversion. So we combined it with a much-needed holiday. Our first plane took us from London to Los Angeles non-stop and here we had to change planes to continue on to Fiji. Normally that would have been a simple transfer within the departure section of the airport. But we were diverted to another exit and found ourselves in the concourse. Our luggage was inside and we were not. The struggle we had trying to get back to where we should be was titanic. Airport security is very strict in the whole of America and of course a couple of strange brits asking to go through the departure door without checking in meant that we were potential terrorists. After a fourteen hour plane journey we were very tired.

So we tried to reason with security and ended up in front of a very unpleasant adviser who didn't buy our story. Our plane was due to take off in two hours with our luggage on it and here we were on the wrong side of the divide. No point in losing our temper. We asked very politely to see the airport manager, which was accepted, and explained to him our predicament. Luckily for us he believed the story and we were quickly transported to the Fiji bound aeroplane. Ten hours later we arrived in Fiji's main airport whacked and weary.

Here we hired a car and discovered that our accommodation was on the other side of the island. two hours later we found the five mile dirt track that led to our destination on the beach and arrived there even more fagged out. It was all very informal and at that time it was night. There was no restaurant, just a barbecue where one cooked for oneself. The man in charge looked at us rather strangely and offered to sell us some food. However we were too tired to even think of eating and he showed us to our hut. In the middle was a large four poster bed with a mosquito net draped over it. We were advised to keep that over us at all costs.

We slept for 12 hours. It was the middle of the morning before we awakened. Lying on the bed we noticed that were several large hornets flying free in the room. We thought nothing of it, dressed and left the hut to find some breakfast. The view of the sea was tremendous, large waves crashed onto the sandy beach and the sun shone brightly from the sky. It was a view of a South Sea Paradise. Moving to the central hut we discovered the reason for the strange look. Every person we could see was either a teenager or a very young twenty-something. It was a haven for surfers, young Americans, Australians and New Zealanders, here to try their prowess on the massive waves in the vicinity.

The owner was in his forties and actually looked quite relieved to see a couple of old farts arrive. We said our hellos to those who hadn't yet reached the sea and tucked into eggs and bacon for breakfast. As others came along wet and barely clothed we said hello to them too and soon got into conversation with our new neighbours for a week. It was fine. They were quite happy to see Grandad and Grandma arrive on their territory. In the evening barbecues that followed we made many young friends. We told tales of France and the rest of the world where we had visited and they hung on our every word. Surfing was their only love in life but they recognized that there were other places, other things to do.

Returning to our cabin we found that the number of huge hornets had increased enormously. Indeed we could see nothing but hornets . They hung on the nets, the bed, the table the sink, everywhere. If we had gone in we could have been eaten alive. We dashed back to the owner's hut, hoping not to be pursued by a hive of angry hornets. 'Shit, again?' he said, And then he took two large bottles of spray, put a net over his head and entered the cabin. We watched from a safe distance, as they buzzed angrily. You could tell they didn't like it. After five minutes of continuous spray hundreds of hornets lay dead or comatose on the floor. He went back to his lair and produced a large vacuum cleaner into which the insects disappeared. 'That's finished' he said 'They won't bother you again.' And they didn't and neither did any of their cousins, uncles, or offspring.

We explored much of Fiji in our stay there. We went along to the marketplaces, we swam in the sea but didn't go far enough to be taken by the rip tide. (that's for a later story). The most interesting was our trip by boat into the interior to meet a Fiji community. We booked for it at the cabin. And were told to be at the company office at 10 am without fail in the next town. We arrived and looked for an office which turned out to be an overturned container. There were a number of us, again mainly young. On the way we were warned what and what not to do and to appoint a leader who would make a reply to the speech of welcome. He would be the chief of the visitors for the day. Step forward Grandad as Mr Chief while Maggie became Mrs Chief. I was given a garland of flowers to put round my neck. I dedicated it to Bolton.

We arrived at the massive Central community hut. There were young toddlers outside. It was all very formal and solemn. The Chief of the community welcomed us all to the tribe and I responded by saying how honoured we were to be there and thanked him for receiving us. Then there was the community choir which sang several local tribal songs and a display of tribal dancing. The singing was a sight better than our village rabble. Harmonisation comes naturally to Fijians. In France we have to fight for it, and it doesn't always appear. We all clapped enthusiastically.

Then the obligatory photographs, first with everyone and then just the chiefs for the day with the sous-chiefs of the tribe. I treasure that photograph. At a sign that the preliminaries were over the ladies laid out their tables around the hut to display their wares, most of which they had knitted or made themselves. We were urged to buy since this was the tribe's only means of income. We did. It was time to return to the town and to relinquish my symbol of chief for the day. I must admit that I relished the Bolton Boys and girls accession to tribal chief and his missus.

And that was Fiji. We both learned a great deal about the customs and everyday life of the people as well as lessons on humility and understanding. We took the plane to Australia and Brisbane where I had a keynote speaking engagement at Rockhampton University 100 miles up the coast. Then another in Brisbane itself, for some reason Australia couldn't get enough of me, before we had to leave for New Zealand and the first of the PALLACE events.

PALLACE rampant

The Auckland, New Zealand, conference took place at the time that the Americas cup races were also sailing the surrounding seas. Maggie came with me. The yachts in the harbour were magnificent and the rivalry between them at sea was tense, especially between America and New Zealand. But it wasn't the yachts that took our attentions. It was the massive ocean liners that had lined up on the docks. Each one could take at least four thousand passengers and there were those that could house eight thousand. We had seen them in Southampton harbour, but to see six of them together in Auckland was like looking at a city in the sea.

In the PALLACE discussions we achieved some harmony among the groups represented there. We came to a common understanding of what the project was trying to achieve in terms of international understanding and the particularities of the project development. With such a small grant there was no money to pay people for working on the project and so each partner was working voluntarily and contributing from its own resources. Far from satisfactory but the principle of international harmony was strong and none of them withdrew at the beginning. Each partner would perform the tasks allotted to them. As the months went by, the individual projects came together, Finnish children from three schools started to talk with seventeen schools from South Australia about community development.

That is until there was a change of political party in the Espoo city council and they withdrew because it wasn't supported financially by the Commission. The Brisbane axis threw in a project they were developing to create a newly built community with the technology to communicate with other communities around the world. Some contact was made with Beijing, whose delegates attended all the conferences. The Auckland partner developed a module on the subject for teacher trainers and established a link with France. There were other such links, though the intensity inherent in the original proposal was diminished by the fact that people were not being paid.

Later we caught the plane to Adelaide to meet with one of the PALLACE partners at home. Again we were treated like royalty and housed in a beautiful hotel by the Tasman sea. Each day we would be taken to a different venue , a school, the university, a college, the city council where, at each, I gave a brief outline of the PALLACE programme and what it was trying to achieve. The

123

welcome was cordial and the interest in the project sky-high. Australian schools are used to twinning with schools abroad and the idea of linking with the Finnish schools to exchange ideas on the council of the future appealed to their outward-looking agenda. They were also planning a lifelong learning festival similar to the Japanese model.

Maggie and I were also treated to excursions to wineries, the mouth of the Murray river and a circular tour of the city. I had no doubt that Adelaide would do its bit and more for the project. There were later meetings in Brisbane, Adelaide, Edmonton and Edinburgh to exchange ideas and consolidate actions. Documents and learning materials were created and tested. Partners interacted in a spirit of cooperation and learned from each other. At the end we submitted our results to the Commission. These were then confined to a Brussels basement, never to be seen again. I tried to resurrect the idea by submitting another application but this was to another department and the world was not their concern. The dream would have to wait for another twelve years before it could be resurrected. But that's another story for another time.

While in New Zealand we had taken the opportunity to visit other places on the North Island. We hired a rent a wreck and drove it three hours north from Auckland to the beautiful sub-tropical 'bay of islands' where we took a boat out the Russell on the opposite peninsula. We watched the pods of playful dolphins following the ship and threaded through small islands and sea -formed arches by the shore. Russell is a quiet town, quite pretty and looking like a middle class haven for people who like isolation. In the nineteenth century it was quite different, reputed to be the roughest and toughest in the south seas. Smugglers, bounty hunters, pirates, prostitutes and low life of every kind filled the taverns and terrorised the people. No-one was safe from being Harassed, killed, mutilated, or raped. The only reason for living there was that it paid well.

We had a drink at one of the notorious pubs and returned to the opposite shore. The bay is also close to Waitangi, the building where Captain Cook and the Maoris came to an agreement to hand over New Zealand to the British crown. This was an excursion to be remembered. Another was made to Rotorua the town built on an active volcano. Here we saw constant geothermal activity. The park where small rivulets of volcanic activity bubbled up in the ground and the fields of bubbling lava. Everywhere the smell of sulphur, even in the hotel where most rooms were heated from the depths of the earth, volcanic bathrooms and kitchens. It was a fascinating experience, to be remembered for its attack on the olfactory senses, especially when the hotwater tap was turned on. It reminded me of an IFIP visit we had made to Iceland. We also visited underground caves lit by hundreds of glow-worms and the Otorohanga Kiwi House & Native Bird Park where the very shy iconic New Zealand bird makes an appearance only in the evening.

Crocodiles

From Adelaide we flew up the Far North of Australia for a holiday among the crocodiles of Kakadu, a UNESCO world heritage wetland of two thousand square kilometres and three hours to the East of Darwin. On the way there we saw twenty feet high termite cathedrals, hundreds of towers of active insecthood at the side of the road. We had hired a hut for four days at one of the camping grounds while we explored the area. For naïve brits who had never seen a crocodile or the flora and fauna in an Australian National Park it was an eye-opener. We took the small boat that sailed the wetland past huge, menacing, recumbent crocodiles and through acres of beautiful tropical countryside. We saw birds that existed nowhere else, huge wing-spanned avians, Darter birds that resembled the pterodactyls of the Jurassic period.

We saw five thousand year old aboriginal cave paintings, and went to Jim Jim Falls, a towering waterfall under which it was possible to bathe where the crocodiles had not yet reached. We fished in the lakes and we were chased by a crocodile when we were stupid enough to leave the camp at night. We were lucky. Those crocs move fast when they are hungry. This was lifelong learning at its best in an unfamiliar environment where it was prudent to follow the rules. Before leaving Australia we spent a day in Darwin and learned about the devastation caused from the bombing by Japanese planes during the war and the even greater devastation caused by cyclone Tracy that flattened the whole city in 1974. The sunset market was a vast marketplace selling more than fifty Asian dishes in more than forty restaurants by the quay. Even our taste buds were learning lifelong.

A Thailand rest

The last lap on our round the world trip was to Thailand, and what treasures we found there! We weren't interested in the much applauded beaches. It was the culture we wanted and we got it by the spade full. Our hotel in Bangkok was on a standard suburban street but the difference was its vitality and vibrancy. Tailors would be plying their trade on sewing machines out on the pavement, the noise of traffic and the press of people were overwhelming. In the evening, stalls would suddenly appear selling everything from umbrellas to shoes to every manner of clothing. They would be there until midnight and then disappear into the night. We made the most of our five days there, taking a boat along the river to see the waterside slums mixed with palatial residences. We went to the market in the river only accessible by boat, we must have seen a hundred buddhas, each one different and some as big as a house, some in gardens and others on plinths in the many parks.

The means of getting around were the tuk-tuks, a sort of motorised bicycle with a pillion seat for another two people on the back. It was noisy but managed to move around much more quickly than the cars could. We took an excursion to Ayatuttha, the old capital some fifty miles north of Bangkok that was razed to the ground by the Burmese. What unimaginable beauty remains! More buddhas, a couple of them enormous, in size. The restored houses were built in a style quite unfamiliar to us and painted in bright colours, predominantly red. Elephants roamed at random, many of them dressed up as if going to a party, and the traces of a thousand years of history, stone buildings, statues, Chedis, exquisite stone buildings in shapes seen nowhere else, temples and more were all around. As an exercise in lifelong learning it was, like everything we saw in Thailand, fascinating.

But the big attraction in Bangkok was the royal palace. It was beyond beautiful. a collection of colourful buildings all different from each other and most of them visitable. We hired one of the many guides to take us round and explain the fascinating history of this Elysium. And of course we took multiple photographs of our stay in Bangkok and district.

Then we flew to Chiang Mai in the North of the country. Another heaven on earth. Is there no end to these places. They certainly put Bolton into the shade. My dad was wrong. There are places worth seeing outside of England. Thousands of them and all picturesque beyond anything to be found in Britain. The hotel was in the centre of town surrounded by a park with Buddhist icons. It was charming. It was also noted for Thai massage which is meant to lower the pressure on the brain and relax the muscles, thus giving a stress free inner peace. We both tried it. I don't know about Maggie but I didn't lapse into la-la land, though I enjoyed it. We booked a trip into the hills and were taken by bus to an elephant centre by a river. It was a unique learning experience.

We learned about elephants, how to harness them and train them. The elephants performed tricks for the onlookers, such as sitting on their hind quarters with their feet in the air and making quasi-singing noises to music. I have to confess being extremely ambivalent about this. Elephants are majestic, intelligent creatures and to use them as entertainment for human beings seemed to me to be an unwarranted human exploitation of the animal world. But maybe I am being a little oversensitive. At least it provided food and water for the hill dwellers.

We fed the endearing baby elephants who were pushing their trunks through the fence, and at the end of the show ascended onto a howdah on the back of the largest of them. Maggie, who is uncomfortable with heights was unsure but we

126

squeezed her between me and a portly gentleman and she calmed down. The train of elephants took off, wading through a fast-flowing river and onto dry land further down where we disembarked to stage two of the proceedings

This entailed boarding a raft to transport us down the river. We all climbed aboard the rafts, which were a lot more sturdy than the ones that castaways use in adventure books. They even had seats. It was a very pleasant feeling just floating down on the water. Except that the water was also full of young children, mostly girls, up to their chests in the water, and trying to sell their goods. It was sign of the poverty of this area of Thailand. Of course I bought, as did others but the thought of those poor girls doing this day in, day out played upon me. It may have been the difference between eating and starving but that didn't make it any better. It taught us humility and a certain guilty thankfulness for our relatively pampered way of life.

We arrived at the landing for the third stage which was a ride in a bullock cart to the restaurant where we would eat. This was fine with me. Bullocks have been used to pull these carts for centuries all over the world. In more sophisticated places they have been replaced by cars and lorries. We arrived at the restaurant and were treated to an excellent meal of Thai food. And that emphasised my inner regret wondering what those poor young girls would be dining on. It was dark when the bus deposited us in our hotels. I spent the night in contemplation of the difference between the riches of the developed world and the struggles that millions of poor people have to endure. The things we take for granted and the world we see only every now and then.

LILLIPUT reborn

Two days later we caught the plane to London, then to Paris and finally to Perpignan and the train home. For the second time I had circumnavigated the Earth. It was time to get back to work. We had indulged ourselves for far too long, and the pile of commitments had reached the sky. The Lilliput project was now in full flow and the seven partners from Denmark, Ireland (Dublin), Scotland (Edinburgh), Norway (Drammen), Czech Republic (Olomouc), France (Toulouse) and Sweden (Gothenburg) were awaiting my orders. So we called a meeting at Napier University Edinburgh to parcel out the responsibilities. The aim of this project was to create learning materials on lifelong learning in fourteen separate modules, each one with several topics, an introductory module, how to propagate it in a city's many stakeholders plus others on economics and politics.

Different partners were allocated one or two modules each and I was in charge of two, plus harmonising all the others into a coherent whole, and making sure that everyone was singing from the same hymn sheet. The method was also decided. It would consist of an introduction to the module, what and why it is needed followed by written exercises that a 'learning leader' (a teacher, leader or lecturer) could use to teach the particular content, followed by a kitbag of visual aids to help further understanding.

If that doesn't make sense it isn't important. Most of the partners didn't understand it either, or didn't have enough knowledge of lifelong learning or pedagogy. I ended up writing or modifying most of the learning materials, creating 300 hours of exercises for using in classrooms, universities, companies, City halls and other places of learning. The others then translated the modules that concerned them and tested them with real live learners. It was quite complicated.

Australia revisited

In 2002 Maggie and I were once more off to Australia, this time to the tropical region of North Queensland where I had a speaking engagement on a mission to bring the principles of lifelong learning to Cairns, its major city. We travelled a week in advance and spent it in Port Douglas, a smaller prettier town fifty miles to the North. It was from here that the ship to the Barrier Reef left and of course we took it. What a privilege to visit the world's largest coral reef and before it started to suffer badly from extreme climate change, not to mention the human destruction caused by the Adani Coal mine exporting fossil fuel to China.

In effect I had been there in 1999, when I had had a ten minute scuba diving lesson on the way and was set loose on the coral on arrival. That was both wonderful and scary. I am not a good swimmer and suffer slightly from claustrophobia. I marvelled at the variety of fish of all colours and sizes on the sea bottom, all the while wondering if I would ever leave this watery prison. This second visit, this time with Maggie was far more formal. On the way we were shown short films and given lectures on the reef, its origins and the dangers it was now facing. We were taken to a docking centre where fish large and small came to the surface to be fed by the crowds on deck. It was still an experience, especially for Maggie, but for me quite an artificial one.

The next day we were taken on an excursion into the Daintree rain forest where we boarded a boat for a ride along the river. It was like all the films we had ever seen about the jungle. Dark, tree-covered, full of wild life, especially crocodiles, and eerie but beautiful in its own way, and different from the sider open spaces of Kakadu. Twelve hundred species of flowering plants, eight hundred different rainforest trees, spectacular orchids, strangler figs, exotic palms and hundreds of unique creatures inhabited this lush green world.

We half expected Tarzan to swing out from the trees on the opposite bank and land on the boat quickly followed by Cheetah. He didn't and neither did the ape. The owners are missing a trick there. It could be a holistic display. We also visited the mouth of the river and saw the signs warning against bathing because sharks, crocodiles, lethal jellyfish and it seemed every known predator to man were waiting impatiently for the first stupid human being to try their luck. We didn't bathe though probably many more macho lunatics have.

This was a week to remember, because the next day we took the Kuranda railway, a train that climbs vertiginously up the side of a gorge to the Atherton tablelands at over a thousand feet. Half way up it stopped for breath and people got out to admire the view. This is the one time we saw a Cassowary. It is a shy bird something like a very small ostrich and even many Australians have never seen one. He walked out of the bushes and, on sighting us, scurried away back from whence he came The train continued and reached the top where there were restaurants, aviaries and other attractions.

The aviaries were amazing. Every bright colour under the sun and more than thirty species. One entered into the huge cage with them and I have copious shots of Maggie with a double-eyed Fig-parrot or Macleans Honey-eater on her shoulder, a Golden Bowerbird or Pied Monarch on each wrist and seemingly speaking to them. But another treat was to come, but perhaps not for Maggie. The way down was not by train but by sky cabin above the canopy of trees. In response to her anathema to heights, she had her eyes closed all the way down, while I admired the flora and fauna. It was a breath-taking ride.

On the last day we were on our way to Cairns in a hired car when we spied a crocodile farm at the side of the road. We explored further and found it to be a lake full of crocodiles with a couple of people standing in the water making them do tricks. Neither of them were Steve Irwin, the Australian botanist who made films of his exploits with Australian wildlife, and especially crocs. The spectator gallery was high above the lake to protect the gaping masses, like us. From the lake we had a running commentary about how crocodiles were probably one of the most ancient species on earth and how they had survived several extinctions of other species from the distant past, including the meteorite landing that saw off the era of the dinosaurs.

These two were in the water feeding the crocodiles as if they were tame dogs, and only if the animal would make a death roll to earn it. This is not a career I would recommend to my grandchildren if I wanted to see them every Christmas, or indeed anyone else's. A few years later Steve Irwin was killed by a crocodile. I wondered if those two are still standing in the water.

The Cairns conference went well and that was followed by another in Brisbane. While in Brisbane I caught up on their contribution to PALLACE. I was taken around the new 'learning community', shown the old 'learning corridor' and updated on a 'learning festival' being organised by the university. Some parts of Australia were well advanced in lifelong learning city development. The trip ended, as usual with a few days with the Baileys and the Chardonnay.

In October of the same year we were blessed with another addition to the Longworth family. Adam was born in Southampton to David and Mandy. So now we were grandparents to a lovely girl and baby boy to perpetuate the dynasty. What more can one ask for? It certainly increased the number of times we crossed the channel to meet the family, even staying in posh hotels during Christmas since, surprisingly, their prices had lowered.

Chapter Sixteen

Stirling Work

'The whole purpose of Education is to turn mirrors into windows.'

Lilliput was the last project I carried out as visiting professor to Edinburgh. My good friend Professor Mike Osborne at Stirling University saw the potential in this young sixty seven year old and I signed up as visiting professor to that university. We had submitted a project to identify the lifelong learning indicators that would allow schools, universities, companies, adult education institutions and local authorities to transform themselves into learning organisations. Other Universities in Ireland (Limerick), Italy (Catania), Norway (Drammen) and France (Toulouse) joined in the fun. It was called Indicators. It started in 2003 three months before my fateful visit to the hospital And we had our first meeting at Stirling University. It was pretty straightforward. I would write what I called learning audit tools. This how I described the schools audit tool in the jargon.

Learning Audits

'The audit itself is not simply a questionnaire. It is a carefully-worded instrument to engage the stakeholder in debate with itself about its own future as a quality learning organisation, and its relationship to others in the city/region and beyond. The lifelong learning rationale is embedded in each action element of the audit tool, in order to help stakeholder management and staff understand what a lifelong learning organisation within its sector will be like and how it can make that transformation.

Schools become closely involved with the transformation process through questions soliciting opinions, information and comment, and exercises developing internal and external debate. The 'stakeholder audit' tool we have created for schools therefore has five purposes, all of which are connected with meeting these criteria in a learning region:

1. It will enable schools to measure their performance as 'learning organisations' within a learning region.

2. It will explore all the parameters which enable a modern school to address the vast number of changing needs and demands of all its own stakeholders – parents, governors, teachers, children and members of the community around it – in a 21st century lifelong learning society.

3. It will examine the contribution the school might make to the construction of a learning region in which it can play a part and from which it can benefit.

4. It will act as a basis for comparisons with schools in other regions

5. It will stimulate discussion and debate among staff, students, parents, governors and the surrounding community

We have tried to make the Schools Audit both flexible and useful by dividing it into sections dealing with different aspects of its activities. Please note that this is a tool and not just a questionnaire. Its purpose is to stimulate thinking, debate and a determination to take action through discussion, study and action. This transition affects all parts of the administration, often in quite fundamental ways, and the change process it will engender will take months and years.'

So what we are trying to do is bring schools in this case into the twenty first century on a European scale but bearing in mind cultural differences in each country. The same with Universities, Adult Education, Companies and Local authorities. Phew. That wasn't too bad was it. I promise not to burden you further. If you really want to know the content of the audit it can be found on my website www.longlearn.info together with hundreds more learning materials.

They probably didn't understand a word or get past the second paragraph, but the audit questions explained it all anyway.

A hearty interlude

The Lilliput project and the general workload had obviously taken its toll because the fifth life descended upon me and I was carted off to hospital for three by-passes to my heart. I didn't actually have a heart attack but, according to my cardiologist it was imminent and it's to that decision that I owe my relative longevity. So far. I was in the hospital for ten days followed by four weeks in a recovery institution where they made me pedal static bicycles, swim ,walk daily round a lake and eat lousy food. They do things thoroughly in France. It was the month of July and August 2003. The rest of France was experiencing a heatwave not seen for a hundred years and old people were dying like hornets in a Fijian hut.

So in my temperature controlled bubble in the hospitals I was missing out on all that fun. Of course Maggie and several of my friends came to visit me. And they sometimes brought titbits of real food but I had no computer to pass away time's rolling moods and for much of the time I was somewhat bored. When I was finally allowed out into civilisation I asked my doctor what I was allowed to do 'No tennis' he said 'no running, no cycling. You can, you must, walk, but not too far and not up hills (in the Pyrennees? You must be kidding!).

You can sing in your choir but take it easy and eat sensibly.' I had lost fifteen kilos of weight and Maggie's nursing skills came in very handy. He didn't say anything about golf so three months later saw me on the first tee at St Cyprien golf course for my daily walk. From then on I swapped tennis for the gentle sport of belting the hell out of a small white ball. I had four lives left and intended to keep it that way.

I was allowed to work and continued to travel to project meetings in Dublin, Kaunas, Edinburgh and Pecs before writing the Lilliput project report for the European Commission and completing the new book I was writing that year called 'Lifelong Learning in Action. Education for the 21st Century.' Which surprisingly sold quite well, as far as academic books ever sell. It is often said that academics write books for other academics to read, and it is true, but this and my books had been translated into Spanish, Lithuanian, Chinese and Italian and that covered most of the world's reading capital.

Coals to Newcastle (NSW)

In between this meeting and my sojourn in hospital we had actually made yet another visit to Australia and New Zealand. It was getting as if we were thinking of emigrating, which was the last thing on our minds. But the prestigious association of Australian universities had asked me to give the keynote speech at their annual conference in Newcastle, New South Wales and I didn't know how to say no. So off we both went in our airship to land in Sydney and caught the train to Newcastle.

After I had done my bit and attended the conference we stayed an extra day to look round the place, and indulge Maggie's search for whales. They were reputed to be on the move up the East Coast. Newcastle reminded me a little of Bolton, which of course is another way of saying that it didn't have much to offer. Which was not quite the case because it is on the seashore from where one can walk out along the promenade to the typically Australian name of Yorkey's Knob. It is also the centre of Australia's most famous wine growing area, the Hunter Valley. And that's it for Newcastle.

Up the Coast

There were far more interesting places up the coast towards Brisbane 500 kilometres away, where I had another engagement. So we hired a car and drove up the New South Wales coast towards Queensland at a hundred kms per hour, the official maximum speed. We reached Port Macquarie on the first night. The following day Maggie went out in a whale watching boat to fulfil her dream. She arrive back 4 hours later not having seen even a spout. This, according to the boat's skipper was the first time this had happened. So now we knew who it was who jinxes every whale watcher. Once the undersea communications media had started to monitor where Maggie was, all whales were placed on curfew within hundred miles.

The other highlight of our stay in Port Macquarie was the Koala sanctuary, where sick koalas were made whole again. It comprised a field with several eucalyptus trees in which these timid lovable creatures could hide, a sort of hospital where the patients were hiding from the doctors. Maybe we need more of those around the world. We caught a glimpse of three or four peering out at the world and a couple more on their way to the operation room. If such cuddly creatures didn't exist someone would have had to invent them – probably from Disney.

We had booked into a hotel in the famous Byron Bay for the following night and continued our journey northwards in that direction. We took lunch at the 'Big Banana' an Australian name for a kind of museum where all things banana could be found. It was indeed a bit bananas but, as was our wont, we learned a lot about them. We also had a demonstration of hydroponics, a method of growing crops without using soil, just water and nutrients. After a lunch of bananas in different guises we renewed our journey and eventually arrived in Byron Bay by five pm.

It has the reputation of being the coolest place in Australia not in temperature but in the approach to life of its citizens, the wellness capital of the country. The publicity blurb says 'the region is known for its spectacular beaches, unique shopping and dining experiences, world-class festivals, and vibrant community spirit.' So that's why went there as well as visiting the lighthouse on the eastern-most tip of Australia. Difficult to experience all of this in one evening and one morning before we had to be on our way, but it was a pleasant enough place. We soon reached the border between New South Wales and Queensland and found our residence after driving through the gold coast, little Japan as it known in Oz because many of the high rise buildings facing the sea were funded by Japanese entrepreneurs. And the Japanese visit it in large numbers.

Another life gone

From Brisbane we spent a day with one of the nurses that had trained with Maggie in Southampton Hospital. She lived in Maroochydore on the sunshine coast where the waves are as high as houses. And this is where life number six was lost. The two families settled down on the beach but, being naïve and simple-minded, I wanted to swim in the sea among the huge breakers.

There was an area set aside for bathers and patrolled by life guards, but the breakers were larger further along the coast and that is where I stupidly went. Having several tons of water thundering onto one's head is a fine thing to do, but the sensation palls after the brain has been battered for more than ten minutes, and it was time to wade ashore. Except that the riptide formed by the breakers had a tendency to whip one's legs away and wash a body back under the battering. I tried several times to break through but the result was just the same. I was getting exhausted and in the first stage of drowning. I could see Maggie and her friends on the beach. So I gave them the one armed wave that denotes I needed rescuing. They waved back, thinking I was telling them what a good time I was having.

For the next ten minutes I was waving frantically for help, as what seemed like another hundred tons of water descended on me each time I tried to escape. I had swallowed enough water to sink the Queens yacht and my strength was at its lowest. I made one last effort and luckily another group of people noticed that I was in trouble, happened to have a long rope and a young man came to the rescue hauling me like drowned possum across the rip. I thanked him profusely and made my way, exhausted, to where Maggie was happily chatting. 'Did you have a good time dear' she said, while I collapsed on the sand in front of her. I learned later that more than a hundred people drown each year performing that very activity. And being equally brainless. I wouldn't be surprised if it contributed to the heart problem. I count this as yet another life almost lost and was now down to three.

To Sicily

Our second Indicators meeting was in Catania in Sicily a couple of months after I had left the sanatorium. We compared progress and re-assigned responsibilities, modifying and explaining those aspects that partners found difficult. European projects have to cope with cultural differences. After the meeting those present decided to climb to the top of Mount Etna which at that time was scattering fire and ashes all over its flanks and beyond. We hired a car and drove up the road to the restaurant half way up – that is at six thousand feet– passing piles of molten lava that had been thrown out of the mountain top. Here the road ended and it was possible to continue by train. Sadly I could go no further. My height limit, according to my doc was one thousand feet and here I was at six. It would have been unwise to go further.

It probably was unwise to reach six thousand but some people never learn, even when they are preaching lifelong learning. The rest of them took the train and returned with tales of derring do among the lava beds. We then descended to a village on the flanks of the mountain and partook of a meal consisting only of mushrooms of the region. It was delicious, especially the porcini which I had never eaten before. They were heavenly. We returned via the village of Taormina and what a delightful village it was. One long street of beautiful houses and shops leading down to the most perfect Greek theatre overlooking the Straits of Messina. Tourist perfection. We were fulfilled.

Exploring Sicily

I took Maggie there again when she joined us in the third Catania meeting six months later. Of course we took extra days to explore this marvellous island. Our first stop was at Syracuse, formerly a Greek City built centuries before Christ and a history book all by itself. The architecture is stunning, there are palaces, fountains, catacombs, baroque churches, an indescribably brilliant cathedral on the main square. And that's just the hors d'oeuvre. There was also the Italian sense of enjoyment and carefree living.

Further East we drove to Noto, a UNESCO world heritage site. I may have waxed lyrical about Syracuse but Noto is even more interesting. The old city was razed by an earthquake in 1793 and the new Noto is an entirely Sicilian baroque construction in its entirety, built on a grid system with a soft rock that gives everything a honey colour. Breathtaking churches galore and cafés, restaurants and cuisine to die for. We spent hours walking round the streets and exploring the interiors until we finally collapsed into a restaurant and then went to bed tired but happy.

Inspector Montalbano

By this time we were getting culture weary. We moved further south and East into Inspector Montalbano country. First Ragusa, then Modica, built on the side of a gorge and a bugger to explore because everywhere there are steps and staircases not recommended for aged people with weak hearts. But the cathedral of San Giorgio is a gem of Sicilian architecture and the restaurants are generous to the point of obesity. We only had time for one more cultural wallow in this magnificent region of Sicily and to visit one more wonder of the ancient world before we had to return home to meet reality.

As a farewell treat the town of Agrigento would do nicely. It was a Greek town in antiquity and the remains of Greek buildings were mostly gathered on a hilltop site near the town. This was yet another archaeological jewel. Temples galore to the gods and heroes of Greek mythology, Hercules, Vulcanol, Thesius, Theron, Juno, all in excellent shape except for the lack of roofs. As in the Parthenon in Athens, the pillars are still there in all their strength as if challenging the modern world to match their longevity and their vitality. We can thoroughly recommend this part of Sicily, not just as place to relax but also as a beautiful learning experience that will mellow your soul.

Canada

2004 sneaked in through the door without our noticing it. We had as usual spent Christmas in the UK with our wonderful family and returned home the heavier

137

for it. All was well. David teaching in Gosport, his partner Mandy working the telephones, Charlotte growing into a beautiful young girl and Adam now just two years old and lively as a jack rabbit. Jeannette had moved to London and was working for a large multinational company while living in a flat near to Hampton Court. This was the year we finally decided to go to Canada to meet my long lost cousin in Ontario. We had met when she paid a visit to England when I was ten but I could not for the life of me remember how she looked. She was now seventy nine years old and I was sixty eight.

Why Canada? She was the offspring of my mother's sister who was sent by my grandfather to Canada aged nineteen in 1920. There was no work to be had in Bolton at the time. She prospered, married and had one daughter whom she called Lois. Lois too had also prospered and had four children who each also had three or more children so that the Ball Canadian dynasty reached well into the thirties. But how to recognise her when we landed in Toronto? And how would she recognise me. I was no longer a ten years old Bolton scrubber and neither was she a twenty year old swinger. I need not have worried. There standing in the concourse of the airport as we arrived was my grandmother. The spitting image. Genes don't lie.

They lived in a town some hundred miles to the north of Toronto – distances are all relative in Canada. We were both treated like royalty. Ferried everywhere to meet the family which had dispersed widely, as North Americans tend to. One part of the family lived on the shores of lake Huron a hundred and fifty miles away, another daughter in the hills only fifty miles away. Her son, Tom, was in Vancouver two thousand five hundred miles away and the others within driving distance.

We saw them all, daughters, son, grandchildren, great grandchildren and even a few babies from the next generation. For two single children like us with just two children and two grandchildren it was all a little overwhelming. The welcome we received at each house was also overwhelming, but these relations were seeing their British family for the first time and curious about whether we looked like ordinary human beings or cabbages from outer space. I drew up a chart of the Ball family abroad for them to see, and included the Canadian contingent. This astounded them. They were Canadian through and through and had never given a moment's thought to the family on the other side of the pond.

We left for a short visit to Tom and Kathy, my remaining relatives, in Vancouver. Here we were taken to see one of the world's most beautiful cities and we vowed to keep in touch as one does. This time we meant it and have done so ever since. Finally Maggie too has Canadian relatives and now it was her turn. We hired a car and drove the thousand miles to Dawson Creek up in the wilds of

British Columbia and the beginning of the Alaska Highway, built during the second world war in case of invasion by the Japanese.

It was like a frontier town with access to a vast wilderness only to be found in Northern Canada. We drove hundreds of miles along gravel roads to see the lakes, the enormous trees and along the Alaska Highway. The immenseness of nature's wonder encapsulated in this landscape. It was a privilege to be there. We got on well together. Maggie and Joan found family togetherness and John and I found common interests in music, especially classical and more especially the opera bouffes of Gilbert and Sullivan of which he had the whole set.

The Icefield Parkway

Came the time to leave. We intended to travel to Alberta to look for Maggie's other relatives and in particular the name of her uncle who died in the first world war which would be on a plaque in Banff. So we drove another eight hundred miles through rolling hills and magnificent forests to Jasper and the beginning of the Icefields Parkway, a travellers delight. Here we explored the spectacular countryside around the town before leaving our log cabin.

The parkway is breathtaking. Near Jasper it passes the early stages of the river Athabasca where it tumbles down mountainside and gorge on its six thousand mile journey to the Yukon, the Mackenzie river and into the Bering Sea. There is more water here travelling at, it seems, a hundred miles an hour, than any river we have seen. It is a watery spectacle involving thousands of litres of water every minute. Further down the parkway is the nursery of another mighty river, the North Saskatchewan which winds its way east over much of Canada and eventually into Hudson Bay. As a geographer I found it fascinating to map the course of these rivers which are ten times longer than any to be found in Britain.

Along the parkway too there are waterfalls, glaciers and wildlife – bears, moose, elk, bison, mountain goats, wolves, cougars to name but a few. We saw them all except the wolves. And views to make us gasp. Such as the photogenic Lake Louise, surrounded by snow-covered high mountains and a watering place with luxury hotels and restaurants. A few miles further by Canadian standards, fifty by normal, is the town of Banff, high in the mountain scenery where a Dutchman built the first Fairmont luxury hotel, a majestic building that costs the earth to stay there.

It was here in 1912 that Maggie's great uncle upholstered the chairs in the hotel and rode his horse down the main street. The last time he rode it was 1918 as a soldier in the Canadian Cavalry in the vicinity of St Quentin in France. He is buried in a war grave there. But there is also a tribute to the Banff cavalry in the city and Maggie found his name there. That is what we came for. A day later we flew down to Calgary deposited the car and flew home. When we returned home we found a parcel of all of Gilbert and Sullivans' opera bouffes. We knew who had sent it Unfortunately Canada has a different hi fi system and they are just a little jerky.

Indicators completed

Back home there was work to be done on the Bolton boy's bid to change the world of education for the better. The Indicators project was in full swing and there were further meetings in Limerick, Drammen and Toulouse. Finally the audits that we thought would transform the delivery of education throughout Europe and provide a new highway to a more effective and saner lifelong learning perspective were tested and completed. And filed.

LILARA explained

I wrote the report to be sent to the European Commission. It only remained to apply for another project to implement it and thus LILARA was born. Learning in Local and Regional Authorities. This one was aimed at implementing the indicators we had just completed within the organisations they were designed for. And which would satisfy their learning needs if the new educational order, outlined in Lilliput and Indicators, was to see the light of day. In the words of the project description to the Commission.

'The focus of the LILARA project is to use the results of INDICATORS and other projects to research and satisfy the needs for training and learning in Local and Regional Authorities and their institutional stakeholders. By creating, testing, modifying and making available a number of learning programmes it will assist the development of a wide variety of staff in Lifelong Learning Organisations, Regions and Cities. This is not just a dissemination project to let people and organisations know about the existence of learning materials. It actually researches the need through a learning needs analysis, finds relevant materials, creates new materials, and disseminates them through the web for all authorities to use.'

Sounds reasonable enough. So, having defined what a lifelong learning organization is, it now remains to assess the extent of the need for education among those who are implementing it and then supply it both in cities and regions. It is based on the premise that Learning Organisations, Cities and Regions are not the preserve of any one member state. They affect the economic, social, cultural and democratic future of every city, town and region in Europe. The project also envisaged a conference. The partners were the same as Indicators plus Pecs in Hungary.

140

Frolics in Eus

Life in Eus was quite time consuming. The clique that we had led astray gave weekly dinners at which there was much singing, a euphemism for the noise that could only be heard by the neighbours, and the drinking which caused it . We also set up a wine-tasting society in which the host would buy the wine, set it up as a blind tasting, and the rest of us would guess its provenance. It could be red, white, rose or, as I did, an aperitif wine. It was great fun. None of us had a clue and couldn't tell the difference between a red and a white never mind a Cabernet Sauvignon, a Syrah and a Merlot. But we had great fun trying, each one requiring at least two or three fill-ups to make a decision. Spitting it out? Forget it. We would never make oenologists.

Quite apart from our membership of the choir our social calendar increased exponentially. We belonged to a circle of music lovers established previously by Jo, a British ex-opera singer with whom we became very friendly. On the first Sunday of every month one of the members would host a musical evening, choose the music and provide the chairs for people to sit on chez eux. Occasionally there were live events with pianists, guitarists and our two opera singers providing the entertainment. Until this year this has continued and is being organised by Maggie and me. The musical choice always has been eclectic, much of it is classical, a ballet, an opera, but the choice is entirely the host's choice. We were not averse to Pink Floyd, Jazz evenings, even pop. It attracted around twenty five music lovers often packed into whatever accommodation was available. The pandemic of 2020 finally put a stop to it after 28 years of unbroken musicality.

Croisée d'Art

Maggie became a painter. She learned everything there was to know, went to painting lessons, bought books and magazines and adopted her own style. Though I am not a connoisseur of the visual arts it seemed to me to be good, though her friend, who had been painting for years was the Picasso of the two. They always entered into the local painting exhibitions with a view to making a bob or two by selling their wares. The big occasion was always the 'Croisée d'Art' the Eus village super-show every first weekend in June when the villagers opened their houses to the artists so that they could display their masterpieces.

It is well-known far and wide and visited by thousands who had the extra task of climbing the steep streets to get to their destination. It was very successful as a spectacle but not as a pathway to economic self-sufficiency since very few were actually bought. Catalans are well-known for their frugality. The variation of styles was extensive, anything from recognisable landscapes and portraits to the latest in undefinable blobs. Eus prided itself on its avant-guard traditions. And it wasn't just paintings. Peculiar pewter mugs and strangely shaped dishes were proudly presented as creative, visionary art which may, or may not, exist only in the minds of the perpetrators.

La Brigade Internationale

Not to be outdone I formed a dance band. I had bought a Yamaha piano in 2002 and every now and then would practise. But for 'La Brigade International' as we called ourselves after the people who went to Spain to fight against Franco, it was serious stuff. It comprised a Welshman on the drums, a Dutchman who played the Saxophone, A Frenchman on the double bass, an English guitarist and me, following in the footsteps of my dad sixty years on. We practised the quicksteps, foxtrots and waltzes we knew from yesteryear but we soon learned that the region's proximity to Spain meant that the locals preferred the more South American rhythms. So we expanded our repertoire to the cha-cha cha, the rumba and the pasadoble as well. We had our share of strange requests. Such as the man who had won a pasadoble competition some 40 years previously and, at the end of every dance, asked us to play another pasadoble.

We played gigs at many locations including the square in our local metropolis of Prades (population six thousand) to an audience of hundreds and during Festival weeks in the villages. Because of its name many people thought we were ersatz communists trying to herald the return of the new Stalinist world order. The band lasted several years and then the saxophonist went to live in Portugal, the drummer back to the UK and the guitarist, who been a busker in Yorkshire in a past life decided to branch out on his own. La Brigade therefore met the same ending as the original one.

Back to LILARA

LILARA continued on its educational course. We had meetings in Stirling, Pecs and Limerick. The middle one is stunning. It is at the point in Hungary where Christianity meets Islam and the mosques are built opposite the churches. I wrote the audits that would be translated where necessary and sent to the punters in the schools, colleges, universities and local/regional authorities. Each partner had a specific responsibility for one of these, to administer the audit received, write up the results, translate it into their own language, and organise a seminar locally for the participants, report on that and then join the conference to be held in Limerick.

The final result was planned to be not just the audits to discover interest but also a learning needs audit that every local and regional authority could use to stimulate its own employees but also those of the their institutions, including companies. It involved getting people to identify which aspects of lifelong learning they thought they needed more awareness of if the municipality was to adopt lifelong learning principles, which many were already beginning to do. They included twelve targets for learning in a local authority such as basic knowledge, wealth creation issues, Educational Issues, Contribution Issues, Cultural issues, Environmental and sustainability issues and more. The respondents simply had to tick whether this was high, medium or low as an issue for them and were given the opportunity to say why if they wished to do so. Simple stuff. A course would then be provided. In Sicily the university held a seminar in a school in one of the towns close to Catania and produced some interesting feedback.

In Stirling we liaised with the city leaders to ask its four thousand employees to complete the audit online. About five hundred did which was rather disappointing after they had all been asked by the mayor. We assessed the results and built a seminar around them for the city employees. Only twenty turned up , the others pleading pressure of work, but that was OK since the room we were using wouldn't take five hundred. Similar activities took place in the other partners. The final conference was attended by a capacity a hundred people from around Europe. They listened to the presentations and participated in exercises to strengthen the understanding of LILARA tenets.

A final addendum to this is that interest was also shown in Victoria, Australia and they paid for me to fly there to explain it to the relevant government authorities. Which I did and received a resounding confirmation of interest such that they intended to follow it through in all their townships. Looks like the boy from the backstreets of Bolton should have become an Aussie. At seventy years old that wasn't really on the cards. I would probably have been redirected to the Nauru immigration detention island.

Seventieth Birthday - Rome

Life continued and down in the sticks of the South of France we adopted another stupidly bright custom. We would all take a trip abroad when either of us had a birthday ending with a ten or a five. That started with a mass emigration to Venice for one lady's sixtieth which was so successful that we made it a permanent feature. It was now 2006 and my seventieth birthday. Where should we go? Why Rome of course, the Eternal City. After all there was a daily flight from Girona airport just down the road. So Rome it was, accompanied by twelve hangers on who had come for the free meal and to admire the splendours of the city, of which there were too many to count.

We all threw coins into the Trevi fountain, ran up and down the Spanish steps, poising at the bottom to see the house and explore where John Keats the British

143

poet lived. It took me back to my English literature days at school. We walked round the Forum, circumvented the Colosseum, queued to enter the Vatican city with its paintings by Raphael and the stunning ceiling painted by Michel Angelo in the Sistine chapel, toured St Peter's and its square, said hello to Castelangelo and the Pantheon. Wherever we looked roman history was staring us in the face. Wherever we strolled there was a monument to Rome's ingenuity. It was pervasive and just to be there was a tribute to lifelong learning. The birthday dinner took place in a restaurant in the Trastevere area where the Italians eat. If you haven't been to Rome a veritable treat awaits you.

The year before we had sold our last house in the UK, taking advantage of a hike in prices, and we were now homeless there. In future, when we would return for Christmas or the grand-childrens' birthdays, we would need to find other accommodation, usually in hotels but occasionally in the houses of friends who were away for Christmas. It was a little saddening. We were still British in our minds and supportive of the then government because of its commitment to Education, though we could not condone the atrocities being committed in Iraq, mostly by Americans but also, by proxy, by the British. It was a year of gradually distressing news.

These were the heady days when educational development for the future was being supported by government bodies. Economies were strong and the need to prepare for change because of the effects of innovation, climate crises, lifestyle adjustments, technology and a whole host of other transformational events was a challenge that only better education could solve. George Bush was crowned for a second term, Tony Blair for a third, Hurricane Katrina flattened New Orleans in retaliation, the US and Australia declined to support the Kyoto protocol on global warming and there was, what's new?, trouble in the middle East. On the bright side Charles finally married Camilla. Hooray, Britain was saved. The education message **was, however, not always getting to the places where it was most needed, the schools and communities who could most profit from it. Only in certain countries like Finland where education was well funded and innovation encouraged was there the necessary transformation of mindset.**

Eus sings

In the magical land of Eus, the daily grind of living in paradise continued apace. Maggie's painting was rapidly reaching Gainsborough standards and she was selling more but for low prices. They will only reach millions after her death. My band was playing an increasing number of gigs including charity fund-raising concerts. For example we played for Médecins sans Frontières at the Eus Maison de Temps Libre, or village hall, and raised eight hundred euros. We tended to play for free and the fun of creating music and that is probably the main reason why we were in such demand. At same time our choir presented its second 'spectacle' or musical drama on the history of the village according to the creative minds of its two geriatric authors.

I should say a couple of things about this choir. It is a village choir and according to its dear leader, conducting it is a little like searching for the philosopher's stone – that is trying to produce golden notes out of distinctly base musical metal. As she remembers it, not even the greatest alchemists in Europe ever found the secret. But they had a great time trying, and she also has trying time. Practice night is often a case of never mind the notes, feel the music. Close proximity to tonality becomes one more triumph, as does one less groan from those whose only familiarity with pitch is at the Perpignan Rugby ground. But to be a little more respectful, the quality is not as low as all that. We sing in competitions and at the local *rassemblements* with and against other choirs and we are far from the worst. Which of course is saying very little!

The choir is finely and evenly balanced between sopranos, altos, tenors and basses and in each there is an equally even mix of those who hit the note, those who think they have hit it and haven't, and those who send out a search party for it with little idea of where, or how, to find it. Tone-deafness is an occupational hazard for an equal number of people in each section. Some members are there more because it's hugely preferable to watching French TV (vomiting in the toilet would be preferable to that), and perhaps, too, for the free wine at the end of the proceedings. In spite of this, some songs we get completely right, more by good luck, I suspect, than any particular magic. Others we get almost right and there are a goodly number of tunes around which we are continually fighting a rearguard action, if not activating an undisciplined rout. Sometimes we think we have got it surrounded but somehow it escapes to fight again another day.

Driving in the Conflent

The driving here also tends to leave room for improvement. Most brits tend to believe that all French are lunatics on the road. Down our way we have the French drivers' French driver. Like most cars in the region my car boasts the scars of battle - scratches and dents gained while stationery in the supermarket parking lot, a missing side-view mirror from a Honda that seemed to want to occupy space on my side of the road and a shattered hub cap from a tractor with an appendage as wide as the road it was driving on. Drivers in France are never required to retake a driving test at any age and driving licences last unto death, and sometimes after, without need for renewal. I understand that it is part of the French obsession with the rights of man.

Thus we have blind, deaf and batty geriatrics in charge of potentially lethal instruments of death with the right to create carnage wherever they drive, and infant child racers with all the confidence of youth, but none of the ability to justify it, together with all the wannabe Lewis Hamiltons in between. We have a fairly narrow road leading from Prades to our hamlet. Most drivers use the centre of the road so that they can travel at high speed without dropping into the concrete water ditches on both sides. This does not allow of course for vehicles travelling in the opposite direction. It's often a game of dare. Which one of us will give way first? Somehow it works, though I have had to replace my rear view mirror more than once. There are very few collisions though sometimes one might end in the ditch and have to call for the local farmer to drag the car out. This tendency to invite carnage prompted me to write 13 laws of Catalan driving, as follows.

1. If you are behind another vehicle, overtake. This is a matter of honour. Following another vehicle is a stain on your (wo)manhood

2. Always wait until just before a bend before you overtake. This keeps oncoming traffic on its toes and maximises the surprise factor

3. Never brake until the very last minute. The insurance company will always make the other driver pay for rear bumper collisions

4. Solid white lines are just broken ones where they have mistakenly forgotten to put the gaps. So, once more unto the breach, lads

5. If you have a passenger, engage him/her in animated conversation with lots of hand movements and eye contact. Do this while driving fast. Put him/her in the back seat for maximum effect.

6. Never signal your intention. In this way you keep the other drivers guessing as to which way you will go. If you do decide to signal always forget to turn the blinker off. This causes maximum confusion for minimum effort.

7. If you are female, you can do anything you want on the road. All mirrors, especially the rear-view mirror, are placed there so that you can ensure that your hair is straight and your mascara hasn't run.

8. The recommended gap between you and the car in front is three microns. If it has a foreign number plate it is two microns or less.

9. Ignore all speed limits. They are there to annoy you.

10. Overtake as if long lines of traffic are exactly the same length as a single car. If a car approaches from the opposite direction, swerve into line only at the last minute. Remember the other guy will always give way.

11. The shortest distance round a corner is straight across it. This maximises both petrol consumption and annoyance to other drivers

12. On narrow roads, always drive at speed in the middle. Make way for cars approaching from the opposite direction just at the point where the front bumpers are about to meet. Extra points if the other car lands in the ditch. Blind bends are particularly interesting places for this rule and may require some speedy manoeuvring. Extra points for catching his rear view mirror

13. Better dead than cissy

PASCAL

But enough of this frivolity. Let's get back to the action. In 2007 I wrote the final report of the LILARA project to the European Commission. It was accepted of course and then put on a shelf in a Brussels building. It was up to us to disseminate it widely, which we did. But probably not widely enough to make a real difference. In the meantime I had become involved with a global organization of universities and some companies called PASCAL with headquarters in Melbourne, Illinois, Glasgow and Pretoria in South Africa.

This gave a much wider opportunity to disseminate our research work on lifelong learning and learning cities. For this organization I was, among other things, asked to visit Botswana University in Gaborone, Africa to spread the good news. This I did, having meetings with the Botswana Government and delivering two seminars at the University. It was highly successful and for the week I was there I was treated like a royal visitor. I also took advantage to renew my acquaintance with Capetown. What an incredible city with the Table Mountain overlooking an exciting city against an azure sea. I was only there for two days, so I did the bare tourist necessities including a trip on the hop on, hop off bus and a rise to the top of the mountain. There is so much more to see and do there.

PENR3L

I made yet another application to create a network of lifelong learning partners in each European country that would preach the word locally. The sort of job that Paul did in the new testament to market Christianity but with less reliance on letters and more on seminars and distribution of the learning materials created in the other projects. We called it PENR3L for reasons known only to us. That too was accepted in 2007 and we had a jolly time gathering together all our contacts in different countries and developing conferences in Barcelona, Kaunas in Lithuania, and a final one in Limerick.

We also brought PASCAL into the mix so that it would get global attention. It ended with 'the Limerick Declaration' which I had written and now needed to present before the mass ranks of attendees at the conference in Limerick. This was an important document in the annals of European lifelong learning and was distributed widely. I present the first part of it here to demonstrate the urgency of keeping in touch with developments in European education. If it seems a little uninteresting to non-educational readers I would point out that education is the single most important activity that human beings can engage with and it needs to be lifelong if humanity is to survive on this planet. However you are, as always, at liberty to skip this rather lengthy peroration.

THE LIMERICK DECLARATION.

We recognise the urgent need for local and regional authorities to meet the changing economic, social, political, environmental, cultural and management challenges of 21st century life. We believe that the solution lies in a better understanding of the underlying regional dynamic which balances the global and the local, develops the social capital already existing in most communities and fosters innovation, creativity and growth. This can only be achieved by a large increase in continuous and lifelong learning for management, professionals and councillors, eventually extending to the citizens themselves. In short, cities and regions must become learning cities and learning regions, developing their human, intellectual and community potential for the benefit of all, and engaging all stakeholders in this task.

We, bearing in mind the importance of learning throughout life, declare that we will foster and develop new knowledge, expertise and resources to help create learning cities and regions well able to meet the future with confidence, imagination and success. In particular we believe that the following list of strategic directions will help local and regional authorities to construct stable, prosperous and sustainable learning regions that will benefit all its institutions and citizens.

Exploiting the resources and expertise of Higher Education Institutions, thus helping them to fulfil their third mission in the Bologna process

Mobilising the energies and potential of other public and private sector stakeholders for social and economic growth

Fostering innovation, creativity and vision in people and organisations

Capitalising on diversity as an investment, valuable for economic , human and intellectual growth

Adapting and using already existing tools and materials to increase lifelong learning opportunities for all citizens

Requiring all institutions and workplaces, including the local authority itself, to become learning organisations with continuous improvement programmes for all employees and high quality benchmarked standards

Developing interaction between the local and the global to create investment opportunity

Continuously improving employability and skills to meet the changing requirements of the world of work

Releasing the talents, skills, experience and knowledge of the community in active citizenship projects

Using the media imaginatively to publicise and celebrate the learning region internally to its citizens and externally to its customers and potential investors

Enabling people and institutions to become actively involved with environmental protection projects

There were then four pages of addenda which spelled out exactly what each part of civil society could do to make all this happen but I won't bore you with the details. They are in the website www.longlearn.info for those who have a yearning to understand more.

The last throw for 2007 was the publication of my book 'Learning Cities, Learning Regions, Learning Communities.' Associated with it are several hoursworth of learning materials on the internet. Professor Finnegan, who wrote the Preface, said that it contains:

The origins, development and main characteristics of the learning cities and regions concept and the reasons why it is so important in today's world.

The many tools and techniques usable by cities, towns and regions and their stakeholders to energise participation and help create a culture of learning

A proposed global role for cities and regions to help combat the blinkered ignorance, binding poverty and militant terror that my ultimately engulf us all

He has read it so it must be true. He also said that it was written by one of the 'world's foremost thinkers' for which I thank him. The problem is that the world does not always listen, unless it is repeated many times on the television.

Chapter Seventeen

Glasgow University

'A person can have all the education in the world and learn nothing'

This was my last project with Stirling University. I had gained it some excellent European publicity and in return I had obtained the personal status symbol of a Wikipedia writeup, which can be looked up at any time on the internet. It is for sure shorter than this book. In the future my European project work would be with Glasgow University, to where my friend Professor Osborne had emigrated.

Crash, Wallop

Then in 2008 came the crash, and panic all over the world as stock markets tumbled. Everyone blamed everyone else for it but in truth it is always caused by greed and one or more countries exceeding what it would be wise to do. In this case it was caused initially by the Bush Government selling houses to those that could not afford to pay for them but countries around the world had to deal with the backlash. It certainly affected the amount of money available for projects. But I had completed many projects successfully and, for the first time for fifty years I was more or less unemployed.

Vienna, City of Dreams

Which of course gave us time to catch up on family matters and other more pressing things like celebrating Maggie's birthday. She was seventy in 2008 and we all bundled off to Vienna, including my cousin Renee and her partner from England. What a City! There is so much to see and do, and the architecture is stunning. Much of the centre resembles a film set for a period drama. There were fourteen of us and we visited the copious art galleries, the amazing Lippizaner horse display in the iconic Hofburg, Schönbrunn castle, a baroque masterpiece with superb grounds, the 18th century Belvedere palace, the Architectural beauty of the town hall and so on without end.

The city of Mozart, Beethoven, Strauss and so many of the greatest eighteenth and nineteenth century composers was in full bloom. We had Sachertorte in the coffee houses and booked for a concert at the Musikverein which proved to be Andre Rieux and his orchestra playing Vienna waltzes without end. The actual birthday dinner wasn't in Vienna. There was a water bus to take us several miles down the Danube river to Bratislava, and the party took the ride past the riverside castles and the grand mansions to the quay at our Slovakian destination. I had booked it at the First Slovak pub, which wasn't a pub but a restaurant. This was the one meal I had to pay for and which all our guests came to eat. A long way to go for a free meal, but what extra hors d'oeuvres there were in the previous days.

The meal itself was an eyeopener. The first course was a garlic and cheese soup in a bread bowl. It wasn't obligatory to eat the bowl but some of us did, and by so doing filled their stomachs too full to enjoy the specialité de la maison, the Slovak

152

hog, which came almost whole and required the birthday girl to slice for everyone. The comments were rife and I have a photograph of Maggie, knife in hand, playfully threatening one of the guests. We exited the pub stuffed but ready to explore the evening highlights of the city, another mid-European gem.

Then came the problem of getting back to Vienna. Dusk was falling, there were no river boats and only one bus for which there was an enormous queue. We were some of the first people at the bus stop but that didn't count for much when it arrived. There was mass assault on the entrance. Thankfully we all managed to get on board but it was close run thing.

The Eus Home Cinema

On our return we took up our life in Eus again. But the times they were a-changing, even in deepest France. Our saxophonist left us for a life in Portugal with his son, who had a holiday home there. He had already started showing signs of dementia by playing bum notes at crucial times. Next the guitarist decided that he wanted to plough his own furrow. And so 'la Brigade Internationale' was no more.

However, the britgang was still operative and the dinners ever more raucous. And les amis de la music had passed to new hands, ours. We organised the seances in everyone else's houses, and our own. Here the upstairs second storey became a theatre for thirty plus people. We carried up all the chairs in the house and carried them back again afterwards. We hoisted the tv screen up high, adjusted the wifi to its highest et voila, here was the Eus home cinema. Pink Floyd's the wall was performed there, the disc version not the live one. We showed operas, brass band music, ballets, jazz concerts and had live concerts, whatever came into our heads. It was very popular among the cognoscenti who attended it. .

Came September and it was to the UK for the grand-childrens' birthdays which fell closely enough together for us not to need to return. We travelled slowly through France via La Venise Verte, the green Venice, an area in the Charente of canals and trees through which one can be boated by a French gondolier, not that the boat is anything like Venetian. It is very relaxing experience in an area that is quite unique in France. I took many photographs and they all came out green, thus confirming its name. We arrived in the UK where things were constantly changing. The grandchildren were twelve and six, David was moving out of the house and Jeannette was graduating back to her first love, taking up a post with a childrens' theatre with its headquarters in Newark.

On our return to the bottom of France Maggie, who was not finding enough to do to fill her restless soul discovered Cancer Support France, an organisation to help

153

Anglophones weather the ravages of cancer. With her friend Penny she helped to build up its organisation in the south of France, offering a telephone service, translation facilities and many other kinds of help to English speaking people with cancer. It was a satisfactory surrogate for her inability to work in hospitals.

Canada once more

2008 morphed into 2009 and, for the first time at the beginning of the year I had no commitments to the European project. It would have do without me. It didn't last long as we shall see. I did however have a PASCAL meeting to attend in May in the University of British Columbia, Vancouver with attendant presentations, and this became the focal point for another Canadian adventure with Maggie and our cousins. We arrived in Vancouver in mid-May, just before Maggie's seventy first birthday and stayed with cousins Tom and Kathy for two weeks. Three days of that week were taken by my presentations at the conference but the rest was ours to own. And what fun we had.

We were taken to all the places around the south of British Columbia, Harrison Hotsprings , Hope, Whistler , the port of Vancouver, Stanley Park and a ride up the coast to horseshoe bay. There was Victoria day, long forgotten in the UK, but a national holiday in Canada and an opportunity for all the bands in the district, of which there are many, to puff and blow their instruments while parading along the main street. It was all great fun. We were taken to Tom and Kathy's holiday residence in the Rockies for several days and travelled by Tom's boat through the lakeland there. We barbecued our way to obesity. I managed a game of golf with Tom at one of the strangest courses I ever played – all slopes and water hazards. They were the hosts beyond compare.

Next it was the time for Maggie's cousins to entertain us. They had moved from Dawson's Creek to John's family house in Ladysmith on Vancouver island, an area as large as the British Isles. Canada is a vast country. More cosseting. John drove us to most of the most beautiful spots on a beautiful island. Lake Cowichan, through the Qualicum parks where we could hide inside massive douglas fir trees to Tofino on the West coast where we could look across the Pacific ocean to Japan five thousand miles away, down to Victoria and back. Then the following day through Chemainus, the logging town that lost its livelihood but rebranded itself by inviting the island's artists and sculptors to paint huge murals on all the walls - and transformed the town into a three million visitor a year spectacle.

To Butchart Gardens one of the most beautiful flower parks in the world. We saw about one hundredth of the island which is wild in more than three quarters of its land mass. Finally John and Joan drove us to Northern tip of the island, a five hour trip, to Port Hardy where the Britanny Ferries ship would sail us up the west coast sound to Prince Rupert, the end of the Canadian National Railway. More whale watching for Maggie since this is a favourite spot for them. Alas word had got around the whale fraternity that Maggie was here and they once more declined to make an appearance. The blue of the water the green of the trees, the brightly painted huts along the shore, and the spectacular sundown made this a voyage to remember.

Prince Rupert is not very attractive. It is a terminal which lost out to Vancouver a hundred years ago. But it is the starting point for the spectacular Skeena Railway, which traverses the Coastal range and the Rockies to Jasper in Alberta. And that is why we were there. All the carriages are built for viewing the amazing scenery in this part of wild Canada, the rivers the lakes, the snow-capped mountains and the vast curtain of forest on the way. It was an experience like no other. The train stopped at logging stations and for a night at Prince George half way. Then on toward Jasper. At our request it stopped at a small town called Longworth so that we could have a picture taken of ourselves underneath the town sign. That's what I call Canadian service. I can't imagine it happening anywhere else.

At Jasper we disembarked to be met by Maggie's second cousin and her whole family. They had booked a log cabin at the hot springs just out of the town. The following day we wallowed in hot water, not too hot, and then took the cabin car up the mountain above. What a glorious extravaganza of snow-filled mountains, lakes and small villages which epitomised Canada for us. Later we were taken to their house to revisit Edmonton where we spent several happy days exploring more amazing sights of Alberta.

Then back to Jasper, where we hired a car to traverse the icefield parkway to Banff again. The next day we descended to Calgary and took the plane to Toronto to meet my Ball relations once more. We were taken to the casino where one of the daughters worked. Spent a lot of money on the machines. And then put my last dollar in the last machine as I left. It coughed up five hundred dollars. Which I couldn't spend because we were leaving the following day. I gave it to my cousin. Sadly she died two years later in a care home. Her husband followed her a few months later. They were both ninety.

Climbing the Canigou

In August, David and the grandchildren came to visit us in the South of France. It was an opportunity to do the things we wouldn't ordinarily do. For instance we climbed the Canigou (9000 feet), the mountain we see every day from our front door. We all piled into a jeep that took us to the refuge halfway up and then it was up to us to walk the rest of the way. Adam, 8 years old, ran up, David, 48 years old, walked up and the old 75 years old fellow crawled to the top, the result of too many project meals in posh restaurants.

Adam ran down, David walked down and I then hobbled down. It was the third and last time I have climbed the mountain. Next time I'll wait until the helicopter arrives, though it hasn't ever been seen. Maggie and Charlotte didn't make it because Charlotte was suffering from vertigo, but she made it to 8000 before retreating. In the next days we explored the caves in the Cerdagne, a hanging valley to our West, visited the soon to be UNESCO world heritage site at Villefranche, went to the beach at Collioure and had a boat trip in the med. Among many other things. There's much to do in paradise. That's why we live there.

Sicily and Italy – more history and beauty unleashed

2009 was a year of constant travel. After our exploits in Canada we were on the move again this time to fulfil our friend Linda's 60th birthday party which she had scheduled for West Sicily, the bit we hadn't explored. The core of the gang attended, this time staying at a hotel in Trapani near to where the Ryanair plane had landed. It was an agreeable town with narrow streets and an esplanade but without much evidence of history. It seems that we would have to hire a car that would accommodate six people for that. We did.

Not everyone is as interested in beautiful buildings, history and sight-seeing as we were. This was more a boozers outing for the cheap wine, culinary experience and a change of air. But we managed to persuade the crowd to visit the hotspots of religious and touristic beauty. Places like Erice, just up the road, an ancient town built up at 1500 ft with a view of the whole countryside so that the people could see their enemies approaching and take appropriate action. It had battlements and, at the time we visited it, a racing car rally with a noisy commentary in rapid Italiano.

Monreale

The next day we explored two of the marvels of Italian history The monastery of Monreale and the city of Palermo. Both were fascinating. **The cathedral and cloisters at Monreale particularly. You don't have to be religious to recognise the splendour and elegance of a cathedral. And there some that go even beyond that. Monreale is one such. We have, in our lives seen gaspworthy buildings, but this one gobsmacked us as soon we entered through the door. A wonderland of richness and magnetic delight. Even Linda and Alan who are the apotheosis of atheism had to sit down so impressed were they. The upper part of the cathedral's interior is completely covered in gleaming gold mosaics; more than**

156

6,000 square metres of mosaic. They were almost certainly created by craftsmen from Constantinople, and the art and architecture was spectacular. In the apse, above the altar, there is a huge image of Christ Pantocrator, draped in a blue robe, his hand raised in blessing and surrounded by depictions of saints.

The central nave is lined with glorious pictures from the Old Testament. One of them, a stunning sequence of scenes of Noah's ark, with animals being coaxed on and off the boat, and passengers crammed in like Ryanair customers peering through windows was exquisite. In the side naves were scenes from the life of Christ. For a small charge, you could buy a ticket to view the *tesoro* - the treasury of the cathedral - to get a closer look at some of the mosaics, and to visit the cathedral's panoramic terrace. We took numerous photographs and continued on our way to Palermo stunned and silent. After that Palermo seemed grey although it is one of the most iconic of Italian cities, sullied by its history of mafia atrocities. We walked the streets from one majestic building to another and had a meal in one of the many restaurants. Then we walked some more until we saw a church devoted to the templars. We entered and there we saw a mini-Monreale, an exact copy in miniature of the Cathedral. That made our day even more worthwhile.

To Puglia

Maggie and I had to leave the party the following morning because I had a project meeting in Bari on the East coast of the Italian mainland. We flew to Rome and then over the Apennines to our destination. Yet another immaculate Italian city. The place is full of them. There is a perfectly preserved Norman quarter dating back a thousand years and the town, built on a grid pattern in the 18th century, is very chic. My meeting was at the universum, a sort of university for those who missed out when they were younger.

The meeting was for a PASCAL project, PURE, to identify the links between industry and education within a region which would enable it to prosper in the future. It covered the whole of the Puglia region in South-east Italy. So while Maggie was exploring the Norman quarter and getting some serious shopping in, I was holed up in the city's conference centre listening to presentations from the local education and business gurus. I said my piece about the importance of creating learning regions before any of this could take place and got a warm applause which seems to indicate that they listened.

It remained to write up a strategy to make it happen, which would be then sent to the Puglia Regional Development Headquarters in a few days. But first thing the following day we were out on a tour of the region stopping off at various institutions to hear their testimony. Maggie came too for the ride. The coach travelled down the main road to the south stopping off at Brindisi, a ferry port to Turkey and Greece, and Lecce a University city in the far South. I didn't see much of the town but the university had allocated 2 students to take the non-participants, including Maggie, around the town. She reported back that it was beautiful.

The coach trundled on, turning to the West and came to Taranto on the instep of the heel of Italy. This was an environmental disaster city that had relied on an enormous iron ore plant now in its death throes. The carnage was everywhere, polluted water, dumped rubbish from the plant over several square miles and desolation everywhere. We also learned in the college hall that the Italian nuclear fleet had also been based there, that it no longer existed and had dumped therefore it spare uranium into the sea. The passionate speaker was an environmentalist challenging us to solve an unsolvable problem.

As an outraged supporter of a green economy I was prompted to suggest a few remedies including better education and a government effort to clean the place up. Other people made similar remarks but the truth was that few organisations, including government, were in a position to implement a rescue because of the global recession. The poor people of Taranto would have to continue suffering illness and degradation until things improved. On our way back to Bari, shaken by what we had seen, we were taken to see the Trullies, small circular huts that acted as holiday homes. Our report was written and submitted to the regional authority, but I have no idea whether or not it was implemented.

50 years wed

2010 was notable for being our 50th Wedding Anniversary which was held in Southampton with many guests comprising those we had known and befriended in the UK over those years. The boy from the backstreets of Bolton and the girl from the two up two down in Deane had made it so far. It was both a romantic and an emotional celebration. My remaining cousins, old friends, including George, my mentor in the early IBM days, and of course the whole family, dressed up to the nines to celebrate the occasion. My wife as always looked radiant and even David wore a tie. I wore a white jacket for the one and only time. I wasn't taken for the wine waiter but it was a close run thing.

Jeannette gave a short speech and David a longer and very witty, one. Charlotte and Adam looked very grown up. If what they said is anything to go by, we have successfully brought up an intelligent and caring brood and their brood in turn have followed in our footsteps. It was a moving and wonderful occasion and we received many golden presents to remember it by. The wine and bubbly flowed freely and the dancing afterward reflected the state of inebriation of the dancers.

Sojourn in Madrid

It was also my 75th birthday and according to tradition had to be spent somewhere other than home or the UK. So a party of 10 brave souls holed up in an apartment block in Madrid, near to the Plaça Major, the city's huge and most beautiful central square. One of my guests was John Osman, the former BBC correspondent for Africa and then Russia. He is the only person I know to have had more adventures in foreign lands than us. Like all good journalists his capacity for alcoholic beverage was enormous, as was that of his wife Virginia, also an ex-scribbler for the Daily Telegraph for her sins. In Madrid we were welcomed by Jesus Rueda, a former colleague of mine from the IBM Education Centre. He had retired back to his home town and willingly escorted us all round the sights of the city. For which he earned his and his wife Annushka's place at the free birthday dinner in the poshest restaurant in town. So, grâce a Jesus, we saw the Royal Palace, The Prado Museum, The Puerta del sol, the Gran Via and more. At the restaurant, served since 1790, the 'spécialité de la maison' was suckling pig for which it was justly renowned. And it was indeed delicious, unless you were vegetarian or Veganly inclined.

Eurolocal

It was another busy year. I had a PASCAL project in Ostersund in the middle of Sweden which required a few weeks of preparation. And I had been asked by the European Commission at the end of 2009 to submit a project request that encapsulated all the lifelong learning materials we had created in the previous projects into a single website, together with any others we could find within Europe. This I did, and co-opted three partners from Italy, Germany and Hungary. And we got it.

It envisaged ten project meetings and workshops in various parts of Europe and a conference to complete the task as well creating four new audits, developing new tools and publicity to identify new information, modifying existing materials to fit the requirements of the website. I said that it would be complex and it certainly was, By the time it started in early 2010 I was seventy four years old and eager to get this finished ready for retirement at seventy seven. It was to be my swan song. Mike found an excellent web designer and we were on our way.

The European Eurolocal project to gather together all learning materials into a knowledge storehouse on Lifelong learning and learning regions and cities in Europe started with a meeting of all partners in Glasgow. Here each partner was given a slice each of the continent for which they were responsible, for finding

activities that could be included in the website. As the help document stated, to collect the knowledge that enables Europe's cities and regions to become learning cities and regions. These would be uploaded into the Eurolocal website that was, even then, being created. To assist them in this I developed two initial tools, one to identify the topics and activities we wanted to include, and secondly a help document listing the types of information we needed to put into the website. They included

1. Self-learning materials. Audit tools, course materials, personal and organisational development tools, learning needs analyses, videos. consultation tools etc that can be used to raise the level of participation of people and organisations in learning region/city development

2. Finance, Development Strategies, Skills Development, Active Citizenship, Innovation and Creativity, Culture and Heritage, Communication – any initiative that would help a region to understand the steps to be taken in order to become a learning region or city.

3 Papers, Books, Research and Development Reports, Charters, Projects and Outcomes, Presentations, Monographs etc that will expand knowledge of learning region and city development and highlight the need for learning in people and organisations

4. Initiatives to increase the contribution of schools, adult education, universities, business and Industry, local authorities, libraries, museums, communities and people in learning region/city life and growth. Includes international cooperation and learning organisation

5. Local, Regional, National and International networks, organisations, associations and groups concerned with learning region and city development. Includes useful websites and web references

All these had to be uploaded: So a set of instructions on how to do this followed. There were 3 workshops to help them to enter details of the information they received and to test the tools, among other things. Like I said complex, and not always easy to accomplish since they had to identify the organisations that would provide such data. My patch included the European Commission's organisations and I did the rounds of the departments that could help, including the Committee of the Regions, the Directorate Generals for Development and for Education and Youth and more. I spent several days in Brussels seeking these out and interviewing the people responsible.

It was the first of these that offered the most feedback. Initially they knew nothing of the learning materials we had developed, the concept of a learning region or the projects we had already completed. Which shows how inward-looking some of the Commission departments were. But they soon saw how we could help each other in Eurolocal and sent their staff to all our meetings.

More Canadian Capers in France

2011 appeared without us noticing. Apart from the exigencies of the Eurolocal project which entailed a bucketful of travelling it was also notable for receiving visitors who had never before darkened our door. First Maggie's cousin brought his Philippino partner to wonder at the marvels of our countryside. He had housed us several times during our infrequent visits to Bolton and so we regaled them both with the wonders of Carcassonne, the delights of Villefranche and the fleshpots of Vernet-les Bains. Later in the year it was the return visit of Tom and Kathy from Vancouver, and we intended to outdo their hospitality to us.

Neither of them had ever been to Europe. So we did France as a starter for ten. The first week was local – places we took everyone and already mentioned in these annals, including Carcassonne which is a good one and a half hour drive away. For those who have never been there the main attraction is called la Cité. It is reconstruction of the old city, according to the creative mind of Viollet le Duc in the times when the Cathars held sway. The Cathars are the gentle religious sect that was rapidly taking over the area when the naughty Catholics were playing hardball.

Most of the local aristocracy supported this new religion but that was declared to be a heresy by the pope. Innocent by name, sinful by nature, guilty by action. He commanded the then King of France to do something about it. So the badly named Philip the Good sent an army of Northern thugs under the command of the psychopathic Simon de Montfort to do the dirty work. In the end the Catholics won by the simple expedient of burning lots of Cathars alive. That was then and this is now. It is the second most visited place in France for its narrow streets, twee shops, ramparts, a castle and oodles of restaurants.

Next we took them to Rocamadour, another humdinger of a town 3 hours further north in the department of the Lot. This is vertical town on a rock face. The citizens live below, the ecclesiastical part is half way up the rock face and the Castle sits on the top. It is very gaspworthy and nearby is a large hole on the ground said to be made by the devil but is actually the cause of limestone collapse. One can descend and make an exit by boat. So we did. We spent three days in that beautiful part of France. Next further north we took them to our favourite castle in the Loire Valley, Chambord. Now that's a real eyeopener.

Built by Francis the first in the 15th century after a derring do visit to Italy, it still has all its stones intact. He never actually lived there but he paid the bills apparently. We managed to squeeze the castle of Cheverny in too.

Finally to Paris which excited Cathy so much that she kept shouting 'hello we are Canadian' out of the car as we rounded the Arc de Triomphe. We were lucky not to be arrested for breaching the peace. We stayed in an apartment that belonged to their pharmacist back in Vancouver. We did Paris in six days, Chateau de Versailles, Montmartre, the Invalides, Eiffel Tower right to the top, La Defense , Notre Dame. They got the lot, so much so that they caught the plane back to Vancouver dewy-eyed and in shock.

Chapter
Eighteen

UNESCO Consultant

'The Object of Education is to teach children how to educate
themselves throughout their lives'

The Eurolocal project lasted two and a half years, eight meetings in Pecs, Limerick, Munich and Glasgow and a final conference in Switzerland by the Murtin lake. A mountain of information found its way onto the website, most of it useful. It was at this conference that I met Jin Yang, a Chinese dynamo seconded to the UNESCO Institute of Lifelong Learning. He was one of the speakers. And immediately my plans for retirement bit the dust.

It was 2012, I was seventy seven years old. The people in UNESCO had taken note of my books on learning cities and I was regarded as a world expert. They were developing their own global network of learning cities. Could I please help? The Bolton Boy was once more entering a new adventure into global educational politics as a consultant to UNESCO. I went to the UNESCO Institute of Lifelong Learning headquarters in Hamburg to be formally shriven before setting out on another adventure.

2012 was also notable for other activities. We had been invited to go with Alan and Linda, our Yllician drinking friends, on safari in Namibia and South Africa. They had spent 3 years in Baphutotswana as advisor to government on environmental education. How could we refuse? So off we went via Etihad airlines via Abu Dhabi to Johannesburg once more followed by a short hop to Windhoek in Namibia where we hired a car. Namibia is mostly desert but it is a wonderfully crowded desert chock-full of interest.

Namibia

Formerly one of the few German colonies, which was taken over by South Africa during its Afrikaans period of Apartheid, the people are quadrilingual, speaking German, Afrikaans, English, and their own tribal language. Puts Britain's monolingual culture into shame. We drove on the first night to a hotel on the way to the North of the country. It was luxury incarnate. Fourposter beds and meals to satisfy Desperate Dan except that there was no cow pie. So we luxuriated for a night.

The next day we drove for 8 hours up a dead straight road to the Etosha national park where we hoped to view the exotic wild animals in their own habitat rather than in a zoo. We stayed in Rondellas, typically circular huts with all the mod cons and dined in the central restaurant. We would rise early at 6am, definitely not one of our normal habits, and travel around the vast park in the car in the certainty of seeing different species. We were not disappointed. Elephants by the hundred, wildebeestes by the thousand, Giraffes by the score, Kudus, springboks, zebras, a rhinoceros, and no end of warthogs. Among the birds there were goshawks, hornbills, bustards, flamingos and vultures. It was a wonderful 4 days filled with interest and lifelong learning for a Bolton boy and girl.

164

Victoria Falls

And the trip wasn't finished because we had booked a hotel in the Zambia side of the Victoria falls, on our way to our next destination. We were welcomed at the hotel entrance by six make-believe warrior Zambians complete with spears, sjamboks, grass skirt and assegais, we could only enter by offering the entrance fee which wasn't very much. They sang songs and danced to their own traditional music. This too was lifelong learning at its best though we were somewhat disappointed by the falls themselves since it was the dry season and the volume of water was low. Still, I have a picture of Maggie showing David Livingstone the way there.

We took a boat trip on the Zambesi which steered well clear of the hundreds of hippopotami in the river and got up close to the elephants until they too started to bat their ears to tell us to back off. Up river there was a large herd of elephants old and young having a great time swimming in the river and spraying water over each other like young hooligans in a swimming pool. At our luxury hotel the gibbons in the trees were busy stealing anything they could find that wasn't locked down. Our stay there was all too brief. There was much more to see but we had a date with our friends near the Kruger national park and a plane to catch.Crocodi

More Africa

Kruger was wunderbar. We revisited our friends the elephants and the giraffes and added new ones such as buffalo, a leopard and hyena and a clutch of baboons with their young clinging desperately on the underbelly of mum and dad. Alligators and mongoose added to the fun. The leopard, as leopards are wont to do, had hoisted his prey high into the tree for all to see, much to the approval of the vultures and eagles. We never saw a lion in the parks but we did at our next destination by a lake south of Johannesburg. It was a magnificent white lion sadly in a cage but with a large area to roam in. Here too was a crocodile farm where crocodiles were reared to eventually be transformed into purses and bags. This was not what we came for. But I have a photograph of Maggie holding tiny baby crocodile 6 inches long and wishing she wasn't.

UNESCO again

Time came to return to the warm embrace of European and Global affairs. The Eurolocal project had come to an end and the learning materials were on the website for everyone to use. My attention was now turning to the UNESCO Learning Cities project. I paid several visits to headquarters in Hamburg and gave them the benefit of my learning city wisdom. But UNESCO's main thrust was to provide the indicators that would define a learning city, only it didn't want to call them indicators.

If it was to attract cities from around the world its remit was much wider than that of Europe alone and must cover many different cultures and countries from the muslims of the middle East to the poverty stricken African cities to the Catholic cities of South America to the Cities of Eastern Asia in China, Japan and Korea for example. All very different from each other in outlook and culture. It aimed to establish a 'brand', something similar to the World Heritage sites, which may be called UNESCO Learning City if that city could demonstrate its commitment to satisfy certain preconditons to be more or less determined by our indicators. Moreover these cities would eventually work together within the Global Learning Cities Network. It described it thus

The Global Learning Cities Network

The overall aim of the establishment of the GLCN is to create a global platform to mobilise and exemplify cities in the international community to effectively use all its resources in every sector to develop and enrich all its human potential for the fostering of lifelong personal growth, the maintenance of harmonious social cohesion, and the creation of sustainable prosperity.

More specifically, the objectives of the GLCN are as following:

1. To proclaim and champion the importance of lifelong learning and building a learning society in cities;

2. To develop, promote and assure compliance with the principles of the Charter of Global Learning Cities by the member cities;

3. To develop a Global Learning City Index and assess and award a 'Global Learning City' brand (or kitemark) to those cities which show exceptional progress and achievement as Learning Cities;

4. To facilitate research into the enrichment of the concept of learning city, and its essential characteristics, as well as their effectiveness in building a learning city through the dissemination of research findings;

166

5. To organise policy dialogue and peer learning activities among member cities through international conferences and seminars on building learning cities as a strategy for promoting lifelong learning;

In other words to do many of the things that I had already been urging Europe to do but on a global scale. So just at the time that Europe was beginning to rein back on the Learning Cities concept, UNESCO was now taking up the flag at a global level. I believed that I had much to offer to this agenda. I had developed charters, proclaimed the importance, facilitated and carried out research, organised international conferences, and seminars, produced indicators and linked cities together in the PASCAL project. The only thing I hadn't done, because I didn't have the means or the clout was the official brand. So, at seventy seven, I threw myself into this task with all the enthusiasm of a twenty five year old. Everything would be to prepare for the Launch of the GLCN in Beijing, October 2013.

So where's the problem? Well the main problem was the speed at which we were allowed to move. In UNESCO there has to be concensus on everything between the countries and cities that would take part. And, as everyone knows it's difficult to get certain countries to agree to anything. For example the USA Senate has thrown out measure upon measure that conflicts with its own view of things. And nor was it a member of UNESCO, since Bush had quit it in a fit of pique, when it did something he didn't agree with. Obama had not found the support among the republican senate to overturn that, and in any case he was busy trying to arrange his re-election at the time.

China was the foremost backer of this initiative. So Jin Yang and I worked together, consulting with indexing organisations all over the world to produce guidelines that learning cities could abide by. We met with experts in Brussels, Beijing, Hangzhou, Hamburg and many other places. We surveyed reams of material on indicators from Business and Industry, Government and international organisations. We eventually produced eighty three indicators, which of course was far too many for UNESCO who wanted a maximum of twelve. In the end we got it down to forty three but with three categories, six actions and three more preconditions. Expressed within the UNESCO logo, they included sustainable development, cultural and economic prosperity, personal and community empowerment and attention to all aspects of education in the city. The others were indicators that broke these down into the evidence of progress within those recommendations.

Seventh life

Midway through this period, at the end of 2012 I had my seventh life. My cardiologue had been monitoring an aneurism in my abdominal aorta for some years as it grew wider and wider. Then he went on holiday just as it was threatening to burst and re-distribute my precious blood all over my insides. Luckily there was another cardiologue on duty and I was quickly transferred to St Pierre hospital where the surgeon inserted an upside down Y shaped thingymibob through the femoral artery and into place where the aneurism walls were weakening. Its called an endoprothese, it's like stent, and the bottom of it fitted into other arteries to keep it in place. He said that would last 8 years (it's now 8!). So just two lives left now. Unfortunately it started to leak after 3 years. The story of the blob of glue to stem the flow and my eighth life is told later.

Preparing the UNESCO Conference

2013 was another busy year for an aging fellow. At the beginning of the year I flew to Beijing to meet the organisers of the imminent Learning Cities conference. Jin Yang was there of course and so were others from the Lifelong Learning Centre. The hospitality was overpowering, only marred by the pollution in the air. I made acquaintance again with the Professor who had managed the Beijing contingent in the PALLACE project and spoke to high-ranking officials from the Chinese hierarchy in an enormous hall with one whole wall celebrating ' The Preparation Conference of the UNESCO Learning Cities Project' in huge letters. At least we knew why we were there!

I was shown around the many beauty spots of the city including the forbidden city which was about to be opened up to VIP members from around the world. Bolton Backstreet Boy a VIP? Surely not possible. We were shown the former Emperor's Summer and Winter Palaces, marvels of luxury and debauchery in a very Chinese way. We were taken to a section of the 2400 mile long Great Wall to the North of Beijing and, despite my surgeon's entreaties to take things easy, I climbed up the vertiginous steps to one of the Guard posts where I was presented with a certificate and an engraved memoire of this prodigious feat.

The arrangements for the conference were discussed in rapid Chinese, which meant that I could only make a contribution when asked in English. This was to be a blockbuster of an event to demonstrate China's contribution to world peace and no doubt its new greatness given that the USA was still sulking about the fact that the United Nations included nations they didn't like and therefore withdrawing its contribution to UNESCO. China was now the paymaster for educational development at a global level.

To complete the visit, I was flown to Hangzhou, the garden city of China, to deliver some speeches about learning cities to a group of teachers and politicians and then allowed to fly home, fatigued but bowled over by what I had seen and done.

Journey to Krakow and Back

In May it was Maggie's 75th birthday and Kathy and Tom came from Canada to help us celebrate it. Their first visit two years previously had given them a taste for more Europe and we obliged by making a grand tour starting with Arles in the South of France where the Roman amphitheatre had them gooing and ready for more history. There aren't many Roman remains in British Columbia. We followed this up with a trip along the French Riviera via Monte Carlo, where we spent several hours admiring the luxury yachts in the harbour, the casinos, the palace and re-followed our former footsteps to the Hotel de Paris. This time there was no IBM to pay the bills so we moved on through Nice, the fantastic views over the Mediterranean Sea near to Beaulieu-sur-mer to Menton, near the Italian border for another overnight. The weather was perfect, the sun shone in all its glory and to quote a certain M Voltaire, everything was for the best in this best of all possible worlds.

Venice

But we hadn't even half-finished the oohing and aahing. Off we went along the Ligurian coast of Italy past San Remo and Genoa, stopping off for lunch at Milan and continuing to Venice. Well what can a couple of West Canadians say about Venice. Like every first visitor to La Serenissima they were gobsmacked. We stayed in a small hotel just outside the city and did the day and a half quick visit. Not even half enough time, but they saw the Doge's palace, the Bridge of Sighs, St Mark's square and its Basilica, sailed the grand canal under the Rialto bridge, and over to Murano to see Venetian pottery in the making. Finally, suffering from beauty overload we ate in a small bistro and sample the Baccala Manticato and the Chichetti. Since this was our third visit we were quite blasé but Tom and Kathy went to bed eyes glazed and knackered.

But Venice was not our destination for the birthday girl. We continued through the mountains to Vienna, via Baden, the spa town where Beethoven is reputed to have written the 9th symphony, the one he only heard in his head because of deafness. More gobsmacking in the Hofburg, the St Stephan Cathedral, the Opera house etc in the one day we spent there and onwards and upwards into the Czech Republic to Olomouc and the Bishop's Palace, a pretty town where Maggie and I had spent some glorious days during the Lilliput project 10 years previously for lunch. Eventually arriving at our destination in Krakow, Poland, where the Polish kings are buried and which is reputed to have the largest market place in Europe.

Welcome to Krakow

As we arrived the heavens opened. I have seen many storms. In terms of the amount of water falling from the sky, nothing like this. We parked as close to the hotel as possible where all our guests, who had already arrived by plane from France, Germany and Britain, were peering through the window. In the ten seconds it took us to reach the door of the hotel we were sodden creatures. Stupidly I had left the rooftop airlets open and Tom had to dash out to close them, get our luggage and dash back again. The suitcases were dripping inside and out, the fabric bags had apparently drowned and Tom stood in the vestibule sloshing water all over the carpets. I would have helped but I was too beggared to swim after driving all that way.

As a city Krakow is amazing. The marketplace lived up to its reputation and the architecture was stunning. It was a photographers delight and I took 900 pictures of churches (150 of them), rivers, buildings, people, restaurants, and the salt mines we visited two days later. This latter was enormous - an underground city in itself 9 layers deep with its own hall of mirrors, monumental sculptures galore of Polish history and life in the mines cut out of the salt for more than two hundred years. It was a very evocative place, a city of memories carved into the salt. But the most evocative of all about Krakow is its history during the second world war. Auschwitz-Birkenau is just up the road and is visitable if one has the stomach for it. Several of our company did but we didn't, an omission which I regret.

The Jewish quarter contains the remnants of the pogroms and atrocities and just by it, there is a large square containing nothing but large chairs one for every thousand jews who were annihilated. It is accompanied by a series of pictures, one of which was Herr Schmidt, the post war German Chancellor showing his remorse at his country's shortcomings. For Maggie the tour of Schindlers factory, the German who rescued so many Jews, was her favourite experience. Tom and Kathy knew nothing of this. They are years younger and the second world war on the far side of Canada didn't register. It certainly did now.

But Krakow isn't all gloom and doom. Indeed it's a very upbeat place. Dressed horses pulling elegant carriages take visitors on tours around the town. The marketplace is riot of colours and noise. It is also surrounded by excellent restaurants at reasonable prices. Hawelka, where the birthday ceremony had its being, is one such. We all, that is 19 of us, having come a long way for the free meal, were determined to have a good time. And we did, helped by a Polish dancing group dressed in local costumes while a man, wearing a green velvet coat and sky blue hat and carrying a stick which we think was supposed to be some kind of weapon, rode his wooden horse round and round the tables shouting unintelligible oaths. Not having much idea of Polish history we obviously couldn't understand the significance but it was very entertaining.

Return via Prague and Karlovy Vary

Came the time to leave and we now had to drive back, but we took a different route by cutting across the North of the Czech Republic , through Moravia to Bohemia and another of our favourite cities, Prague. It was crowded with visitors just like us. The castle, the Cathedral, the Charles Bridge, the awesome square with the clock where wooden figures pop out every half hour to tell us the time, Wenceslas square, centre of the Czech uprising against Russian rule. Everywhere was a squeeze but didn't hide the fact that Prague is a very beautiful city. After two days of being shoved around by the massed ranks of holiday-makers we moved on to the spa town of Karlovy Vary, formerly the German Carlsburg, and yet another Czech beauty spot.

In this and in the other years when we have explored the many UNESCO world heritage sites in this wonderful country we have noticed that they all have one ugly building in a prominent position, either a Hotel, or a shopping centre or a block of flats in dark concrete. These are the Russian built monstrosities during the occupation after the war. We moved on into Germany and yet another gaspworthy town in Bamberg with its colourful fairy tale buildings, its Bauhaus by the river and the inevitable castle on the hill above. Finally we drove to Cologne to our cousin Alan, European member of my mother's Ball family, who lived with his German partner there. Here we said good bye to Kathy and Tom. We had enjoyed their company for almost a month and driven them more than 3000 miles to see the high spots of Europe.

The Family in Paris

No sooner had we returned home and established some semblance of normality in the house than we were off again to Paris. Meanwhile I had visited Hamburg twice more to help fix the agenda for the launch of the Global, Learning Cities Network. The Paris jaunt was a family affair. Our son David had some time previously met Emily and they had a third son, called Olly, He was three years old and the rest of the party included his other two children, Charlotte and Adam and of course Maggie. We stayed in a farm to the South of Paris in an area crawling with castles and stately homes, most of which we investigated as well as all the prime sights of the city, including the Musée D'Orsay, Notre Dame, the Invalides and a walk up the Champs Elysées.

This was the grandchildrens' first visit to Paris and I think that they were suitably impressed, though I can't be sure about Adam. He doesn't do emotion and of course Olly was too young to know where the hell he was.

The UNESCO launch

Came the conference. Maggie and I flew there with a two day stop in Dubai to offset the jetlag and a tour of the City with a friend who had a house in Eus. In Beijing the pollution had miraculously disappeared. In the same capacious hall in Beijing there were speakers and high level participants from all over the world, delegates from many nations all in their national costumes. It was an impressive sight from the platform. The same wall proclaimed the same message without the word 'preparation. After the opening welcome speeches, Jin Yang, myself and others from the Hamburg Institute spelled out the proposals for the Global Network to the audience. And each of us took questions. Then everyone went into discussions in groups. The conference lasted three days with contributions from the great, the good and the not so good from many nations, Prime Ministers, Presidents, Ministers of Education, even a few dictators. Had they not been given a voice they would not have come and therefore the project would fail.

I joined Maggie in the audience for these latter presentations and was presented to each leader in turn afterwards. The boy from the back streets of Bolton was getting quite blasé about this, the girl from Deane less so. She had passed one of the days trying to show a taxi-driver how to use a map in order to get to a palace. He had never seen one before. In the end the motion was passed and the UNESCO Global Learning Network was born. Our work had borne its first fruit. The task now was to make it work.

Hangzhou again

But meanwhile I had been chalked down to make another presentation at a conference of Chinese councillors, once more in the garden city of Hangzhou 400 miles to the south. Maggie and I flew with Jin Yang and a few other luminaries from Germany, Canada and Australia to present on Adult Education which isn't really my field. However I put it into a talk on Adult Education as lifelong learning and received a standing ovation. These Chinese know how to make a boy feel good. This was my second visit there. In the first, during the preparation I had spoken to local teachers. This time it was to city leaders. Afterwards we were treated to a slap-up Chinese meal, nothing like the Chinese takeaways to be found in Britain, and taken to the large square in the centre of the city where an open-air concert was being laid on for the citizens. As honoured guests we had front row seats.

It was an amazing display of modern Chinese music and taken from western style musical manners and mores. Firstly a group of about seventy teenage girls appeared on the massive stage all dressed exactly the same, seeming to be one person seventy times. They sang some Chinese pop songs all the while performing a complicated series of manoeuvres as they sang. The decibels were quadrupled by a huge hi fi system place where no-one could see it. It could probably be heard in the next city. Then a young man about eighteen years old, obviously the local heartthrob, appeared on stage with a microphone to his mouth, sang a different song and engaged in more dancing as he was passed from girl to girl. He must have thought he was in Chinese heaven.

The stage cleared and a mixed and older choir now made claim on the space. Again all in like for like costumes though the men wore sporty trousers and the ladies didn't. Although the songs were unknown to me they were pitch perfect and harmonised to the nth degree. Like the previous troupe they got a resounding applause as they were then taken over by the younger contingent ranging from three to seven year old boys and girls armed with brushes, pails, hoovers and water buckets.

This was not at all like the mistake prone performance of an English infant school. It was done to perfection as they sang songs about cleaning the house at the same time sweeping the floor, polishing the mirror, setting the table, washing the dishes and every household chore one can think of. Here were the budding housewives and husbands of the future practising early. It was all great fun and the audience cheered wildly. How many hours they had spent rehearsing all this I don't know but not one thing went wrong. After this impressive display of Chinese togetherness we move to another part of the square where we were given childrens' toys akin to rubic cube complexity, demonstrated how to use them, and we all made fools of ourselves.

Then it was time to make our way to the lake which is the icon of the garden city. A huge boat in the form of a Chinese dragon was at the wharf and there was an elaborate system of boarded walkways where one strolled above the lake. My Canadian colleague, a friend from several conferences around the world, was even older than me and beginning to wilt a little but he recovered on the boat trip that completed this part of the proceedings. They were by no means finished with us. Chinese hospitality is very thorough and does not recognise fatigue or age.

Our next destination was a Buddhist temple which we approached along a path strewn with carvings of the prophet, all different in the rock walls along its length. The happy Buddha, the sad Buddha, the laughing Buddha, the twin Buddhas. The temple grounds were full of people, praying, clasping hands and lighting candles. It was surprising to us that so many Chinese people still worship in the old ways. We had assumed that such rituals were no longer allowed in the

173

modern China. Maybe they just hadn't got round to it. 1.4 billion people is quite a handful to manage.

Xi'an

After such an intense series of activities Maggie and I decided to have a holiday in China on our own. We flew to Xi'an with a very specific objective. This where we saw the real China. 50 storey building after 50 storey building all exactly alike, homes to millions. Air Pollution everywhere. In Xi'an there are two ancient buildings in particular. They are called the Drum Tower and the Bell Tower. They are just one hundred metres apart and we could only see the one from the other through a sooty gloom, so dark in midday was it. We went to both and were entertained in one of them by a drum concert involving many different kinds of drum. The drummers were all teenage boys and girls, all in costume of course, who beat out a wide variety of rhythms with great gusto. In the other one we were treated to a demonstration of ancient Chinese instruments of all shapes and sizes performed by young people who, frankly, looked as if they would rather not be there.

We eventually found the Bell in the gloom and rang it to ensure that we would have good luck and long life. The Chinese are still very superstitious in this way, despite attempts by the government to bring them into a modern world. In the evening we went round the marketplace. Music and noise everywhere, it was an experience which we would choose not to repeat even though it was such vibrant place. We saw many animals in cages, destined for we knew not what. Food we could not always recognise was everywhere in every shape and size and with every flavour and colour. We tasted at the behest of the stall keeper. Some was extremely tasty and others unbelievably inedible. We were never sure of its provenance.

The following day we were bussed to the place we had come to Xi'an to see, the fields of the terra cotta warriors. I have to say that we have seen many sights and experienced many rare visions but this put everything else into the category of banal. We entered the first great hangar and were confronted by row upon row in pits stretching back as far as the eye could see, all filled with effigies of warriors in terracotta. They were so lifelike. No two were alike. It was a sight the like of which we had never seen. We learned that they were made, everyone different, to act as guardians to the first Chinese emperor Qin Shi Huang in 276 BC because he believed that they would guard him in his afterlife to prepare him for the next cycle. These were only discovered in 1974 by the farmer who owned the land and tried to plough it. We met him and he gave us a memento to remember him by.

But this was not the only hall. There were three others, containing one hundred and thirty terra cotta chariots with five hundred and twenty horses, and a hundred and fifty cavalry horses. In all some eight thousand warriors have been found and it is believed that there are many more lying under the surrounding soil. Indeed the total area of the necropolis is thirty eight square miles. There is clearly much more to be found here.

According to one source the last resting place of the emperor is buried with palaces, towers, officials, valuable artefacts and wondrous objects the size of a football pitch. A hundred flowing rivers were simulated using mercury, and above them the ceiling was decorated with heavenly bodies below which were the features of the land. It has never been excavated perhaps because the mercury is poisonous, but the official tale is that of concerns about preservation of the artefacts. The lacquer covering the paint can curl in fifteen seconds in the dry air of Xi'an and flake off in just four minutes.

Jeannette in Hong Kong

Our last port of call on this momentous trip was in Hong Kong, where our dear daughter Jeannette was, by coincidence, spending two weeks with her childrens' theatre. It was my second visit but the first was for one day on the way back from Australia. This time we had three. It really is yet another iconic city, on the waterfront with the skyscrapers so close together that they seemed like one long building. The strident signs of mammon were on every building, proclaiming its commercial importance through the enormous advertisements on every building which at night could be seen from across the water. Everything seemed to be devoted to economic merchandising, from the well-known tram system which climbed the mountain behind to end at a department store selling everything from clothes to toys to toiletries.

We took the hop on hop off bus to the other side of the island where there was a market place, and returned past the enormous apartment blocks one after the other. The main street was a series of indoor and outdoor emporia. We took Jeannette and her colleagues to dinner in the conference centre built especially for the handover of the colony to Chinese ownership. While it is an exciting and dynamic place to be, and I am sure that we missed out on its many delights, I have no longing to return there. We returned, again via Dubai and London to Perpignan and home. We rescued the dogs from our friends. This had been one hell of a visit and one hell of a year. It seemed only commonplace to spend Christmas as usual with our family in Southampton.

Chapter Nineteen

Festivals

'The more you read, the more you know

The more you learn, the more places you'll go'

Cork again

By comparison 2014 was tame. But with yet more travelling. I had been invited to speak at the Cork lifelong learning festival every April since 2011 and this was no exception. The Cork lifelong learning week is unique. It is a whole week when every educational and social service organisation offers free access to learning opportunities from language courses, to choirs, to tours of the university to free sessions on mindfulness – and more than eighty more. The city becomes a universal university for a week and each year more and more people take part. I had had a small hand in making it happen and was a regular visitor to do my bit. Once more Maggie and I turned this visit into a marathon, this time an Irish one.

Maggie is half Irish and had been urging me to tour the country instead of just visiting a city and leaving for home. So we hired a car in Dublin and took a convoluted way to Cork that seemed to include all the castles in the centre of the country. At the festival we participated in the many learning opportunities on offer, visited the nearby Blarney Castle where I kissed the stone, hoping for a miracle at seventyeight. It isn't an easy thing to do. Basically you lie on your back and pop your head a long way down a drainpipe hole. It certainly set my head off in a wheelie and took me several minutes to stand up again. Then they told me that in fact the hole you just gambled your life on was formerly a latrine. Not funny, unless it does what the label says and transforms you into a great orator. It didn't.

Festival Highlights

But I did orate at the festival. Three times . Once to a large audience of educators, secondly to convince the councillors of city and county of the advantages of applying to become a UNESCO Learning City. (They bought it, not particularly because of my irresistible salesmanship skills but more because the city wanted to put one up on Dublin.) The third contribution was at the Friday night – pub poetry night, chaired by Seamus Hosey, an iconic Irish educationist. I read out one of the poems I had written in the last year. It competed unfavourably with the silver tongued Irish poets who really did have the blarney gift of the gab. But there was polite clapping from one section of the audience where Maggie was situated. Bless her.

Our return journey took us along the south Coast where we saw the farm from which President Kennedy's family originated, shook hands with his sculpture, passed by Waterford and Wexford and re-visited the cemetery where Maggie's ancestors were buried in county Wicklow. We then returned the car to its rightful owners and flew home to Perpignan courtesy of Aer Lingus. Back in time for the poppies and to sing for eggs in the village choir.

Conflent Fêtes

May is the month when the South of France downs tools so that it can better prepare for a summer of active hedonism in the Midi. May-day is quickly followed by VE day by Ascension Day by *Pentecôte,* each of them a wonderful excuse to *'faire le pont'*, that is to use up the days between the actual *fête* day and *le weekend* as an extra holiday. After all, it's hardly worth going in to work for just two or three days is it?

Thus, as April gives way to a work-free May, the festivals begin in the Conflent villages. Each village, and there is a lavish abundance of them, has its own Saint's day festival, and those that unfortunately fall in the winter make up for it by holding festivals in the summer time too. It's a matter of honour to attract the most tourists to your celebration. These summer festivals are usually weekend long celebrations of music, eating and drinking with the odd *kermesse* and a few *petanque* competitions thrown in.

The music is loud, very loud. My God, you should hear it loud, so don't forget to bring your ear-plugs. Oh and bring the wife, mistress, parents and kids as well - they'd love it if only for the noise. Here's how it works. For the Friday evening overture, the rock band piles its biggest and most ear-splitting ghetto-blasters one on top of the other in the village square. There until 10 pm they sit in a silent and often eerie contrast to the ancient stones of the surrounding buildings.

Ten pm arrives and the silence is abruptly shattered. The band arrives, pipes in a few electronically enhanced chords by way of welcome and then launches into a frenzy of noisy motion. It stays that way until two or three o clock in the morning, while the happy but deafened villagers caper and prance like cats on hot coals. The older, and wiser, take up station *behind* the stage.

One number blends into another until it seems that the actual notes are irrelevant, which of course is true. Teeny-boppers, young mums and dads, older and should-be wiser heads all hop, jig, skip and swing in a seventh heaven of ecstasy. People communicate their basic requirements - would you like to dance with me, I badly need a drink, that sausage looks extra-ordinarily tasty - by sign language. But it is all great fun for everyone. The houses vibrate alarmingly, the food tables groan extravagantly and the local wine flows abundantly.

The youngsters dance the ear-splitting night away, the middle aged try energetically to recreate their faded youth. The village wrinklies, well equipped with the wisdom of age, smile on indulgently - they are probably now understanding how they came to be so deaf. And they know only too well what village festivals can do to the body. In the distance, not only the village, but the whole valley, rocks rhythmically to the music of the festival.

Saturday morning is usually silent - not merely in contrast to what has gone before but largely because of it. The middle-aged rockers of the night before lie in their beds, every movement of their aching bodies emphasising the mentally painful realisation that confronting the passing of time demands a high toll fee. The youngsters lie in their beds because they are youngsters and that is what youngsters do, and only the wrinklies move timelessly and wordlessly about the village, grateful for the luxury of an unaccustomed silence. They can't hear a thing and the flashing lights have played havoc with their eyes, but .. well, that's part of being old, isn't it? But that does not last very long.

In the afternoon all is bustle again. It is the time of the *petanque* competition, when all the brave macho men, dressed in a variety of hats, show their prowess at throwing metal balls in the proximity of each other in the village boulodrome. The *pointeurs* project their *boules* hopefully to a position somewhere near the *cochonet* (translated, and regarded, as 'little pig'), and the *tireurs* do their best to destroy the pretty patterns they make. Everything is *serieux* – the loss of an end is a *catastrophe* or a *désastre*, the winning of it a *triomphe*. French male pride is at stake and the prize is *la gloire* for yet another year.

Until quite recently women did not enter this contest - it would not even have occurred to them to do so in a male-dominated village society. Then, one or two of the more brave and liberated female souls tried to enter and were of course banned. But even in this remote spot the malign influence of the modern world cannot be denied access, and the *petanque* competitions are now grudgingly open to all. Even *étrangers* may enter. And so the rules are rigged to have preliminary rounds in the hope that this will lead to an early elimination of the running sore of women and *étrangers,* thus enabling our heroes to continue as before. More often than not this ploy works, but it has been known for either or both to continue into the final rounds, and, horror of horrors, some *étrangers* have had the temerity to win against the odds. If they are male, this is gritted-teeth acceptable.

But the idea that a female, worse a female *étrangère*, might win is anathema. The shock to the collective male village ego would engender such a deep sense of shame that it would ruin the whole festival weekend To my knowledge this has not yet happened, but it can now only be a matter of time before the last vestiges of village masculine dignity are torn to shreds by the new enlightened world order.

The afternoon competition done and the annual champions acclaimed once more, the Saturday evening festivities repeat the pattern of the previous evening's excesses - loud music, frantic dancing, copious food and free-flowing wine. Sunday morning is a time for reflection. The village awakens with the retribution of a mass headache and goes to church in search of spiritual solace, tranquillity and grace. The pews are full of serially throbbing heads and aching bodies, betrayed only by the half-closed eyes and the occasional grimace of distress. But they must attend because, even at this painful time, tradition obliges the priest to bless the whole festival and to dispense low-cost and high-profile communion and forgiveness to an unusually quiescent congregation.

But afterwards, the power of prayer once more demonstrates its capacity to surmount human weakness. Now sanctified and shriven, the men of the village organise a *grillade*, or perhaps even the traditional Catalan version of this, the *cargolade*. This repast entails the immolation of hundreds of *escargots* over a charcoal fire. A British-educated stomach might begin to get alarmed at this, especially after the experience of the previous two days. Buckets and buckets of unlucky arthropods are collected weeks before the festival.

Leaves are overturned, walls are examined, for slow-moving objects within three kilometres of the village. There is no hiding place despite all their efforts to blend into the village scenery. Those that escape, and there must be some to act as the Adams and Eves of next year's party, are probably brainier than most of the villagers. Those that don't are subjected to a diet of thyme and milk to cleanse them of any waste or toxic matter. For the snails this is time of peace and reflection when food and drink no longer has to be laboured for. But the reckoning is at hand.

The unfortunate nemiatoads are then spread out on a metal net to prepare them to meet their doom. They are reputed to have aphrodisiac properties. As the flames complete their culinary task, it is now time for the younger men of the village to demonstrate their uninhibited masculinity by eating them in bountiful quantities. The average Briton might think that one is too many - but for these young men, eager to prove their macho credentials to the opposite gender, 50, 100, 150 is normal.

Some have been known to eat more than 250 snails at one sitting, thus demonstrating to all and sundry a) their staying power, b) their potency and c) their stupidity. Females tremble at such feats of voracity, but they have little need to worry, since any aphrodisiac attribute the snails may have had is soon dissipated by the inevitable effects of over-indulgence. Full stomach never won fair lady – and certainly not one full of creatures that produce slime trails, 'twas ever thus. The young men faded miserably, often urgently, from the scene. For the wiser villagers the *cargolade* continues in more sedate fashion with pork chops and the spicy sausages called *merguez*, which, again if consumed in too large a quantity, can have much the same effect as the snails.

Before the last of the festival hops, there is a performance of the *Sardane*, the traditional dance of the Catalan regions. For this, the larger villages will hire a *cobla*, a group playing the traditional pipes and instruments of the region. The smaller ones will use scratchy records played on an ancient gramophone set – the type grandma used to have. The *Sardane* is not an easy dance for the uninitiated. It is performed in a circle in which people join hands, men's supporting the ladies. It starts with four basic simple steps, hands joined by the sides.

After 84 beats (one must learn to count before dancing the *Sardane*) the arms are raised above head height and the dance proper commences with a complex series of steps repeated over and over again. As it reaches its climax the music subtly changes to a more vibrant rhythm, and an animated high-stepping commences. This too is performed within a similarly complex pattern of steps but the trick is to give the impression of temporarily floating on air, everyone landing at the same time. It isn't easy. It is an impressive sight when done well, though village festivals are not always the perfect stage for precision.

Men and women dance together unselfconsciously, justly proud of their terpsichorean heritage. It is a beautiful and timeless expression of a whole nation and one hopes that it will survive the predations of these cynical times. Even in this frenetic day and age the local towns and villages organise Sardanes in the evening so that workers can indulge their tradition on their way home. It is difficult to imagine that happening outside the Westminster underground station or the Greenock shipyard at knocking-off time. Often, unsuspecting tourists are dragged into the fray, their clodhopping efforts to match the steps of their tutors contrasting strongly with the delicate and elegant steps of the cognoscenti.

However, back to the Conflent village festival. It ends, as it began with an ear-splitting rave-up. Those with energy remaining - the tennis players, the under-30s, the hyperthyroidic and the simply masochistic - party the night away, happy in the knowledge that not only are they having the best time since the last one, and before the next one, but also that the whole valley is reverberating with them in their pleasure.

Swansea

At the end of May I had another rendezvous to advance the UNESCO learning cities project. The city of Swansea also wanted to be a part of the future. They had sent two delegates from the university to the Beijing conference and were now asking me to help with the application. Separately I was also working on the first twelve memberships and that had entailed another quick trip to Hamburg.

181

So, once more this seventy eight year old was travelling to a conference in Swansea University in late May to speak about the project to the city worthies. I took the Ryan air flight to Bristol and hired a car, calling in on the way at Alan and Linda's house, who had returned to Wales from Eus two years previously. It was an emotional reunion and Alan took me round his Roman village of Caerleon of which he was very proud.

In Swansea the following day I was given a tour of the city and its environs to meet the people who were trying, and often succeeding, to make a difference. We even made stop at the Llanelli Scarlets rugby club, one of Wales finest, to learn how they keep their players fit enough to bash the bejasus out their opponents. The plan was to transform Swansea, city and county, both of which had many problems because of the loss of its traditional industry into an 'entrepreneurial learning city' starting in primary schools and working up to adult re-education. I made a presentation of the UNESCO project and suggested how to word the application to achieve success. And I included a ten point checklist of how to achieve their ambition by re-modelling their organisations into 'learning organisations.' For the curious and/or the gluttons for punishment this can be found in the last chapter.

Volcanoes and Ed Bailey

For our annual visit to the grand-childrens' birthday bashes in September we decided to have a look at the Volcano region of France. It's not generally known outside of the country that there is a range of extinct volcanoes down its central core. So here was another opportunity for lifelong learning to explore and we booked a hotel in one of the villages. Just before we had had a visit from Ed Bailey the long lost best man from Australia. His life had turned upside down. His wife had died two years previously and that was followed by a botched operation on his eyes which had left him blind. I had gone to meet him at Barcelona airport and whisked him back to chez nous.

One can imagine the reminiscing that was done in the few days that he was here. We were both back in the fifties with Johnny Ray, Elvis Presley, and Guy Mitchell and with the skiffle group we had created to sing the songs of Lonnie Donegan. For dessert we would recall the unitarian meetings we had attended, the plays we had starred in, the Units dance band we had formed and the cycling tours we took. Even though he was blind he could still play the piano and did. Incessantly. It was good to see him in France even if he couldn't see us and a wrench when he had to go back with the knowledge that most probably we would never see each other again this side of the pearly gates.

Back to the Volcanoes, it was quite charming with lots of pretty villages to visit. Then to Honfleur where Henry the fifth first invaded in his bid to ravage

Northern France. It is the prettiest of them all and worth spending a couple of days or more. Over the Pont de Normandie to Le Havre and we were on our way to blighty. Where we celebrated Charlotte's 18th birthday with a slap up meal at a posh pub and paid for her car with the money saved up in the investment we had taken out on her ten years previously.

Mexico City

2014 wasn't over yet. There remained yet another UNESCO outing, this time to Mexico City, for a planning meeting for the award of the UNESCO learning city badge. The meeting itself was like all meetings were, are and will be. I did my bit with a defective projector that wouldn't show the pictures. Each of the twelve new applicant members gave a presentation, committing themselves to the Global Network of Learning Cities and expressing their dying gratitude to UNESCO. And we all went on a jolly to see the sights of the City. We first went to the historical centre to admire the churches and basilicas that could hold thousands and gasped at the opulence therein. Mexico is a very Catholic country. And it's a long way from Bolton. We bought our little trinkets from the poor vendors on the sidewalk before travelling by bus to the Teotihuacan pyramids near the airport.

The journey of about twelve miles passed thousands of small shanty shacks on the hillsides where the millions of wretchedly poor people lived. There was hardly room to swing a cat inside or out. It reminded me of the pitiful dwellings in Africa. But the pyramids were amazing, built by an ancient civilisation that may, but may not have been, the Aztecs. Experts disagree. Every bit as impressive as the Egyptian piles I had seen when running my IBM seminars but not the same. Different rock, different architecture, different era. I walked along the avenue of the dead to get there and climbed what was long ago called the city of the sun. It was a journey into the history of long ago. The hop on hop off bus tour was a disappointment. It might as well have been through Manchester or Minnesota for the stop-worthy views. But then who am I to criticise after seeing half the world's most dazzling places.

Home Sport

It is 2015, I am seventy nine in March – seems to increase by one every year strangely enough - and the first nine months saw us at home in France. Plenty to do. We bought a puppy. An Australian Sheepdog who requires brushing every hour. We, Maggie more than me, spent hours training the little rascal until he was able to understand the human voice. She is a glutton for punishment. They are said to be one of the most intelligent dogs in the world but this one couldn't speak a word even after all our efforts. As normal, we sang for eggs at Easter and gobbled down the omelette in the village hall afterwards.

We made the annual effort to persuade the garden to grow healthy plants. Maggie was now the big cheese in Cancer Support France for this area and she spent hours and days communicating with the members. There was, for instance a cycle ride to raise money along the Canal du Midi for which several budding tour de France winners entered. At least that would be so if most of them were not in their 60s. So Maggie and I had to organise the route, get the permissions (not an easy task in France) and turn up at the finishing point to present the winners with their medals.

In June, Maggie gave Charlotte a belated 18th birthday present by meeting her for a rampage à deux around Paris. They both relived Maggie's halcyon 1980s days of shameless leisure. Here Charlotte learned how to drink tea in Maxims, shop in the Galeries Lafayette, stroll along the Tuileries and speak three words and phrases in French – merci, bonjour and s'il vous plait.

Back home David and Adam came for the summer holidays. We took them to see Cathar castles, the Orgues at Ille, fantastically shaped rocks moulded by the weather, one of them resembling an organ keyboard, the open air baths of steaming hot water from the mountains, and drove into the high mountains to the small village of Mantet from where allied airmen escaped into Spain during the war.

In the meantime I was playing golf every week in the South of France competitions for the local team of British scrubbers. We played far and wide, all the courses from Falgos and Font Romeu in the Pyrennean mountains to Carcassonne, Montpellier and Nimes, a two hour drive to the East. We played once a week, while the other teams came from golf clubs where they played almost every day. So being British and gifted. the scrubbers won the competition and, although I should be modest, I won't be and whisper the information that, at the age of seventy nine I won the individual player award for the South of France. It was of course a veterans competition but veterans start at fifty years old in France.

Eastern beauties

In September we took a different route up the East side of France on our way to our annual holiday in Southampton. And what spectacular sights we saw. France really is an extraordinarily stunning country. First we drove to lake Annecy and the town of that name, dramatically surrounded by high craggy mountains, beautiful villages and extremely expensive mansions. No wonder it is called the Venice of the Alps. We took the lake cruise of course and ended it in the town, full of picturesque narrow streets, deeply colourful houses, canals and of course, as anyone would expect, a Medieval castle. Gaspworthy indeed. The three days we spent there were like being in a magical filmset.

We moved on to Colmar in Alsace, a part of France we knew well from our visits when we lived in Belgium. No mountains, no lake, but the town is one large fairy tale, an explosion of painted gingerbread houses, eye-catching views and a fascinating range of architectures. We toured the town by one of those silly little open-carriaged trains, like travelling in a Disney picture with the elves and the bearded dwarves. We finished in a medieval restaurant, which, thankfully, served 21st century food.

To complete an eventful journey we called in at the killing fields of Picardy, where the battle of the Somme took thousands of lives. Here Lutyens huge memorial to the dead and its accompanying museum were being prepared for the following year's anniversary to celebrate, if that is the word, the carnage of the Somme. It was a sombre experience but one which people should make to understand the folly of war and the need for countries to work together to make sure it would never happen again. It did of course. And I fear that the current movements towards a world of dictators and serial liars with millions of supporters, will mean that the lessons humanity has learned are about to be forgotten. That is what lifelong learning is meant to avoid but I get that sinking feeling that we are losing the battle. All the more when a certain Donald Trump won the American election in the following year.

While in England we not only celebrated birthdays, Adam became a teenager, but we went up to Newark where Jeannette's childrens' theatre company was based. She showed us round what is a quite pretty place. Not Colmar or Annecy, but it has its highlights. It was good to see the family again. The dog was being looked after by a couple from Ireland. We learned about them from a website called trusted housesitters. They have a long list of people who are willing to look after other peoples' pets . It costs nothing and they get a free holiday without having to pay hotel fees. Seems to work well because since then we have had many more and all have been superb.

Chapter Twenty

Celebrations

'Education is not the filling of Pails, It is the Lighting of Fires'
(Yeats)

A Rugby Match

2016 is eighty years from 1936 and the reader who has got so far will now be thinking that it really is time to throw in the towel and admit that a life of travel and service is well and truly over. Think again, I was just beginning to get started. It started in February when a group of Irish friends in France had purchased tickets for an international rugby match France versus Ireland. Wrong – it wasn't the edifying spectacle when European Rugby's biggest and burliest bruisers slog it out for the privilege winning a grand slam and putting one over the other five teams.

It was instead the Ladies version, if that is the right word for women who fill themselves with the same body-building organic compounds as the men, and it was taking place in Perpignan just down the road. Normally we might have watched it on the TV. After all you get a far better picture of what is happening than sitting on a freezing metal seat in the stands on a cold February night and watching tiny figures on the far side of the field running around like match stick women. Even if you know that there is a ball involved you rarely see it. But it's the occasion that counts, and the beer and the meal afterwards, and the camaraderie. As it happens the French ladies won though that is relatively irrelevant. It was certainly an excellent start to my birthday year.

The birthday parties

Of course much of March would be spent in mad and frenzied celebration. Maggie had booked a posh hotel near to Southampton for the festivity and merrymaking and my family and all my remaining relatives plus the friends from the French gang who had returned to England and some very old acquaintances from our days in Lymington turned up. In the dining room, photographs of me from age six months to age eighty were prominently displayed on the huge mirror. The first one of course showed me in all my infant beauty with not a stitch on. None of the others were like that, thankfully for the guests, but it was an interesting selection of the rise and fall of man.

Everyone dressed to the maximum beauty they could muster. Maggie had a new dress, I had a new velvet coat which barely fitted, such that the buttons remained undone. Charlotte was radiant with her new boyfriend. The bubbly flowed freely and affected the speeches to a meaningless slur while photographs volleyed and thundered their way into later albums. I think that the food was excellent though I cannot be sure. Certainly the birthday cake, with its golf metaphor, was unique.

I was given the marzipan golf club and ball to eat. The others got the cake. My daughter read out a poem I had constructed for the occasion – a Lancashire monologue no less and she added some of her own reminiscences, not all of them benign, but that's my family. They say it as it is, and sometimes as they would like it to be. All in all, we had a great time and at the end said good bye and professed everlasting love. With those who stayed behind, willing to pay the hotel overnight fees, we started again in the evening. The next day didn't happen, at least I don't remember it.

We returned to France just in time to sing for the eggs. Easter was very early that year. And that was immediately followed by the second eightieth birthday celebration, this time before an 80, one for each year, strong mixed audience of French and English in the Village Hall in Eus. An orchestra, or at least the two guitarists who used to be part of La Brigade International provided the music for dancing and singing, and our cleaner and good friend, Lizzie, provided the grub. Except for the cake which was made by the chairperson of the choir. There were long and boring speeches by myself and the other choir person who had become eighty, six days before mine. Though I did make them laugh with this poem wot I ritted about the requirements of staying alive in the eighties. It was also in French.

<u>Rolling back time</u>

A tongue in cheek peek at the world of supplements, complements, implements and devices to keep us alive and healthy in later age.

OMGG my age starts with an Eight
And the signs of dementia might start to gestate
Oh Lordy Oh Lordy just what can I do
To turn the clock backward and build me anew

I wake in the morning and reach for the pills
Potions to cure me of all the known ills
A pill that will help me to thin out the blood
And pills for disorders I'd dump if I could

Another protects me from troubling gout
Plus one for high tension in case I flake out
Don't forget statins to control the plaques
Decrease the prospect of grave heart attacks .

I come down to breakfast and lay out the mix
Chia grains, linseed and vitamin B six
All blended together in one healthy mush
With Brazil nuts, banana, kiwi and such

Then there's the puffer to clear out the tubes

And a strong diuretic to empty the pubes
Prazoles for reflux and pure china tea
Expels the prognoses of senility

Oranges, apples, and five fruit a day
Help to keep all the diseases away
Cholesterol's still going haywire again?
Remember to swallow some strong CQ10

A spoon of turmeric mixed well in goat's milk
Transforms the digestion to Indian silk
Magnesium tablets to bolster the bones
A half avocado to boost the hormones

Levothyroxine to prop weak thyroids
Vitamin D to offset corticoids
Calcium Supplements, walking the dog
Follow these things and you'll sleep like a log.

A brisk weekly golf round to clear out the mist
A walk in the mountains can also assist
These are the tactics I use every day
To roll back time's impact and keep death away

No more forgetting the names of your friends
No more guessing where reality ends
Never again will I open a door
And wonder what I was going there for

Should you be thinking it's over the top
Think of the other ways you can go pop
If to stay healthy you'd really contrive
It's better to do it while you're still alive
© Norman Longworth

Cork Again?

A week later Maggie and I were back in Cork for the Lifelong Learning week once more as the honorary guest who allegedly got them the UNESCO learning city award. I had been there so many times I was beginning to speak with an Irish brogue. We had our photos taken with the mayor, resplendent in his robes and gold chain, before being let loose on the festival. within the learning city. The festival had grown immensely to well over 100 activities during the week, one of which being the accompanying seminar at which I was due to speak together with representatives from other learning cities in Europe, Espoo, from Finland, Swansea, Limerick (which was also establishing its own version a learning city), and two representatives from UNESCO in Hamburg.

The city was also dividing itself into learning neighbourhoods of which the first was Ballyphehane one of its most deprived areas. We joined these colleagues at an event to celebrate the city's oldest lifelong learner, a 100 years lady who had signed up for a course at the city college. The old lady was piped in accompanied by her daughter, grand-daughter and great grandchild., and was presented with an award to remember the occasion.

Uprising

It was a joyful affair, commemorating also the 100 year anniversary of the Easter Rising when seven members of the Irish Volunteers, issued a proclamation proposing Ireland's secession from England and declared a republic. Maggie has a copy of that proclamation at home dating back to the revolution, which seems to indicate that her ancestors were supporters of the rebellion. The British Army brought in thousands of reinforcements as well as artillery and that symbol of British power, a gunboat. With much greater numbers and heavier weapons, the British Army suppressed the Rising.

After the surrender, the country remained under martial law. About 3,500 people were taken prisoner by the British and 1,800 of them were sent to internment camps or prisons in Britain. The leaders of the Rising were executed following courts-martial. The hall was filled with schoolchildren there, firstly to understand the message of the need to learn continuously and secondly to learn about their country's history. The walls were plastered with pictures of the murdered men and some of the children performed a play to drive home the message. It was a fascinating glimpse of Irish patriotism, and, although they all knew we were English we were not strung up on the lampshade.

Despite my nationality my presentation in the City hall's conference room was received enthusiastically, since I was seen to be on the side of the angels and had a valuable contribution to make to the city's future. We also threw ourselves into the festival by attending several events, including a tour of the university, a lecture on mindfulness and of course the pub poetry event, at which I was once more invited to contribute.

The following day we made a journey to the harbour some miles outside of Cork where the Titanic made its last port of call. There is a museum there which gives the whole story and also that of the Lusitania, sunk by a Uboat outside the harbour in 1917 with 800 refugees bound for the USA, and the great evacuation of Ireland during the potato famine in the 19th century. While we already knew about these events our learning curve increased as we explored further. The whole event in Cork made me feel like a 40 year old rather than double that number, and it was good to know that I still had something to contribute. And to learn.

Bologna

Well, we just had to have a foreign expedition to cement the achievement and we chose Bologna for the consummation. And what a choice. It was some forty years since I had been there and all I remembered were the covered pavements. So we drove our BBC friend John, aged eighty six and our old friend Jo, the opera singer, aged eighty four in the car and drove all the way, basking in our youthfulness. What we didn't know when we left was that Jo had started to dement quite seriously. We first realised the extent of her dementia when she kept asking where we were going in the car, and it was confirmed in her behaviour in Bologna.

For example she would go down for four breakfasts, having forgotten that she had already eaten. She forgot her room number multiple times and roamed the corridors, and once she got lost in Bologna not knowing where she was and unable to explain where to find her hotel. Fifteen people turned up for this birthdayfest including our daughter Jeannette and her friend Sally, my German cousin and his wife, and several other friends from France.

This city is a must visit. The central square is a dazzling architectural monument to good taste, with its fountains, churches, restaurants and bars all brightly coloured. John Osman, being an ex-journalist could always be found, drink in hand and reading the Times at one of the bars. We all did our own thing during the day and fed our faces together in the evening.

Trouble at t'Opera

But one of our enduring memories concerns the Opera house. We had noticed that 'The Barber of Seville' was on offer on the Wednesday evening. So we booked the last nine seats by email to see it. We turned up in time on the day to be told that our tickets had been sold. Apparently one has to confirm the booking even though we had already paid. We of course made a complaint and a solution was found. The Royal Box, which had been unused for years could now be cleared for our party. So the boy from the back streets of Bolton, at his 80th birthday outing, became royalty, Maggie his queen and his friends became his lords and ladies in waiting. Of course, as the punters arrived in the lower sections, we waved royally to the crowd to acknowledge our accession to the throne of kings. Until John happened to mention how many aristocrats had been murdered in Royal Boxes. The waving stopped abruptly.

The opera was excellent, even though it was at least the 10th time I had seen it. Jo, an former opera star, particularly enjoyed it. This was her domain, where her former triumphs had taken place and, despite the dementia, she was fulfilled. While Bologna was exquisite, we had to leave for home in our old

Citroen C8 rather than a Landauer and, sods law, it got half way and refused to go any further. We left it to the tender mercies of a garage near to the border and hired a car at great expense to the royal piggy bank. We finally returned Jo to her friend near Carcassonne, thankful that nothing serious had happened. We learned 3 months later that she had been confined to a care home. A bitter end to a glittering career of operatic stardom. Two weeks later I made the journey to rescue my car from the garage in Italy and back in one.

Byrrh

By June I had abdicated the throne and the frenzy of life died down slightly. It made a minor return in August when Adam, now aged fourteen, and David came to visit and we took him to the winery where Byrrh is made. Byrrh, in case you didn't know, is an aperitif wine which tastes a little like cough mixture and was, in the 1920s, the drink of preference of the aristocracy in the chic milieu of the USA. It owes much to the marketing skills of the then owners, since it is basically a herbal medicine masquerading as a fine aperitif wine. Whatever, it originates in the nearby town of Thuir and that is where we went. In these days of mergers and the scramble to dominate the marketplace it takes its place with all the other aperitif wines such as Cinzano, Vermouth, Campari and Martini all under the same management. The tour was fascinating for its insights into the origins and manufacture of a drink well known to the wine cogniscenti. Wr also enjoyed the tasting session at the end.

As an afterthought, I also won the South of France golf trophy for a second time, quite a feat considering my age, and later in the year we made the return visit to the UK via the west coast of France, via La Rochelle, the port of exit of the Huguenots in the 16th century, and the scenic delights of Brittany.

Busy Maggie

Maggie too was having a busy year. Quite apart from organising the birthday events, she was becoming overwhelmed by the duties she had to perform as the local organiser of Cancer Support France. There were the meetings she had to attend, the help line she had to man, the contacts she had to maintain, the exhibitions she had to attend and the concerts she had to organise . It was almost a full time job, except of course that there was no payment. In addition she had agreed to become the church warden of the Anglican church in Vernet les Bains and there were ceremonies to perform, visitors to meet, support services, communication with the Anglican church in Europe and much more.

She also organised the distribution three times a year of the local PO life magazine, the departmental English language booklet, to all the supermarkets, tourist information bureaux, and large retail organisations in the Tet valley. Not to mention selling the poppies in the district at remembrance time and the cooking, washing and housekeeping of a two storey, four bedroom house. But she has such a dynamic store of energy that she seems to perform all these tasks like a conjurer would go through his routine.

Friuli Frolics

2016 wasn't yet finished. In November I received the call from the province of Friuli in Northern Italy to come to talk to the Mayor and other worthies about its future. The idea was that learning cities within a learning region was on the agenda and my advice on how to make it happen was required. I had already been to its capital of Udine twice before, after the mayor had read the Italian translation of my book 'Learning Cities, Learning Regions, Learning Communities.' This was crunchtime for action and I was the catalyst. Part of the presentation is shown on you tube. So, after being ferried around the region to long lost Roman ports and fabulous dark ages churches, I socked it to them for a third time. Having done this I assumed that my working life was over and that no-one would ever want to use my services again. Time to rest in the armchair and mull over my successes and failures.

Taiwan

But life is not like that. At least mine wasn't. Firstly, early in 2017 I had to address a colloquium in Swansea once more with a view to producing a chapter for an academic book on learning cities, and of course had to write that chapter and have it peer reviewed. Which happened, was accepted and the book, edited by Springer, became flesh. Secondly, my old friend Professor Osborne invited me to a PASCAL conference in Glasgow at which I would meet several global faces I knew and some I didn't, and would I also please make a contribution? It's nice to be wanted even as a geriatric, and so I went. At the conference there was a group of Taiwanese politicians and educators.

The conversation with them went like this. 'You Norman Rongworth?', 'Yes that's me.' 'You lote the books on riferong rearning? 'Yes I have written a few.' 'Taipei our Capital is rearning city. That's why we here'. 'That's interesting, what do you do?' We lead your books, We forrow your ideas.' Well it's nice to know that at least one city is doing that but the point of the conversation was that they were having a large conference later in the year in Taiwan, inviting people from the whole of South East Asia and insisted that I should be there to give not one, but two keynotes at not one, but two conferences, one in the city and the other at the University.

Other members of PASCAL were also invited. So, at the age of 81, I was expected to travel half way around the world to speak at a conference. But my curiosity had been piqued and, in a triumph of ego over common sense, I accepted.

On my return home I gave Maggie the chance to come too but she refused. Long haul flights were no longer on her wishlist. So three months later I set out alone to fly to Paris, then to Dubai for 2 days to cut down the jet lag, then to Taipei for glory and the cause. It was fascinating. I had visited Taiwan some ten years previously when I was asked to speak at a conference in Chung Ching University in the centre of the island, and I remember that I was taken to see the last resting place of Chiang Kai Shek in Taipei City before leaving for home. He was the general who had taken the Chinese rebels to Taiwan many years previously and the relations between the island and mainland China were rarely cordial to say the least. Many times the Chinese have threatened to invade and it hasn't happened because Taiwan is protected by the Americans. Which explains why so many aspects of Taiwanese life are so pro-USA, including the music. As will be made clear. But this was different. It isn't a beautiful city. It comprises large ugly apartment buildings to house its vast and growing population. We, that is my colleagues from PASCAL and Cork were treated like kings and queens. It reminded me of Bologna without the charm and elegance.

Apart from the conferences, we were escorted to the city museum, which contained artefacts of great antiquity, to the few open places in the city, which were being used as allotments, and to meet the city leaders and their heads of Education. I was allotted a personal help. A young girl from the university who had been given the task of following me around everywhere I went, not as a spy but as a Daddie's little helper. She took me to a department store where I looked up the electronic goods, expecting them to be cheaper and more advanced than the ones we have here. Which wasn't true and I left with no purchases. At the end we had a concert with the local conference people from Taiwan. It was expected of us to give a turn so that they could see how we lived. So they asked questions and elicited that long ago I had danced to a rock and roll rhythm. Not very well as Maggie will attest. They insisted that I demonstrate this skill.

In a desperate effort to avoid making a fool of myself I said that it needs music. No problem. I should have known they would have a couple of Bill Haley records to hand given their love of America. I said that it needs two people to rock and roll. No answer, not one of them was willing to dance it with me. Saved! Until an even more decrepit old gentleman than me got up and said that he had learned it in the States. So there we two eighty somethings hopped and jived and twisted each other around making utter fools of ourselves. But it was very popular. I never had as much applause for my presentations. So I gave them an encore and sang the Rose of Tralee with the two Irish people from Cork. The following day I started the thirty two hour journey back to Eus.

194

Chapter Twenty One

European Insights

The Aurora

2018 began with a bang. I had always yearned to see the Aurora borealis and so Maggie and I took the plane to Gatwick and another one to the town of Tromsø in the far north of Norway. We would have preferred the Hurtiguren cruise but that cost too much. And what unusual things we saw and learned. The streets were covered with thick ice making walking a potential leg-breaker. We visited an ice hotel made entirely of frozen snow and with magnificent ice sculptures on the walls. We went to a concert given by the Sami people who herd the reindeer, the equivalent of the inuits from Canada and learned more about their language and culture Then came the day we went out to see what we had come for, the dancing lady, the northern lights. This is the story I wrote a week later.

This February my wife and I (note the fake Royal inference.- not bad for a couple of scrubbers from Bolton) flew to Tromsø in the North of Norway in search of the dancing lady, the Borealis, which we had never seen in 80 years of our travelling lives. We did all the usual things, Nordic museum, ice hotel visit, Nordic culture house and so on. But the major event, the very purpose of our journey was the excursion in search of the Northern Lights. We had booked it in advance with an outfit we didn't know.

At the appointed time we rocked up at the trysting house, which we were surprised to find was a youth hostel in the middle of town. We were a party of 12, comprising youngsters from Germany, Hungary, France, Spain, Austria and Italy, all of them more than 50 years younger than ourselves. So we all climbed into a small mini coach to seek her out. The exploration, for such it was – the lady is as fickle as her reputation and often hides behind a covering of cloud – searched far and wide

But what wonderful people these youngsters were. All of them, including a couple of muslims, were proud to be European and welcomed the opportunity to travel with other Europeans of like mind. It was the glue that bound us all together. We may have been Grandad and Grandma to them all but, as we sped around the North of Norway in our little bus, we shared their dreams and hopes and their delight in the freedom to travel and in the camaraderie of being European. As we sat around a makeshift camp fire set up by our great leader (a Brit no less) we discussed the advantages of diversity – of nationality, of culture, of understanding each other, of breaking down the barriers that separate us.

We did see the lady in all her finery and beauty. That was marvellous – but the sheer pleasure of being Europeans together more than matched that experience. It's what humanity is about – learning, listening, understanding, thinking, adapting, creating, doing.' This has happened several times in our journey through life. Meeting groups of young people in Australia, Fiji, New Zealand, Canada, Africa, Thailand, China, Japan and many other places around this beautiful planet has opened our minds, given us wider horizons and fulfilled our own dreams of an open world of peoples working and interacting in harmony with each other. Would that these encounters happened more often.

Maggie's 80th

It was Maggie's turn to pass 80 in May and so we organised a large celebration of the choir plus friends from all around at the village hall, similar to the one two years previously. Same dance ensemble, almost the same audience, our friend Lizzie as caterer, witty speeches of how young she looked compared with her other half and booze available in quantity. I wrote a special short monologue on how we had met. To make you suffer like they did, here it is

She were t'best cadet nurse in t'infirmary
And 'er beauty woulda taken yer breath
Like Aphrodite rising from t'water
Or the beautiful lady Macbeth

Then fate 'appened all of a sudden
It were an airman nearin' 'is end
E'd contracted peritonitis
And were far from bein' on t'mend.

Now Venus when she first saw Adonis
It were love at first sight it is said
It weren't quite the same with Norman
On account of 'im being half-dead

She flashed 'er black silken stockings
Each time she went near 'is bed
Till 'e noticed this young nursing beauty
And it quickly went to 'is 'ead

Well 'e made a miraculous recovery
Came back into t'world o'the free
An' all this were due to our Margaret
And 'er black stockinged Tender LC

Of course there is a French version too, otherwise they would have missed out on the subtlety but I'm still not sure they understood. Maybe the bit with the silk stockings. We really will have to stop having these birthdays. We'll bankrupt ourselves.

Especially when we followed it up two days later with another blowout in the UK. Same place as mine, almost the same audience with a couple of Maggie's former hospital mates, witty speeches of how young Maggie looked by her son and daughter, same overdressed couple, and multiple drinks of alcohol. And the full version of the far too long Lancashire monologue that tells her life story. The alcohol came in useful. I would suggest you take some before reading on.

Our Maggie

There's a famous Lancashire town called Bolton
That's noted for fine cotton thread
It's where Margaret Joyce Whitton were born to
Don and Dora, 'er mum and dad

If yer wondering why her first name is Margaret
Well she were called after t'royal princess
But there were none o' that royal fuss and palaver
They just a put a short notice in't'press

Tha could tell this child were summat special
'Cause when she were wantin' a feed
She'd ask for a menu from her mother
Wi' t' flavours of t'milk she would need.

They lived in an 'ouse near a river
Overlooked by a ruddy great mill
A remnant o't'days when Bolton
Were spinning 'igh quality twill

It weren't like 'tuther Bolton 'ouses
In terraces all in a squash
It were semi-detached wi' a garden
By gum it were reet bloody posh.

Well she 'ad lots o' friends in her ginnall
She were t'queen o' the Callis road crowd
She'd tell all't kids in the street what to do like
And they obeyed, like 'er 'usband does now.

At school she were good at her studies
And were always teacher's best pet.
She even took up ballet dancin'
'er tutu would make the lads sweat

But then she got scarlet fever
No school for almost a year
So she missed out on passing t'eleven plus
And followed a sec mod career.

When she escaped from t' school system
She worked in a factory that made paint
T'smell of the turps made 'er dizzy
It were no bloody place for a saint

Well she'd always 'ankered on nursing
She were a bugger for self-sacrifice
So she became a primrose in t'hospital
Against her daddy's advice

She were t'best cadet nurse in t'infirmary
And 'er beauty woulda taken yer breath
Like Aphrodite rising from t'water
Or the beautiful lady Macbeth

Then fate 'appened all of a sudden
It were an airman nearin' 'is end
E'd contracted peritonitis
And were far from bein' on t'mend.

Now Venus when she first saw Adonis
It were love at first sight it is said
It weren't quite the same with Norman
On account of 'im being half-dead

She flashed 'er black silken stockings
Each time she went near 'is bed
Till 'e noticed this young nursing beauty
And it quickly went to 'is 'ead

Well 'e made a miraculous recovery
Came back into t'world o'the free
An' all this were due to our Margaret
And 'er black stockinged Tender LC

Well t'courtship were done between lessons
She 'ad tons o' nursing to learn
While e' went off to a college
To learn teacherin' so's e could earn

They both passed their examinations
Midwife Maggie and Teacher Norm
Livin' and breathin' in Bolton
Each in their own uniform

They were wed in a Unitarian chapel
They finally got their reward
Th'oneymoon were taken in London
It were all that the pair could afford.

The years passed by in a jiffy
They bought an 'ouse near 'er mum
Maggie worked for a doctor
Till t'children started to come

Jeannette and David joined t'family
Wi' celebrations all round and fanfare
Then add a dog and a rabbit
All under 'er angelic care

Came time to leave rainswept Bolton
Norman had got a new job
So they moved all t'family to 'Arrow
To join t'softy southerner mob.

Now Jason were quite a character
Chasing the fleece made o' gold
In 'Arrer there were two crazy characters
Barmy, if t'real truth were told

While Norm did 'is bit for 'is company
Our Maggie came into ' er own
Delivering babies for London
While t'mothers were all still at home

She were working 120 hour long weeks
Night and day she were waitin' fer t'call
Cos babies don't make an appointment
As to when they'd first start to bawl

They spent 7 long years in't'big smoke
The midwife of distinguished renown
Then Norm went to study for his masters
And they all moved to Lymington town

Lymington's a fine place fer t'yachties
Wi a 900 year famous town fair
Our Maggie became a town councillor
The greatest they'd ever seen there

As Norm were t'chairman o't school governors
They were both worthy town volunteers
They asked 'er to be the town mayoress
The first female in 900 years

But Maggie refused that great honour
'Cos she were t'star of the neurology ward
'eads an' spines were her speciality
In Southampton's hospital board.

By this time t'children had grown up
And they got to career choosin' age
Dave as a teacher par excellence
Jeannette as a star of the stage

But then Norm were posted to Paris
And with a great deal of regret
Maggie said good bye to Southampton
And joined the ex-patriate set

And that's where she learned 'er French patter
Wi' er own personal teacher on board
She became fluent in all things Parisian
Leavin' no word unexplored

Well they explored round Europe together
They were in their travellin' prime
Then USA, Japan and Australia
't'World were there oyster at't'time

Now Odysseus on one of 'is journeys
Ad himself tied tight to the mast
So he could listen to t' siren singin'
As 'is ship sailed gracefully past

Norm's siren brought them to Brussels
Where Maggie managed t 'IBM wives
She showed'em all t'sights and t'museums
And in general took over their lives

Now Bacchus would take well to Brussels
Lots o' fine grub to get at
W'i all that entertaining an' eating
They tended to get rather fat.

Came time to return to old blighty
Maggie went back 'ome again
To Southampton's magnificent 'ospital
Doing research for controlling pain

Well blighty weren't same as it used to be
The excitement and glamour ad gone off
Then Norman got early retirement
And started a career as a prof

'is job took 'im all around Europe,
All around t'world to be true
And Maggie would often go wi''im
To find what he was getting up to

Then t'decision were made quite quickly
They were missing th' European fun
An' as proffin' could be done from anywhere
They buggered off back to the sun.

They still pay visits to Britain
To bask in the family's glow
Checkin' Dave and Jeannette's exploits
And watching the grandchildren grow

So here we now are in this story
A tale of a lady so bold
Who's life 'as been devoted to others
And she's still at it at 80 years old

She works on cancer supportin'
She sings like a lark in the choir
And an 'undred and one other things
She never seems to get tired

It's like a whirlwind 'as got 'er
Doesn't know the meaning of can't
At 80 she's like a 17 year old
With t'energy of a nuclear plant

Now Gabriel is an archangel
He's in a quite different class
But 'e can't hold a candle to Maggie
Our straight for'ard Lancashire lass.

So let's raise a glass to our Maggie
At 80 she's just reachin' 'er peak
You won't find a finer 'uman bein'
No matter 'ow long you may seek..
NL

Maggie in Canada again

Two days later we were on an Air Canada flight to Canada, where we were met
by Tom and Kathy at Vancouver airport. It was another real humdinger of a
holiday, a sort of honeymoon for 80 year olds without all the fumbling. In the two
weeks we spent there they not only gave Maggie another birthday party but took
us for several days up the British Columbia coast, island hopping on the ferries.
The weather was good, the scenery majestic, the food excellent and the
hospitality amazing.

Among other things we walked the twelve kilometres there and back (not easy
for a couple of octogenarians) to skookumchuck narrows where, because the tide
approaches from two directions, the water fashions wonderful patterns and
shapes. Then over to Powell River and Desolation Sound, a sort of bay of islands
where one can see the golden sunset across an azure ocean, Texada island that's
almost been mined flat by American corporations, and a hundred other
delightful stopping places.

We crossed over to Bowen island where two amis de la musique, members of our
monthly music bash in the South of France, hide themselves in the summer. We
travelled to Chilliwack and Hope in the mountains where, in the late 19th century,
a hopeful entrepreneur had built a speculative railway. The enterprise failed but
a multiplicity of tunnels still exist for brave walkers like us to hike through by the

side of a river that cascades vigorously through the narrow gorges. It's an adventure trail and a good way of reducing the effects of the huge meals we were eating.

We ventured into Vancouver to see an Imax 3D film of Canada where the audience swoops down mountains, paddles in lakes, falls out of an airplane and mines for gold. At least that the sensation you get just by watching. And we took the new cable car up the mountain to Whistler. The ladies kept their eyes tightly closed. Up at the top there was a narrow swinging rope bridge across a wide gorge to test the brave at heart. Only one of us crossed it.

We said goodbye to Tom and Kathy after a tumultuous holiday and crossed over the strait to the island for the next instalment with Maggie's cousins, John and Joan. They too offered a comprehensive range of experiences. Sailing a refurbished 1930s smack in the straits in a force eight gale, Goats on the roof (you read that right), a commercial village selling everything under the sun, with remarkable images chiselled by local sculptors, and real live goats on the roofs.

We were taken to a collector of old cars and motorcycles who had the most amazing accumulation of vehicles, including four model T Fords, the Just, which was one of only three cars to complete the 1912 New York to Paris race westwards via Alaska and Russia, a remarkable panoply of old motorcycles, 1950s cadillacs and vehicular contraptions going back to the 19th century. The whole collection was worth billions. We were well and truly gobsmacked by everything we saw on this trip. It was a learning experience and that's important for the wrinklies to keep the grey matter buzzing. And Canadians are super hosts.

Peace at Last – or is it?

The next few months passed peacefully by. We had had our fill of excitement. It was a hot sweltering summer with temperatures up to forty degrees and we spent it hiding from the sun. I had few business commitments and spent my time writing and self-publishing poetry in French and English. I also published three books on the Conflent which perceptive readers will remember is the subregion in which I live in the Pyrenees, one of them of poems in the two languages complete with photographs to stimulate the words. Well, that kept me off the street corners and learning. I had assumed that my working days were over.

Trieste

At Eighty two it sometimes happens that way. But not always. In November I was summoned once more to Friuli, this time to keynote at a conference in Trieste, a city I had never visited and which, at the end of the second world war decided to be Italian rather than Yugoslavian, a wise choice given subsequent history. This too is a noble city with wide marketplaces, narrow streets, grandiose building, historical artefacts going back to Roman times and a panoramic view across the Adriatic Sea. I included extracts from some of the poems in my presentation and took a few books to see if they would sell. The audience enjoyed the presentation but didn't buy the poetry books. I put it down to the fact that they were in English and this was Italy. I learned the following year that the city had decided to apply to be a learning city under UNESCO. Seems that I had still had the gift of persuasion to convert the powers that be.

And that was definitely my last engagement as a working man. Except of course that one doesn't have to work for others. I continued writing my poetry, some of which I have put in the annexe. I began to put it to four part music, which you won't see or hear in the annexe. It's a hobby I still follow. As for Maggie she too continued to serve mankind and make a difference to those with cancer. She is now the one who does the travelling. To meetings and exhibitions and book exchanges and drop-ins, while I walk the dog in the morning and keep the dementia at bay in the afternoon.

Who paid?

Maggie and I have travelled far and wide in our life together, me more than Maggie. And that costs money. So maybe I should add an addendum about reimbursement. Maggie of course has received nothing, and everywhere she has travelled with me comes from our own purse. In the early days when I was working with IBM, it was they who paid everything and also a salary to boot. The double salary I received when working abroad helped us to save a few shillings and to buy a house in France. It wasn't expensive, just 35000 euros.

And we gained from selling our houses in the UK. Since then much of it has gone. With ELLI I was paid the fare to attend the conferences from the profits they earned, but the days, weeks, months and years of creating learning materials was entirely unrewarded. Similarly although I have been a professor at several universities I received no professorial payment from them. I was there to manage their projects and give them the international credit they craved but money for this was there none.

The projects I managed paid the fare to the meetings I attended, but there was little in excess to pay for the development work I did. The idea that working on European projects is a gravy train is entirely false. Every penny has to be previewed in advance, included in the application, and justified at the end of the project if you are to get the last instalment. Thus, for the many months organising meetings, writing papers, books and project materials and the time in attending meetings and conferences I received nothing. Just the fare and accommodation. This is not a complaint. I did it willingly because, in my mind, it had to be done. This applies to the overseas trips to speak at conferences in Australia, Canada, Africa, USA and elsewhere. The organisers paid travel and accommodation and nothing for hours of preparation.

The only exception is the small amount paid by UNESCO for consultancy and a very small income from the sale of my books.. So it has all been done on a small pension from IBM and a UK state pension plus whatever we saved when working.

Chapter Twenty Two

2019 – Year of Affliction

2019 will be for ever imprinted on my mind for the year when I made more contact with hospitals and doctors than I can remember. It started in March with a routine visit to a doctor in Perpignan who diagnosed cataracts. It wasn't a surprise. I had known about it for several years. But now the crunch time came to rid both eyes of the blackness that required stronger and stronger glasses. Much as I take illness seriously I often tried to make light of it with an amusing short story. It doesn't cure it but it helps to lighten the burden. So what follows are the blow by blow experiences of an elderly man's suffering all in one year.

The Farsight saga Part 1. An Eyewatering Story.

Went to the hospital this week for removal of cataracts. How a fast flowing river can get into someone's eye beats me Anyway It was the left one, the one I've never been able to see through anyway on account of it having a stigma. Don't know who put it there. So I rock up à jeun (breakfastless) with Maggie as my carer at 10.15 and we seek out the ophthalmogy department – not an insignificant task considering the size of the hospital. After 15 minutes we found it. The smiling nurse who prepares people for a possible death under the knife told me to take all my clothes off (nurses do that often) – and put on a blue paper outfit that made me look like I was preparing for a Karate competition.

In this half-naked condition I was taken to the waiting cocoon to ponder my fate. It was a busy day, so the waiting lasted longer than usual, even for a hospital, but eventually some guy comes in and asks me my name, address, date of birth and if I knew what I was there for. This last question threw me a little and raised the foreboding level considerably. And there I was thinking this is just a routine cut and paste job. So he asks me to open my eye, look up to heaven and then he dunked it with a river of some chemical that he said would put my eye to sleep. I didn't have time to tell him it had been that way for 80 years already, before he hurried out of sight. Anyway he returned five minutes later with a gaggle of nurses, auxiliaries, helpers and God knows what, all with forced smiles on their faces as if to warn me that this could turn out pretty nasty.

I said what could have been my final goodbyes to Maggie as they stuffed me into an ancient ambulateur and wheeled me through a maze of corridors to what seemed like another hospital far away, but was in fact the location of the operating theatre. From the look on the faces of those coming out of it the floorshow was pretty lousy. Most of them seemed to have fallen asleep. In this new location I was asked the same questions about my origins, my current status and my cognitive awareness of the situation I found myself in, just in case I had morphed into another body. Nurses learn slowly. But hey ho, another twenty minutes wait, and I was bundled onto a hospital trolley and we were en marche to the killing fields, where another crowd of assorted nurses, surgeons and hangers on were waiting to deal the coup de grace. They smiled, a little prayerfully I thought, and I smiled nervously back. They asked if I was comfortable, much in the way I expect they do at Dignitas, and I lied positively.

What seemed to be a waterproof sack was thrown over me as I lay helpless on the trolley and straps, much like those used to restrain patients with violent dementia, were battened down. Finally, my head was placed in a sort of vice, presumably to prevent it moving while the knives and scalpels were busy doing their work in my eye, and the treatment began. This involved much poking, digging, grouting, cursing and groaning by the surgeon (which did little to raise confidence levels) interspersed with oceans of chemicals flung into the eye, presumably to wash out the unwanted bits.

None of this was painful but I did wonder how one eye could sustain all this gardening work. 20 minutes later I heard the surgeon say ca y est, so I asked ca y est? And he answered ça y est, No applause, no fist raising or cheering from the onlookers. Just a ça y est. And so I was wheeled out of the theatre to be replaced by some other poor victim with a problem. I was now the proud cataractless owner of a brand new lens with a blue tint to withstand any passing UVA rays.

Another marathon ride, patch now on eye, back to the ophthalmology department and a refreshing meal of orange juice, yoghourt, dry biscuits and lukewarm coffee. I swapped the Karate outfit for my clothes and toddled off to the secretariat for final orders These included an eyepatch, a parrot to go with it, an offer of a replacement wooden leg (either side), and an introduction to a guy called Silver. Oh and a mountain of chemicals to pour into the eye three times a day for the next month. The parrot's a nuisance – it can't stop squawking 'morceaux de huit' and that affects my sleep. And that's this week's eyewatering story. You needn't believe all of it but most of is faithful to the reality. And the funny thing is – it has to start all over again with the other eye next week!

The Far sight Saga Part 2.

All good stories have a sequel. This one could last forever like a BBC soap. Well a month at least. And so it came to pass on the 14th day after the great left eye-gouging festival, I was summoned to have the right eye subjected to the same abuse. Not a pleasing prospect since this was the one working eye that had carried me successfully through 83 years, hundreds of wickets taken, thousands of runs scored, millions of tennis balls despatched and countless golf balls lost in the trees. But the deed had to be done.

Thus at 5.30 in the morning, long before the first sparrow farted to introduce the day, Maggie, my carer, and I rose into the blackness of the Yllician night to prepare ourselves for the ordeal to come. I took the second shower within 8 hours as ordered and dressed in black just in case. As the blood-red sun made its daily appearance in the East we were Perpignan bound ready for a 7.15 kick off at the St Jean hospital and to meet our happy band of smiling medics. As torturers rather than the victims, they had much more to be cheerful about.

Thus the proceedings commenced as they had done 14 days previously with the preliminary rites of passage - uncertain smiles, the requirement to undress (me, not them) and to don the blue paper kimono once more, ready for battle. Another longish semi-nude wait and the nurse charged with the duty of transporting me to the killing fields arrived. This one did not smile. Indeed she looked worried as if her boy friend had given her a hard time. Even my happy smiling greeting came to naught, maybe because it was a façade and she knew it. So to punish me for being transparently cheerful she made me walk the 10 miles , or so it seemed, to the guillotine, all the while desperately holding up the blue trousers in case they fell down. Not even a tumbril to lighten the atmosphere.

Another long wait ensued as I lay helplessly on a brancard in the pre-preparation chamber while patients were wheeled hither and thither and passing nurses threw sympathetic smiles at me. Monday morning apparently was not the most favoured by surgeons. Especially at such an early hour. Then the hour of reckoning came as a burly red-faced bruiser wheeled the brancard into the torturing space, the one with the bright lights and the people with masks, where only their eyes revealed their inner feelings. Was this to be a good day or had they not slept well in the night? All would be made apparent in the fullness of time.

It did not start well. The surgeon asked me how the left eye was working. The operative word should have been if, rather than how, since I told him that it was in a permanent 1950s London smog through which it was impossible to see Jack the Ripper at 3 feet. This puzzled him at first but he got the drift and, since the bright light was at hand he had a peer into the eye he thought he had previously decontaminated of its cataract. Oops he said in French, we seem to have left some cataract there, as if I were complicit in the error. What shall we do? he said You're the bloody surgeon I thought though I didn't actually articulate the feeling.

Eventually he made up his mind. We'll do the right eye first and then we'll re-do the left. OK? A quick count on my part left me with the distinct possibility of no eyes at all but I was hardly in a position to argue the point. And so the action began. A quick shower of some chemical – it seemed like several gallons – as an hors d'oeuvre. Then the painless digging and grouting and gardening continued in the right eye for some 20 minutes. This was followed by a further 15 minutes of tugging , grunting, knocking and resurfacing in the left – not exactly pain free since this was the second abuse it had received in two weeks, Indeed it felt as if the eye had been removed from its socket for a general service.

210

But finally the surgeon declared himself satisfied with his labour and a mighty soundless cheer could be heard only by me. Two eye-patches, blind pugh model, were installed with not a parrot in sight (We had returned the previous one on account of its constant squawking). But the black spot had been removed and the rejoicing could be heard in Birmingham.

I was returned to my carer, at least I think it was she – could have been anyone. And waited silently miserable, left eye throbbing to a Kenny Baker beat, with this lady and all the other survivors for 2 hours, It was like a silent film of the slaughter of the innocents without the wailing and gnashing of teeth. Eventually the surgeon made a triumphant return like Radamis with all his prisoners to the temple of Isis (Aida) - only without the inspiring music. He professed himself satisfied with his work and sent us all home with, for us, a return date 2 days later. This we duly completed and I was declared still officially alive and functioning. The collateral damage is thrice daily eye baths with 3 assorted chemicals 3 times a day for a month with the right eye and 6 times for the left one.

And I must say that the world according to the right eye is beautifully clear, singing with the colours of spring. I now almost see through walls and mountains. It may even help me to find those golf balls. The left one however is still looking in vain for Jack the Ripper. That was in March. The next chapter started the following month in April,

On Cystisis – to be read only by the less squeamish

Spent four days in bed last week plus a fair amount of time bravely suffering the equivocations of post-infection recovery. Not the most pleasant way of pre-Easter celebrating. Don't know whence it came, this tiny microbe adrift in the vastness of space. Nor do I know why it decided to settle on me as a host for its research findings. Perhaps it wanted to share my vast store of knowledge and wit (and modesty). Whatever, I got it.

So there you are, breaking every world sprint record in a never-ending rat race to the bathroom because your once reliable sphincter has gone on strike. God knows who persuaded it to down tools but it may have been better to carry the toilet around with you everywhere you went. And it's not as if it was all worth while when you got there. Most times not more than a teaspoonful to celebrate success in getting there in time.

And then there are the infection side-effects – the rigor where you seem to have swallowed an iceberg, so cold is your whole body. So you lie under 6 blankets in bed, shivering and shaking like a mad jitter bug dancer while your body goes rigid and all your muscles stiffen and rise up in anger against the ignominy of it all. To the point where the word mortis might almost be a welcome adjective to the condition. And not forgetting the exquisite pain at water passing time - which is more or less a continuous on-going circus. This is especially fascinating when you look down and see that it's all a lovely crimson red colour because you are also passing copious quantities of precious blood from an orifice from which you are not supposed to be passing blood.

It is at times like these that one needs a Maggie, a practised medical bullier who can break down the iron will of the doctor's secretary who insists that everything can wait the 3 weeks when he is next available for consultation. An encyclopaedia of all known ills who can slip slyly into the surgery between patients and emerge with a prescription urine for the testing of and antibiotic for the swallowing. A nursing angel from heaven to remind one of the wisdom of one's choice some 60 years ago.

No longer in the black silk stockings but still an icon of therapeutic beauty. But all good things must come to an end. Slowly the antibiotics have taken effect and the mad rush has diminished to a canter with the invaluable help of a bedside bucket. It took a mere 3 days for the results of the testing to confirm that the culprit was that well known body botherer, Mr E Coli. But I can confirm that I have now taken back control and can even walk the dog without surreptitiously hiding in the bushes more than twice. But it will now take another 2 weeks to ensure that the cystitis does not degenerate into prostitis. Oh joy unbounded. Bring on the antibiotics.

We are less than halfway to good health. Voila part 3, the following month

Vertigo – The Chronicles of a First time Sufferer.

Ever had a crazy motor cyclist doing a wall of death at 500 mph inside your head? It happened to me twice in the past week, and I can now reveal that it is not the most pleasant sensation for a humanoid to experience. Like having one's brains stirred and scrambled inside a car engine. Don't know whence it came or what I had done to annoy the demons of hell, but for me it was certainly the first time in 83 years of living my life on this earth. Anyway, the side effects soon made themselves known in the form a trumpet solo in the head, the retching and evacuation of most of the contents of my body from several orifices (sorry there is no delicate way of describing this phenomenon) the former into a large bowl that Maggie had spirited upstairs as quickly as possible and the latter into the usual place.

The first salvo came at 2am on a Sunday morning, not the best of times to seek solace from the local medical community. Since this Mahomet was in no fit state to go to the A and E mountain, the angry hornets being what they were, Maggie called 15 and tried to describe life on the battlefield in her best French to the half-asleep secretary whose misfortune it was to be on duty. Well it seemed to work because the duty doctor rocked up at 3 o clock, hopefully to dispense advice and salvation.

By this time the motor cyclist seemed to be running out of petrol and I had dared to open my eyes to the light. He asked what I had been drinking just to be sure (nothing alcoholic as it happens even after a Saturday night), looked half-heartedly into my eyes, took my temperature and asked the obligatory questions. Et voila he had a diagnosis – viral gastro-enteritis – they always use big words in times of trouble, it adds gravitas. So he filled out a prescription, identified the duty pharmacy and off went Maggie 20 miles down the road at the dead of night to Vinca to get the goods that would offer succour and relief, including a knock-out pill that, when I eventually took it, immediately went the same way as the rest of my insides had done.

So off went the doc to his next sufferer – apparently he had 15 that night – and back came Maggie. It's great to be married to a ex-nurse. She found another 4 pillows on which to lay my battered head and I managed a fitful sleep dreading the return of the torture for the rest of the night. Morning came and I tried to rise from my bed to expel more of my stomach, only to be punched once again by a head that wandered anywhere in the room but on my body. And thus it was for several days, gradually improving, until by the Friday morning I was able to crawl downstairs for breakfast. The symptoms seem to be beating a retreat. Hardly a single magic roundabout to complain about. Cured – no more circles.

So we rejoiced with the first square meal for 6 days and I even managed to ascend the steps to watch the television that evening. .

Bad mistake. Half-way through the programme the same thing exploded, only tenfold – no motor cyclist but a fully armoured assault vehicle on every neural pathway in the head. Once more the devil had released his fiends to torment me. So the ministering angel that is Maggie once more called upon her new friends in the medical services and this time they didn't mess about. Two burly ambulanciers who might have doubled as night club bouncers arrived to see me off the premises. Trouble was – they couldn't carry me downstairs because I couldn't lie on their stretcher. So the three of us descended the stairway step by step, slowly, with the bruisers on each side and me clinging desperately to the rail.

Off I went to hospital in Perpignan at 90mph in a clapped out ambulance that seemed to run on solid rubber wheels. Throughout the ride I almost wished that it would crash and put an end to it all. So I was dumped onto a trolley into the A and E with the other lost souls of the night many of them crying out to no-one in particular. It was the 7th stage of Dante's inferno and a Hieronymous Bosch painting all in one. I half expected the nurses to be clad in red capes with tales and carrying forks. I still could not lie down – to do so would set off the sirens in my head. The few nurses were overwhelmed and the best they could offer was sympathy and a smile that said 'I'm not sure you're going to get through this one.'

Eventually – perhaps an hour later, a doctor arrived. He gabbled something in fast and furious French, which I was in no state to understand or reply to and so he abandoned me. Five minutes later, by some miracle, there arrived another doctor who spoke perfect English – indeed I think he was English but had strayed into a French hospital by mistake. Either that or I was hallucinating or ascending into heaven.

We were able to converse in tongues and I described as best I could the nightmare I was experiencing. Sadly he didn't seem to sympathise – Doctors in France are not noted for their bedside manner – even the English ones it seems. Perhaps it's not allowed. Maggie however was allowed into the room after an anxious 2 hour early morning wait wondering if I was still alive. The unspoken word was 'stroke', so I was whisked off to have a brain scan – they found nothing – and later to a ward with a bed and an open toilet.

While Maggie drove home at 3.30 am, I fell into the sleep of the exhausted. Until I was awakened at 7 by two cheerful young helpers with a breakfast trolley and given the choice of a bread roll or a biscuit. I took the biscuit in case the orifices opened again. Nothing much happened for the rest of the morning. It was as if

214

the hospital had been evacuated and had forgotten to inform the patients. Thankfully they had remembered to leave a bottle – not for drinking I add. Come mid-day an exhausted Maggie returned after having had 4 hours sleep.

This day was her 81st birthday and she spent it languishing in a hospital room surrounded by bed-pans and a spaced-out husband. Shortly after lunch a doctor finally arrived to ask the same questions I had answered on arrival, perhaps to make sure that I had not morphed into someone else. She said that the rest of the day would be filled with the excitement of medical tests – first the dreaded MRI scan with all its clatter, followed by a blood test and finally an ECG. These tests were duly completed and the result was a large zilch. At least it wasn't a stroke, so they sent me home.

So we knew what it wasn't, but not what it was. I was given papers to give to my doctor but sod's law again- he was off on one of his many holidays as befits a medical man looking forward to imminent retirement. However he had a replacement whom I could see on the Monday morning. By this time I was feeling a little better – walking like a drunken zombie and a head somewhere in outer space – but that constituted better.

The replacement doctor turned out to be a young woman – very efficient and relatively knowledgeable. She asked me to stand on one leg – difficult since I could hardly stand on two, so I fell over. Then I had to walk the line in the same way that drunks are asked to do by policeman. The line I carved wasn't the straightest. However she came to the conclusion that the problem was that crystals in the left ear had gone walkabout. And that my blood pressure was too low most of the time.

I was given the name of a physiotherapist who specializes in mending broken ears and has a weekly clinic in Prades. I have seen him twice now. Both times he puts a hood on my head and tries to gaze into my eyes – not sure why and he's not that pretty - and then I am required to sit in a revolving chair which he whizzes round at great speed several times and then waits to see how long it takes for the head to come back to normal.

He is quite old. I believe that he went to the Gestapo school of torture medicine. Both times I left his surgery feeling worse than when I entered it. I now know about the hell that many vertigo sufferers have to endure and I sympathise with them. Weekly visits to the torture chamber and new blood pressure tablets succeeded in a daily improvement until the visitations ceased at last , hopefully forever. And, a few weeks later I made it up to Maggie by taking her to the UK to see the family.

Meanwhile there was the small matter of the haemorrhaging aorta. I had seen my cardiologue in June and wanted an end to the leaking. So this I what I wrote after the next encounter with the medical fraternity.

The Saga of a Blob of Glue

2019 has not been a good year. I have heroically survived the double evacuation of cataracts in March, the icy rigours of cystitis in April, the circular horrors of vertigo in May. However, a full month passed by before the next offensive and the exigences of an arthritic back in July. This story however chronicles the August assault period in which the spectre of the man with the scythe played a small part.

It is not well known that there lies hidden within my abdominal aorta a Y shaped thingymibob to counteract the life-threatening effects of an everwidening aneurism. In hospital-speak it is called an endoprosthesis. If it were not there I would not be around to write this rubbi – er tale. It was inserted 8 years ago when I wasn't looking, owing to the drugs I had been given. It is nevertheless a thing of great beauty and grace, performing its allotted task with an elegant efficiency.

However for the past seven years it has been less than fully effective. This is because it has leaked. Not in large quantities I hasten to add. Just a few droplets of my precious red stuff seeping into god knows what inside every single day. So in July I had my annual scan and checkup. I showed the lovely coloured pictures produced by the scanner to my cardiologue, who, much to my surprise, decided that the leak should be sealed forever and the blood no longer be allowed to escape from its aortal prison.

Messing about in an abdomen is not an easy thing to do. One does not slice into the stomach with happy abandon, stick some bluetack onto the offending article and then sow it all up again. That's the old way, as many occupants of churchyards would tell you if they could speak. Modern fashion dictates that it should be done by stealth, slyly and sneakily entering the body where the offending ailment is not expecting it through the femoral artery, and pushing the article along hidden arterial pathways to its destination. Surgeons of today are pokers rather than slashers. My cardiologue trusted no-one in the hospitals of Perpignan to do this, even though it was one of them that put the thingymibob in situ in the first place.

So off I went, accompanied by my carer, my wife, to see the chosen butcher in Montpellier, some 160 kms away. There they x rayed, scanned, MRIed my insides upside down, inside out and right way up from every angle. The photos were magnificent, ravishing, thought-provoking. Picasso could not have painted anything more lovely. So we waited the normal 4 hours for the local endoconnoisseur to explain their wondrous meaning unto us. Which, when he deigned to arrive, he did with the confidence of the born showman - piece of cake, be done in half an hour, we shove a blob of glue up this, along that, over the other and plug it in. Just come back in 4 day's time at 10 am and bob's your uncle.

As it happens I don't have an uncle Bob and 10 am was a little early for part 2 so we arrived the previous evening. I slept in the hospital and Maggie in the hotel across the way. It was a fitful nights sleep, full of dreams of grinning surgeons in battle dress armed with scalpels, sabres and Kalashnikovs. On being awakened at 6 am, not an hour I recognize, I was first razed – well you know where the femoral artery is. No surprises there – can't have an infection from anything which might be unwittingly lodged down there.

Then the all over shower with the antiseptic soap and, of course, no breakfast before the human engineering was due to commence. Eventually the hour of judgment arrived. I told Maggie where to find my last will and testament (she already knew) and I was wheeled into the gladiatorial arena. Four masked nurses said a pleasant hello, though their eyes betrayed a certain anxiety, and I was introduced to the two surgeons present, one of whom I recognised from my previous visit, and the other who looked disconcertingly young. I assumed that he was an intern come to watch the great man at work.

So they put me on the experimentation slab, switched on the searchlights and set to work. I was told to lie perfectly still, not an easy thing to do since my back had chosen that very moment to start playing a Mozart overture, Don Giovanni I think, where the Commendatore comes in. I could feel the first cut, offering entry to the delights of my body and some fiddling about with an accompaniment of heavy breathing. After a few minutes the gaffer came to ask if I was OK, while at the same time someone was still poking about down below.

And I realised the awful truth. It was the intern doing the job and it was probably his first ever attempt at guiding blobs of glue through the complex arterial system of a human body. Well they have to start somewhere, and why not an old bugger who has already had a long life. But I would have preferred it not to be me. Time passed – a half hour, an hour, an hour and a half – what the hell happened to the piece of cake in half an hour? How long does it take to push something not more than a yard away whichever route they chose to adopt? From time to time a nurse would come anxiously to the slab and ask if I was OK.

Not much confidence there then. Of course I wasn't alright. My back had finished the last movement of Mahler's 8th – the coda where the percussion takes charge and the loud music hits crescendo, and it was just starting a full blast

217

rendition of the Marseillaise. I told them so and they said it wouldn't be long in a not very convinced way. I don't think they knew about Mahler. At the other end the two surgeons were having long conversations – he seemed to have lost his way. Maybe he had it in the carotid by mistake, why not try the radial artery – that should get you close, or then maybe not. Maybe he was on safari exploring all the arteries one by one while he had a live cadaver.

The torture continued another 2 hours until finally I heard a grunt of satisfaction, or was it a cheer- I had given up all hope of survival by then. They had, or thought they had, placed the glue in the right place in the right part of the aorta, though I would have imagined that it would have set long ago. Now all that remained was to withdraw the pusher, slap each others' backs and uncle Bob would be satisfied even if my own back would never be the same again.

Suddenly there was a cry and mayhem ensued. Nurses started screaming, boss was shouting, young surgeon pressing hard on the femoral artery time and time again. A nurse explained it. On exit, the silly sod had nicked the femoral artery and blood, my blood, was gushing all over the slab, the floor and the surgeon.

Not much I could do about it. I could hardly get up and run all over the floor and paint the room red. Finally, after what seemed hours but must have been minutes, he managed to stop the blood river. And things quietened down. Relieved faces everywhere. I was wheeled back to the ward and left to sleep. The surgeon did not come to see me again. Indeed there was no mention of the shenanigins from anyone. It had been effaced from the records. I spent another night in the hospital and then cleared off with the wife as soon as they would let me. I should have had an IRM scan the following week and then 6 months later but I asked if that could happen elsewhere, since the journey is long and costly and there are perfectly adequate IRM facilities in Perpignan hospitals.

The hospital agreed but didn't sign me up for one in Perpignan. So, I don't know if it has worked. Or if the blob of glue is now stuck to my left kidney. I will have to wait until May 2020 in my annual checkup. But Hey. I'm alive and it's all over …. Isn't it? My back had a brief word with me recently. It said you're not going back to that place again.

The rest of the year was spent in robust health, if we ignore a few back twinges that the physiotherapist tried in vain to correct And I was able to report in September that the worst was over . Except that it was now Maggie's turn to hit the surgeon's table to attend to her waterworks, which were leaking like a broken dam. While her sojourn in the central hospital was not quite so dramatic as mine had been. The aftermath was equally theatrical with nurses turning up

218

on our doorstep twice a day for several weeks. Whatever, I was able to report that life had returned to normal by writing the following bulletin

My Sunday

This Sunday has been like every Sunday there ever was here in the paradise of the Pyrenees-Orientales. Indeed every day seems to morph seamlessly into the next one as it has always done through recorded time. Sunday morning is Maggie's church time. She is a churchwarden which I think means blowing a whistle and evacuating the premises every time the enemy bombers come over. (This observation gives a clue to my age. Cowering in an Andersen shelter during the second world war and wearing a gas mask was a weekly delight for a young lad.) Me, I am awakened by the dog desperate for a pee, as indeed am I, and I struggle down the stairs holding tightly onto the banister while he takes the steps 3 at a time and waits with his legs crossed at the bottom. Eventually I get to the back door to let him spray the garden.

So while Maggie is praying and organising the communion bowls, my prime duty is to transport him to the nearest flat piece of land and throw sticks for him to chase. Two sticks - to make sure he is constantly on the move and I'm not. He's a young dog and needs plenty of exercise. I'm an old dog and need that sort of dashing about like I need a brain transplant – (come to think of it..........!.) Anyway we eventually return home so that I can give him his dentastick and his meat treat (nothing is too good for this hound – even his name, Jupiter, reeks of opulence and entitlement.)

The rest of the morning comprises shouting at my tablet as the interminably bad news comes pouring out of it, swallowing several tons of pills to keep myself alive and trying to avoid doing the morning chores – not always successfully. Oh and writing some excruciating music on my computer – I have this software which does most of the hard graft like inserting notes and testing harmonies. The rest is my fault.

It's mid-day. Maggie, now well shriven, returns from her spiritual cleansing and sets about re-organising the house, doing the things I should have done and didn't get round to, and making the dinner. This lady has all the energy of ten nuclear plants and an erupting volcano combined. She exhausts me just watching her. The whole world is her stage for showing how much she loves life and people and making a difference. I thought that I had a monopoly on changing the world, what with a carbon footprint that would equate to every inhabitant of Africa combined, but Maggie's vision seems to include the universe and beyond.

Anyway, as I was saying, it's dinner-time and we have a busy afternoon ahead thinking of how to fill it. My preference is a siesta but Maggie says the garden must be done, and that becomes law after a brief vote in which the casting decision always seems to go one way. So after a jaw-dropping meal of 5 vegetables and 3 fruit (leaving 2 more for the evening) we don our war garb for the coming assault on the grass, the plants and the bloody moles.

My speciality is mowing the lawn – indeed it's the only thing I do which Maggie trusts me with, other than wheeling the barrow up the road to the rubbish cemetery. So I put on my back brace (age is a bugger), set up the wiring, clip on the mower box and wander up and down, up and down until the grass is at the required height of 3.3 centimetres. That is, where there is still grass since the moles have had yet another late night underground rave-up and forgotten to tidy up. Maggie's gardening combat plan is less brutal. It involves using secateurs to cut bits off plants and then corralling the mess into a wheelbarrow seemingly without touching it. It's a gift not given to ordinary mortals.

The hole-digging, tree-cutting, hedge-bashing is often mine and mine alone. Which explains the horrifying state of the garden boundaries. After a half-hour of toil my poor back starts to shout enough and I look for ways of quitting the scene. But all escape plans between lawn and house are foiled by Maggie's strategically placed wheelbarrow whose contents need transporting for interral into their last resting place. And so, at the risk of further crippling injury, I of course do my duty before abandoning the battlefield for a well-earned rest. Maggie ploughs on like a gardening wonderwoman until she too has to accept the inevitable.

We have both now succumbed to the dictates of age and we partake of a refreshing half-hour afternoon siesta, much to the chagrin of the dog who would much rather we indulged his constant need to play. However around 4pm he gets his wish and, for the second time in the day, to demonstrate his capacity to keep moving without apparently the need to breathe. So it's now 5pm, we are back home again and we have to fill the next 6 hours with purpose. Every first Sunday of the month that decision is taken from us by 'les amis de la musique' a happy band of music-loving nomads who take it in turns to open up their houses for 2 to 3 hours and present a programme of their taste in music. This Sunday is one such and Erik, a happy Dutchman living in Prades, is to regale us with his recorded version of Pink Floyd's Wall from Berlin when walls were a permanent feature of the landscape there. Come to think of it walls appear to be making a comeback across the pond, in Israel, the USA and anywhere there is a bothersome leader. Anyway, back to civilisation, our 'amis' repertoire is eclectic and reflects the whim of the presenter whether it be Classical, Jazz, Pop or, rarely, plain unlistenable.

Thereafter we will return home, lash up an evening meal full of vitamins and healthy victuals before Maggie retires to the upstairs lounge to watch the latest version of Eastenders which she missed last Friday. My task at this time is to light the fire and retreat hurriedly back downstairs before I have to watch grown people squabbling and shouting in a cockney accent. I will pay another visit to my home office to write some more insufferable music, or an excruciating story like this one, or catch up with the need to prepare the annual taxes, as I must do soon.

At 9pm I too clamber up the stairs to the eyrie with my Sudoko book, and Maggie and I agree on which least bad tv programme we will watch until it is time for me to retire for bedtime reading, our nightly cocoa treat and for the dog to have his final pee of the day. Maggie will continue to scrutinise the news and subsequent political chatter until the wee small hours. She is a glutton for punishment.

And that, ladies and gentlemen, is my Sunday. Thrills and excitement from dawn to dusk for the whole family. It's a wonder we are still alive, such is the gruelling fight to survive in this Pyrennean paradise. It is not for the faint-hearted.

Journey into Catalunya

In October , Maggie and I decided to have holiday in the Ebro delta. It isn't that far way. Maybe a couple of hours down the coast into Spain? Think again. Nothing in 2019 seemed to be straightforward. Thus follows the captivating tale of a very peculiar first day of a holiday

A funny thing happened to us on our way to Catalunya. It was the last week in October and we were taking our annual holiday. Late I know but what can you do when every other week is taken by a meeting, a social event, a drop-in, a tragedy, a crisis or hospital visit. We weren't going far. Just next door more or less to the Delta of the River Ebro in Catalunya to see the last of the migrating birds - the ones who are having such a ball in their summer holidays further north that they leave their departure to the very last minute. With a stop-off at Tarragona to view the debris the Romans had left behind when they left 1600 years ago. Just a 3 and a half hour drive down the motorway past Barcelona.

Except that the Spanish government, in its infinite wisdom, had chosen the previous week to imprison the leaders of Catalunya's attempt to abandon their Spanishness and go it alone. And the Catalunyans were not pleased. So much so that they decided to close their borders with France (not that France had any part in it), and to make sure that everyone knew their displeasure by rioting and demonstrating on the main roads. It was not explained why this would improve things but perhaps they had heard that we were also due to visit on that day too.

So, in true military style, we took the advice of Clausewitz and decided to by-pass the motorways and main roads into the region by testing its weak Northern flank

222

in the Pyrenean mountains. In the hanging valley known as the Cerdagne round our way. No dice. The road into the Catalan town of Puigcerda was blocked by a couple of burly gendarmes armed to the teeth with weapons of human destruction. Their intent to thwart our passage to our destination was manifestly evident. Impasse.

Time to rethink the strategy. By now it was lunch time, so we decided to recharge the stomach and devise an alternative master plan. Here, in mid-steak, we made contact with a local, who like me had been bitten by the golfing bug some years previously. We discussed the pros and cons of all the golf courses in the area and, as an aside, probed his knowledge of the countryside., in particular of the existence of little known crossings whereby we might sneak into the forbidden land.

He directed us to a small border village in the surrounding hills where, if we took the right turning, we may have been able to cross the river on a narrow bridge between France and Spain and which quite probably would not be manned by the local constabulary. So we tried it and – bingo – there we were. The only foreign entrants in Catalunya on that day. So we continued on our joyful way to our destination. Except again that the towns on the main route to it were in full manifestation mode and preventing all access to the South of the country. This was made clear on large road signs advising vehicles to travel no further in that direction.

So we changed plans again and drove North West to the small town of La Seu D'Urgell on the border with Andorra, where our map had told us that there was an alternative route direct to Tarragona with fewer awkward dissenters trying to discourage foreigners from travelling along their highways. A bit like going from London to Birmingham to get to Cornwall. In this way, nine hours after leaving home, we arrived in Tarragona.

Where we found the city once again beset by manifesting Catalunyans, and all access to the beach area, where our hotel was, blockaded. What to do again? Maggie had the bright idea of driving to the nearby airport of Reus to ask advice from someone with local knowledge. Not a tactic that I could understand but she was the navigator, so we drove the ten kilometres to the airport. Here we met a helpful young man who was delighted to help us solve our problem, the airport having been short of planes all day.

He constructed a map with a complex system of roundabouts and diversions that he believed would resolve the problem and give solace to our travel-weary minds. Which we followed and ended up in a not very savoury quarter of the city far from any hotel that we would ever want to frequent. The only light in the tunnel came from a pharmacy which was still open and (wo)manned by a very pleasant lady who spoke neither French nor English but was very good at sign language, as is Maggie when negotiating with the dog. Between them they managed to create a map which led us to the coast and hopefully the hotel.

Now readers may think that this the end of the saga. Think again. I swear that the following is true and Maggie will confirm it. We did indeed find our way to the coast but, as sod's law dictates, took a wrong turning when we arrived there. After a few hotel-less miles we dropped in at what seemed to be the first hostelry on the road in order to ask the way. I parked the car across the court yard and climbed out of the car to walk to the door opposite. Before I got half-way a scantily clad young lady came out of the door, approached me, put her arms round me and said welcome. I kid you not. It's true on my mother's honour.

So there I was being embraced by a lady wearing hardly any clothes when Maggie got quickly out of the car to find out what was happening. Whereupon the lady reluctantly released me and led us both to the door of the 'hotel'. We looked inside at the décor which comprised pictures, mostly in pink, of people in various states of undress and several young ladies reclining on settees and evidently waiting for the action.

At this point, after my eyes had reset in their sockets, we had to confess that there must have been a mistake and that, whatever the ladies had in mind, it was not the purpose of our visit. And nor was Maggie looking for employment. There was however a certain boost to the 83 years old ego that he might be capable of taking advantage of the goods on offer. Anyway much to the young lady's disappointment she took us into the back room where a large Greek looking man who might have been a sumo wrestler in an earlier life sat at the desk.

We explained our dilemma and gave him the name of the hotel, whereupon he offered to take us there. An offer we couldn't refuse. And he did. Regrettably he didn't give us any free entry tickets into his establishment should we change our minds. And that dear readers is the first day of our holiday. 10 and a half hours after leaving home we arrived at our Tarragona hotel and 2 days later migrated to the Hotel Flamingo an hour further down the coast. The saga of the delta will be the subject of another story.

I never did write that story. But it was certainly eventful. Seems we had chosen the hurricane season to have our holiday. After a couple of days of fairly mild weather which allowed us to explore the waterways of the delta, Storm Dave arrived from further south and wreaked havoc on the coastline right up to Montpellier in France, destroying everything in its path. It was an interesting adventure. As the rain lashed on our hotel and the wind tried to blow it off the cliff face we decided foolishly to visit the town of Tortosa inland because we had read that there was an interesting must-see cathedral there. We ran into the car and it was as if we had jumped from the bath. In the 2 minutes it took us to find it the pluvial battering had done its worst to our dry weather clothing. Undaunted, after all we are British, we continued on our way. But British or not, it was no weather for a couple of aging geriatrics to be let loose on the road. Maybe. we thought, it would be better 20 miles inland.

Alas for unfounded hope, the rain seemed to be even more impenetrable as we found an underground garage near to the cathedral. We stuck our heads out of the garage door. It wasn't a street. It was a river ankle deep in flowing water. Since we had no wellington boots we threw caution to the wind and dived in. As we approached the cathedral it became knee deep and we wondered if we would have to swim to our destination. We arrived. The place was closed until 3 pm. It was now only 1pm. So what to do for two in this swimming pool of a town. We were the only one foolish enough to be out. Eventually we found a café open. The proprietor looked strangely at us as two apparently alien creatures waked through the door. But she fed and watered us nevertheless for the two hours remaining, probably because no-one else was screwy enough to venture into her establishment.

So we tried again, and much to our surprise found the Cathedral open. I won't say it was magnificent but it was interesting. Maggie and I have been in many such and oohed and awed at the decorative walls, floors, pillars and ceilings. Maybe it was the weather but we weren't turned on by the decor, though we bought a book on leaving, and retreated to the garage where our car was now in 2 feet of water, and rising rapidly. We drove out just in time to find that road signs in the city were unintelligible. We drove aimlessly around passing the same street several times before we found the exit road back to the coast. Traffic as moving very slowly, for fear of drowning though there were a few lunatics who revelled in driving fast and spraying the other cars with gallons of water. Gingerly we navigated the street of the village before arriving at the hotel. The joyride of the elderly decrepit fossils had come to an end.

Christmas 2019

Christmas that year was not a joyful affair. Maggie's uncle Harold, a 99 year old man who, in a previous time of his life had been a Japanese prisoner of war, had fallen ill with a minor ailment and was in Worthing hospital a 2 hour drive from Southampton. We made this trip almost daily to see how he was and what needed to be done for him, since his wife, Doreen, was in the early stages of dementia. We bought him a new tablet so that he could stay in touch but, at his age, he found it difficult to understand how it worked. He died on January 13 not from the illness had but from a bug he picked up in hospital. Maggie had flown out a couple of days before on the news of his deterioration. She stayed there fixing everything for the funeral and informing every organisation that needed to know.

Then came the problem of Doreen. How was she to survive.? Maggie called the social services, who recommended a company that provided daily care services for her. This seemed to work although Doreen was not the happiest of bunnies that people were coming in and out of her house. Harold had done everything beforehand and she was lost to understand why all these people kept coming through the door. In February I flew over to help out and to attend the funeral, which was a sad affair attended only by us, David and Jeannette and 4 neighbours. Doreen was of course distraught. Maggie and I stayed in a hotel since Doreen forbade anyone to enter Harold's bedroom, let alone sleep in it. News came of the lockdown in France within 5 days and we hurried to get back, just making it the day before.

2020 Lockdown

There is little to say about 2020. Lockdowns , masks, distancing and self-isolating became the new norm. We were lucky in that we could walk the dog several kilometres without having to cross a road. Our weekly trips to the supermarket to pick up a weeks-worth of food were our only connection to the outside world. For an 84 year old with chronic bronchitis this was the only way to stay alive. The alternative wasn't acceptable. Maggie too was one of the more vulnerable of bunnies having survived her operation in the previous year. She rang Doreen every day to make sure she was still alive and kicking. However things changed in September. Doreen would fall over quite frequently and injure herself. The diagnosis was that she needed 24 hour care. This she would not tolerate in her own home. She attacked the carer who came to spend the night there and was taken into hospital. From there she was admitted to one of the best care homes in the region. And that is where she remains still longing to go home and asking to be taken there. Being in care is not satisfactory but, at 93 years old, it is the only solution for her.

This history really sums up our 2020 and that of many others. We have been imprisoned by the pandemic and only a vaccine will allow us out on parole. It has been promised for the over 80s soon. We shall see.

The only other excitement is that Maggie was taken back into hospital to undo the operation she had a year previously. That again is not satisfactory but has to be endured. I console myself that I am still active, still have my faculties, can still write prose, poem and music, and await the call to recommence my career as a public speaker who makes a difference to other peoples' lives. I am not holding my breath.

The last thing that the pandemic deprived us of is any big celebration of our 60 years of marriage on Christmas Eve. In the event a one night relaxation of the French curfew restrictions enables us to have four friends for dinner. Each was enjoined to do a turn, play a piece on the piano, sing a song, recite a poem or whatever. Which we did to great amusement and then we sang the night through with Christmas carols and any other song that came into our heads. It wasn't the grand celebration it ought to have been but at least we celebrated. That will be a matter for the future when all this is over.

Reflection

This is my life story. I hope it hasn't been too boring. I have travelled a long way from the back streets of Bolton, and Maggie too, from her two up two down, has lived a life of selfless service to others. The heart bypass I had 18 years ago will not last forever so it's good to get all these things off my chest now. I have one life left. We have both tried as far as we are able to make a difference within the restraints of our upbringing and we both have made our small mark on the world. We both know that we are not the only people in our circumstances and from our backgrounds who have done this. Some have achieved even more.

So what have we learned in this journey from the back streets? I wrote this book not for self-aggrandisement or show, but to demonstrate that making a difference is an opportunity open to everyone no matter their background. Others will do it in different ways, by devoting themselves to healing the sick or caring for the afflicted for example. The secret of success in my mind is the determination to never stop learning. I have an axiom that I have often quoted. 'Once you stop learning, you might as well be dead.' I have been lucky enough to follow it through my lifetime and so has Maggie. Nor have I stopped now that my working life is over.

And in a post truth society, never has it been more urgent in the history of mankind that continuous learning should be a priority for every human being. Real learning, that takes nothing for granted and ensures that the information they receive and the knowledge they obtain is accurate, verifiable, far-ranging and well understood. The pathway to wisdom is a hard one. The science fiction writer Arthur C Clarke said in 'Childhood's End' - 'Everyone will need to be educated to the level of semi-literacy of the average university graduate. This is the minimum condition for human survival.' In our ever more complex world, it isn't science fiction any more. It's a probable fact. And it raises the importance of a thoroughly far-ranging and universal education system that opens minds and broadens horizons in every single person.

We have but one planet, one rock in space, one chance to explore its beauty, to help maintain its biodiversity. It is undoubtedly under threat from irresponsible, self-serving politicians, greedy, rapacious and covetous industrialists and powerful, autocratic demagogues who appear to have no concern for the future of mankind on the planet. Only their own wealth and glorification. If human beings are to survive we need an economic system that maintains and does not destroy - and that presupposes a much more inclusive education system that exists to provide the knowledge, skills, values and attitudes to drive home these simple certainties. A vast increase in Learning Cities working and learning together can help with that.

Maggie and I have been fortunate in that these opportunities have been available to us. We have met people from many cultures, many countries and many races and it has enriched us beyond anything we ever dreamed of. We would not have it any other way. And we believe that we have had the pleasure of contributing to something crucial to the future of humanity. Our journey from the back streets of Bolton has been, in the current jargon, a blaze.

It is said that travel broadens the mind and I like to think that this was one of the outcomes of our perambulations around the globe, despite the carbon footprint we must have made. Certainly we have embraced the idea that our world is an exciting, stimulating, intoxicating, wonderful place. But that is not learning. Learning entails implementing sensible courses of action. We have learned that to keep it as such, all human beings must cherish their planet's diversity.

We are realistic enough to know that our contribution has not been world-shattering but I like to believe that the difference my efforts have made to what I calculate is millions of people, will live on. I dream too of a world where everyone makes the sort of contribution to the common good that we have been lucky enough to be able to do.

Norman and Maggie Longworth
Eus, France, February 2021

Valedictory

It only remains to fulfil the promise I made of showing a few of the hundreds of the Bolton Boy's lifelong learning materials and poems. They are in colour but that is not replicated in a black and white book. It is not obligatory to read this section nor the poems that follow them. If you wish for more the website www.longlearn.info is useful as are the books that end this tale.

Learning Cities and Global Learning Cities

A Learning City is one which invests in quality lifelong learning in order to:

liberate the full potential of all its citizens

invest in the sustainable growth of its workplaces

re-vitalise the vibrant energy of its communities

Enhance the dynamism of its stakeholders

exploit the creative value of local, regional and international partnerships and

guarantee the responsible implementation of its environmental obligations

In so doing it will release the strength and capacity of all its social, economic, human, intellectual, cultural, technological and environmental resources

Prof Norman Longworth

A Global Learning City is one which fulfils all the above and...

Empowers all its citizens to live in harmony with people of other creeds, colours, countries and cultures

Encourages its primary, secondary and tertiary learning providers to participate in the power of international collaborative learning by all their staff and students.

Widens horizons and action by facilitating international dialogues between citizens

Establishes dynamic bilateral and multilateral links with other cities to explore how each one can assist the other

Recognises the global reach of environmental matters and accepts its obligations to the future of both its citizens and the planet

Works with NGOs and INGOs to implement the recommendations of international treaties and obligations

Assists with the development of international trade between cities

Prof Norman Longworth

	A Sustainable Learning City/Region will......	
11	Invite citizens to suggest improvements to the city region's environmental strategies	
22	Engage citizens (especially young people) in active environmental control and clean up schemes eg waterwatch, airwatch, treewatch	
3	Promote cradle to grave lifelong learning policies that continuously address sustainability issues	
4	Monitor and control air pollution within its boundaries	
5	Ensure provision of clean water and sanitation to all its citizens	
6	Utilise clean sources of energy wherever possible	
7	Ensure that sustainability issues are on the curriculum of every school	
8	Encourage citizens to grow their own food where possible	
9	Prioritise the open availability of parks, gardens and other open spaces	
10	Provide affordable sports, health and well-being facilities	
11	Recycle waste sustainably into new energy	
12	Require rigorous environmental impact assessments for every project	
13	Visibly publicise progress towards environmental sustainability	
14	Provide congestion and pollution-free urban transport systems	
15	Conserve its forests and wooded areas	
16	Devise a strategy to take people out of poverty and provide sustainable jobs	
17	Work with other cities world-wide to exchange ideas, expertise and resources	
18	Offer leadership training to all in sustainability issues	

	An Entrepreneurial Learning City/Region
1	Encourages all its organisations, public and private, to become learning organisations
2	Links its educational, administrative and wealth-creating organisations to develop in partnership with each other
3	Identifies and develops the skills, attributes and structures that allow people and organisations to adapt to a fast-changing world
4	Looks outward. Joins international networks to open all its citizens and organisations to learn from other countries, peoples, cultures and ideas. Treats the outside world as a huge additional resource
5	Releases the power of modern technologies in the service of education, business and industry and communities
6	Increases entrepreneurial education in schools and further and higher education
7	Ensures its future through long-term strategies to foster and market innovation and creativity in all aspects of city/region development
8	Embraces and celebrates the wealth-creating opportunities of diversity
9	Engages people and organisations in implementing the entrepreneurial city's policies by unlocking their talents, ideas, knowledge, experiences, expertise and goodwill
10	Communicates the advantages of the entrepreneurial learning city/region internally to its citizens and organisations and externally to its potential customers and inward investors

Prof Norman Longworth

10 Principles of a Learning Organisation

1. A Learning Organisation can be a company, a professional association, a University, a school, a city, a nation or any group of people, large or small, with a need and a desire to improve performance through learning.

2. A Learning Organisation invests in its own future through the Education and Training of all its people

3. A Learning Organisation creates opportunities for, and encourages, all its people in all its functions to fulfil their human potential

- *as employees, members, professionals or students of the organisation*

- *as ambassadors of the organisation to its customers, clients, audiences and suppliers*

- *as citizens of the wider society in which the organisation exists*

- *as human beings with the need to realise their own capabilities*

4. A Learning Organisation shares its vision of tomorrow with its people and stimulates them to challenge it, to change it and to contribute to it

5. Learning Organisation integrates work and learning and inspires all its people to seek quality, excellence and continuous improvement

6. A Learning Organisation mobilises all its human talent by putting the emphasis on 'Learning' and planning its Education and Training activities accordingly

7. A Learning Organisation empowers ALL its people to broaden their horizons in harmony with their own preferred learning styles

8. A Learning organisation applies up to date open and distance delivery technologies appropriately to create broader and more varied learning opportunities

9. A Learning Organisation responds proactively to the wider needs of the environment and the society in which it operates, and encourages its people to do likewise

10. A Learning Organisation learns and relearns constantly in order to remain innovative, inventive, invigorating and in business

Annexe 2: Poems for Learning Lifelong

I have

I have climbed the mountains high,
I have watched the eagles soaring
I have heard the planet sigh
For thoughtfulness imploring
I have smelled the flowers of spring
New birth then re-emerging
And I feel my heart should sing
With the joy of life now surging

I have wandered through the trees
Nature's beauty now admiring
I have listened to the bees
Their diligence untiring
I have gazed up at the stars
Their number calculating
I have touched the gates of heaven
Eternity awaiting

I have sailed across the seas
Horizons new exploring
I have flown to lands afar
Their diversity adoring
I've resolved to never stop
Understanding and discerning
I've determined to embrace
The universe of learning

I have tried to open minds
All people educating
I have travelled round the world
Their cities activating
I have published poems and books
For stimulating thinking
And managed countless projects
For international linking

My journey's almost ended
Inevitable aging
In the fight for education
The battle's always raging
I've endeavoured to create
A world of people learning
And I pray that you will strive
To keep this life's work churning.

For humanity's sake
For democracy's sake
For the Planet's sake

Norman Longworth

Post script (voluntary)

I have seen the modern media
Deliberately misleading
I have fought against the tide
Of ignorance succeeding
I have witnessed those with power
Lying, bullying, cheating
Integrity's sad demise
Democracy retreating

I have seen the hand of man
Exploitation horrifying
I have come to recognise
That our planet's sadly dying

©Norman Longworth

From 'Poems for a safer Planet'

This poem has been set to music for solo or choral SATB

Making a Difference

If you try to find the key that unlocks mental chains
If you try to halt the growth of suffering and pain
If you try to feel your life has not been lived in vain
You have helped to make a difference for the better.

If you try to drive away the bitterness and hate
If you try to teach all nations to cooperate
If you try to warn the world that soon it is too late
You have helped to make a difference for the better

If you try to fill the world with open thinking minds
If you try to bring new sight to people that are blind
If you try to foster hope for much of humankind
You have helped to make a difference for the better.

If you try to build a dream of world-wide harmony
If you try to teach the guidelines of diversity
If you try to create ways to act unselfishly
You have helped to make a difference for the better.

If every living person could liberate their heart
Noting and rejecting those who tear this world apart
This planet could and would be a place that all could share
Because we've made a difference for a world that's just and fair

©Norman Longworth

From 'Poems to help you Learn
Poems to help you Smile
Poems to help you Think.'

This poem has been set to music, Solo or SATB Choral

Whither Now

Whither now for the young of the nations
What will life hold for the next generations
In an uncertain future where nothing is sure
And changing technology makes jobs insecure

A world where climate change paints a bleak picture
Where the poor become poorer and the rich just get richer
A world of six million forlorn refugees
Where corporate greed is killing the bees

Where extremist hatred redoubles aggression
And a dominant media creates new obsessions
None can predict just what is attainable
In a present that simply isn't sustainable

Life's lasting values will strongly depend
On using intelligence in ways that transcend
All that has happened in times that have passed
For change's wild flight means that little will last

The future belongs to those who will yearn
To constantly, easily, willingly learn
Adaptable, flexible, versatile too
And able to keep new horizons in view

To cherish their planet and sustain its needs
Man's tenure on earth is not guaranteed

©Norman longworth

From 'Poems to help you Learn
Poems to help you Smile' etc

Earth's Story -

My name is earth
With my solar siblings
Forever in captivity
We travel through celestial skies
Never asking how or why
The umbilical cord of gravity
Binds us forever to our fiery mother
The radiant sun

I too have a son
His name is moon
His endless voyage round my earthly form
Illuminates terrestrial night
With all-pervading lunar light
Through hollow space and stellar storm
And aids my silent flight

For fifteen billion years
Through violent turmoil and upheaval
We have ploughed our lonely course
Just tiny insignificant stones
In a galaxy of a billion suns
A billion billion galaxies perforce
Since time began
In the empty darkness of the past

But I am different
Perhaps unique among the planets
My atmosphere creates the rain
The surface of my world is rife
With crawling, walking, flying life
It is my pride and my pain
And it troubles me

I am fragile
And easily broken
The challenges I face are magnifying
Those creatures who can't understand
They pollute my air, my seas, my land
I cannot breathe and I am dying
Like my siblings have died
In the cold, dim darkness of the past

That one aggressive sentient species
Gifted, yet thoughtless and ruled by hate
Obsessed by ceaseless growth and greed
Knowing that this can't succeed
In the finite world they desecrate
They show their ignorance
And they are killing me

My name is earth
In cosmic times to come
I will be here
Saddened and denuded
Circling round my mother sun
And they? well they'll be gone
They showed me no respect
They offered only sad neglect
And it is they that died.
And broke my fragile heart with their passing

©Norman Longworth

From 'Poems for a Safer Planet'

The Dream

I had a dream last weekend, a dream I couldn't resist
I lived upon an island where violence didn't exist
No need to seek protection, no weapons to destroy
And happy fulfilled people, an ambience of joy

Aggressiveness was absent It didn't make sense to fight
If ever there was anger it was quickly put to right
People lived in harmony, their minds would always burn
To cultivate the common good and continuously learn

Above all else the secret lay in joyous education
High values were the mission of every generation
Every child a genius their potential to fulfil
Every adult learning, their talents to upskill

But suddenly my dream was changed reality came through
The island nation ceased to have a visionary view
I saw the schools where children were indifferent and bored
I visited the places where violence had soared

The learning joy had disappeared the high ideals no more
Education had become a monumental bore
A million children left behind behaviour had declined
For want of stimulation to activate the mind

No skills of understanding, few values of respect
No self-enhancing attributes to fire the intellect
No sensitive compassion for those less favoured folk
Just cramming for the state exams, the politician's yoke

I told myself this is a dream it couldn't all be true
We wouldn't let our children grow without a world-wide view
And then I woke and found alas the melancholy truth
That education can't inspire the bulk of modern youth

I wish I could pursue my heart to the island of my dream
Where peace and reason still prevail, perception, self-esteem
Where people open up their minds, true wisdom's flag unfurled
And learned to use intelligence for the good of all the world

From 'Poems for a Thinking Nation'

Books for Further Reading by Norman Longworth

Academic books

Lifelong Learning: New Vision, New Implications, New roles for People,, Organisations, Nations and Communities in the 21st Century (Routledge)

Making Lifelong Learning Work: Learning Cities for a Learning Century (Routledge)

Lifelong Learning in Action: Education in the 21st Century (Routledge)

Learning Cities, Learning Regions, Learning Communities (Routledge)

 Perspectives on Learning Cities and Regions (Niace) (With Professor Michael Osborne

Travel Books

Tales of the Conflent (Vol 1) (Amazon)

The Conflent Tales (Vol 2) (Amazon)

Les Histoires du Conflent (French, Amazon)

Poetry Books

Poems for a Thinking Nation (Amazon)

Poems for a Safer Planet (Amazon)

Poems to Help You Think
Poems to Help You Smile
Poems to help You Learn (Amazon)

Notre Monde (French) (Amazon)

Albert (Amazon, Kindle only)

Printed in Poland
by Amazon Fulfillment
Poland Sp. z o.o., Wrocław

87081143R00137